MICROCOMPUTER HARDWARE, OPERATION, AND TROUBLESHOOTING WITH IBM PC APPLICATIONS

MICROCOMPUTER HARDWARE, OPERATION, AND TROUBLESHOOTING WITH IBM PC APPLICATIONS

BYRON W. PUTMAN

Computer Facilities and Communications
University of California, Berkeley

Prentice Hall, Englewood Cliffs, New Jersey 07632

Library of Congress Cataloging-in-Publication Data

PUTMAN, BYRON W.
    Microcomputer hardware, operation, and trouble-
shooting with IBM PC applications.

    Includes index.
    1. IBM Personal Computer.   2. Microcomputers.
I. Title.
QA76.8.12594P88   1988   004.165   87-14576
ISBN   0-13-581943-1

Editorial/production supervision
    and interior design: *Theresa A. Soler*
Cover design: *Photo Plus Art*
Manufacturing buyer: *Ed O'Dougherty*

IBM PC is a trademark of International Business Machines, Incorporated.

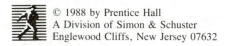 © 1988 by Prentice Hall
A Division of Simon & Schuster
Englewood Cliffs, New Jersey 07632

Printed in the United States of America

10 9 8 7 6 5 4 3 2 1

ISBN   0-13-581943-1   025

Prentice-Hall International (UK) Limited, *London*
Prentice-Hall of Australia Pty. Limited, *Sydney*
Prentice-Hall Canada Inc., *Toronto*
Prentice-Hall Hispanoamericana, S.A., *Mexico*
Prentice-Hall of India Private Limited, *New Delhi*
Prentice-Hall of Japan, Inc., *Tokyo*
Simon & Schuster Asia Pte. Ltd., *Singapore*
Editora Prentice-Hall do Brasil, Ltda., *Rio de Janeiro*

To Elaine

For pretending to believe that this is absolutely
the last one.

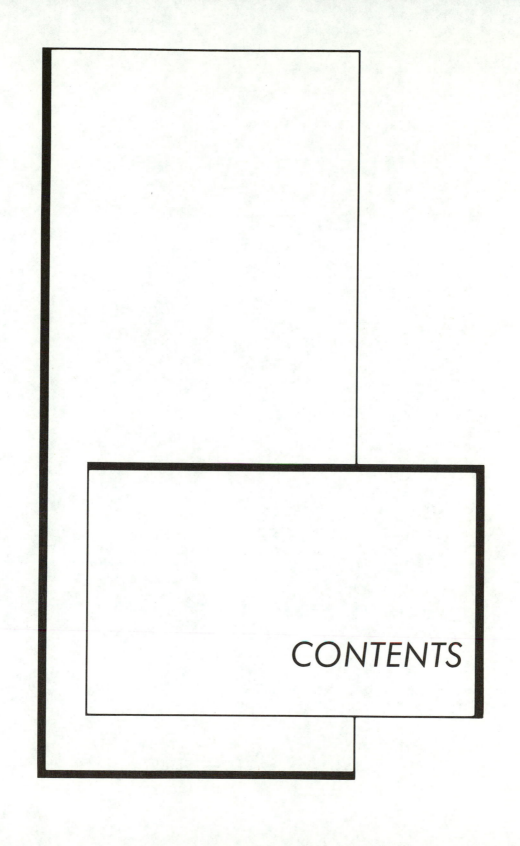

CONTENTS

6   THE DRAM SUBSYSTEM AND EXPANSION SLOTS   125

7   THE VIDEO DISPLAY   143

8   THE FLOPPY DISK SUBSYSTEM   167

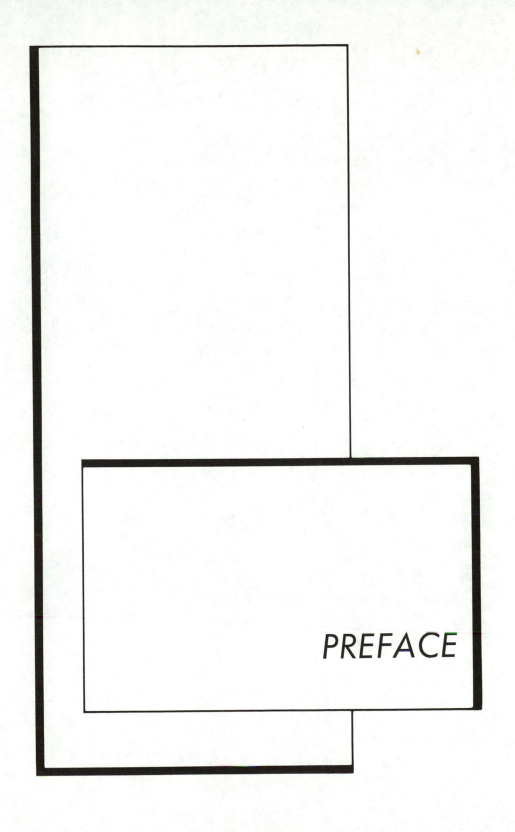

PREFACE

This book is intended to satisfy the needs of the electronic technician, systems software designer, research scientist, or other individual who requires an in-depth knowledge of understanding, troubleshooting, expanding, and interfacing microcomputer hardware. It is a modern, systems-oriented introduction that produces the additional benefit of acquainting the reader with the world's most popular microcomputer system, the IBM PC.

The functions demanded to support three-bus architecture are considered as the fundamental requirements of all microcomputer systems. Concepts such as fetching and storing data (memory read and write operations), wait state generation (to accommodate slow memory and I/O), interrupt processing, and direct memory access block transfers between RAM and disk are examined in a tutorial manner.

In addition to its tremendous popularity, the characteristic that makes the IBM PC an excellent vehicle for learning microcomputer systems is the open architecture philosophy adopted by IBM. In creating and manufacturing the PC they have withheld no secrets; IBM has published documents describing every aspect of the PC, from the schematics of the hardware to the BIOS assembly language listing.

The microprocessor is an astounding device—so flexible and powerful that it invariably gains much more than its just share of attention in textbooks pursuing microcomputer technology. No one can deny that the microprocessor dictates the limitations and personality of a particular microcomputer system. However, the microprocessor is only one of the many complex intelligent devices that form modern microcomputer systems. Among these other devices are the direct memory access controller, programmable interrupt controller, programmable peripheral interface, programmable interval timer, CRT controller, and floppy disk drive controller.

The only prerequisite to a successful completion of this book is simply a solid working knowledge of basic electronics and digital circuits. This knowledge-base supports a three-tiered approach of theory, applications, and troubleshooting. Each component or subassembly is first discussed at a block diagram level where the functional description of each group of signals is discussed. The device is then integrated into a subsystem that performs a distinct function. Finally, symptom analysis and troubleshooting are discussed.

Chapter 1 introduces the terminology and universal concepts associated with general purpose computing systems, and Chapter 2 acquaints the reader with three-bus architecture (the address, data, and control/status buses) and the generic microprocessor depicted as the master of the system bus.

Chapter 3 illustrates the standard configuration of the IBM PC. Included in the discussion is the important relationship between the hardware, BIOS, operating system, and applications program layers.

Chapter 4 employs the concepts introduced in Chapter 2 to perform a detailed analysis of the CPU subsystem: the 8088 microprocessor, 8284 clock generator, and 8288 system controller. Emphasis is placed on understanding how the 8088 interfaces with the memory, I/O, video, and mass storage subsystems.

Chapter 5 studies the intelligent LSI support devices in the PC system and the functions that they contribute: the 8255 Programmable Peripheral Interface, 8253 Programmable Interval Timer, 8253 Programmable Interrupt Controller and the 8088 Interrupt System, and the 8237 Direct Memory Access Controller. The chapter concludes by integrating the 8088 processor subsystem and the LSI support devices into a functional block diagram of the system board.

Chapter 6 explores the DRAM subsystem and expansion slots. All aspects of bit-oriented DRAM memory systems are considered: row and column address multiplexing, RAS and CAS generation, and refresh cycles. The unique refresh operation of the PC is discussed by examining the functions of Timer-1 of the 8253 PIT and Channel-0 of the 8237 DMAC. The expansion slots are considered from the point of view that they are driven by an extremely powerful microcomputer chip (in reality the system board).

Chapter 7 introduces the monochrome display adapter and monochrome display. The functions of the 6850 CRT controller, dual-ported video-RAM, and the character generator are studied. Great effort is taken to define the responsibilities of the system processor and the CRT controller. The elements of a video display are illustrated including a block diagram of the monochrome display.

Chapter 8 describes the floppy disk subsystem. The floppy disk drive adapter board consists of an 8272 Floppy Disk Controller, Digital Output Register, and standard MFM data separator. The interaction of these circuits with the floppy disk drives is discussed in detail. After the electro-mechanical assemblies of the floppy disk drive are examined, the standard index, radial, azimuth, and spindle-speed adjustments alignment tests and adjustments are illustrated.

Chapter 9 is dedicated to troubleshooting. The individual tests of the firmware-based Power-On-Self-Test are examined as aids to isolating system board failures to a bad component or group of components. The routines of the IBM Advanced Diagnostics Disk are also employed to verify hardware failures to the subassembly level, and DRAM and keyboard faults to the component level. Finally the technical and financial aspects of subassembly repair are considered.

Appendix A details the binary and hexadecimal number systems which are used throughout the book.

Appendix B explains the ASCII code and control characters.

Byron W. Putman

ACKNOWLEDGMENTS

A special thanks to the staff of Workstation Hardware Support at UC Berkeley—especially Vincent S. Bocchieri for his fine research efforts.

I would also like to thank the following companies for their illustrations and photographs:

Lynx Inc., Dair Computer Systems, John Fluke Mfg. Co. Inc, and Tandon Inc.

OTHER PRENTICE HALL BOOKS BY THIS AUTHOR

DIGITAL ELECTRONICS: Theory, Applications, and Troubleshooting

DIGITAL AND MICROPROCESSOR ELECTRONICS: Theory, Applications, and Troubleshooting

RS-232 SIMPLIFIED: Everything You Need to Know About Connecting, Interfacing, and Troubleshooting Peripheral Devices.

MICROCOMPUTER HARDWARE, OPERATION, AND TROUBLESHOOTING WITH IBM PC APPLICATIONS

7

THE ELEMENTS
OF A COMPUTER
SYSTEM

The first two chapters in this book provide the systems and microprocessor background required for a detailed study of the IBM PC. In this chapter we give an overview of the devices that constitute a *general-purpose programmable computing system*.

1.1 COMPUTER SYSTEMS: MAINFRAMES, MINIS, AND MICROS

Computers are usually classified into one of three groups: mainframe, mini, or micro. The factors used to classify a computer are the physical size of the machine, the number of bits of data it can handle in one read or write operation, the size of the physical and logical memory it can address, and the speed with which it can process data. As technology has progressed, the distinction between the three groups has become much more subtle. *Mainframes* can handle multiple word lengths of data between 32 and 64 bits; *minis* have word lengths between 16 and 32 bits; finally, *micros* have word lengths between 8 and 32 bits.

Mainframe computers are found in environments where tremendous quantities of data must be stored, retrieved, and manipulated, and where high-level mathematic and statistical applications are required. Banks, insurance companies, and manufacturing concerns all rely on mainframe computers to handle heavy data and *number crunching* (processing). Mainframe computer systems are really constructed from many different independent computers. The central computer in the system does all the actual data processing. Other computers in the system are used to do front-end processing (the preprocessing of data) and communications tasks. Mainframes can support 100 to 1000 simultaneous users.

Mainframes gain their great speed by employing *Emitter Coupled Logic (ECL)* circuits. ECL is a logic family that is appreciably faster than TTL or CMOS because it employs nonsaturated logic levels. Instead of switching a transistor on and off between saturation and cutoff, ECL switches between two voltage levels in the linear portion of a transistor's characteristic curve. This eliminates the need to overcome the base-collector stray capacitance, greatly reducing propagation delay. ECL uses a -5.2-V power supply, and typical output voltages are -0.9 V for a logic 1 and -1.75 V for a logic 0. Although it is unquestionably the fastest logic family, ECL has many drawbacks: It consumes great amounts of power, has a low noise threshold, and cannot be highly integrated.

Minis are used in small business environments that require the manipulation of only moderate amounts of data. Perhaps the largest users of minis are colleges and universities. In an academic environment, minis are used to support students in programming classes, for text formatting and electronic mail, and in small-laboratory research. Other applications of minis include control computers used in factories and loading docks and automated electronic test systems. A typical mini can support 24 to 48 simultaneous users.

The *microcomputer revolution* is one of the most far-reaching technical breakthroughs in history. Micros are found everywhere. They are used in business, education, research, and communications. Small businesses that could not justify the price of a mainframe or mini can easily afford several micros. Businesses use micros for inventory control, accounting, personnel management, data base management (i.e., the storage, manipulation, and retrieval of large pools of information), word processing, and forecasting. Individuals often use micros for the same applications as those used by small businesses.

Large businesses that own many mainframes and minis use micros for personal workstations. These micros are connected to the mainframes and minis to appear as normal terminals. A person with a micro who has such a mainframe or mini connection can share vast amounts of data with the other users in the system. Thus a micro user has the best of all worlds: an independent personal workstation capable of running sophisticated applications and a channel to transmit and receive important data communications from all the users connected to the mainframe. Users in such a network can send and receive electronic mail, share peripherals, such as printers, and access electronic bulletin boards that display company news and events.

Although the microcomputer is presently the dominant force in the computer world, a new kind of supermicro called the *workstation* is quickly consuming both the micro and mini markets. Workstations are, in fact, a merging of micro and mini technology to create 32-bit personal computers that are capable of supporting minicomputer operating systems (such as UNIX). These workstations are specifically designed to be directly connected to vast computer networks. This enables the workstation user to gain access instantaneously to huge data bases on mainframes, share expensive system printers, disk storage, backup facilities, file systems and utilities, and other important system network resources.

1.2 BASIC ARCHITECTURE OF A COMPUTER

All computer systems, from mammoth mainframes to lap-top micros, share the same basic architecture. This architecture entails four major blocks: the central processing unit (CPU), memory, input circuitry, and output circuitry. Figure 1.1 depicts the classic block diagram of a computer system. It is important to understand that the devices and circuitry used to construct the blocks in Figure 1.1 vary greatly among different computer systems. The intent of this chapter is to describe general concepts that apply to all computers, regardless of age, size, or capability.

The CPU

The circuitry needed to implement a CPU in mainframes requires many circuit boards of components, whereas microcomputers contain a CPU in one Large Scale Integration (LSI) IC called a *microprocessor*. The CPUs in mainframes and microcomputers perform the same function; the difference is that the CPU in a mainframe computer is thousands of times faster and more sophisticated than its microcomputer counterpart.

The CPU can be thought of as containing the heart and brain of the computer system. CPUs typically contain the following logical blocks: arithmetic/logic unit (ALU), registers, control and timing circuitry, and microprogrammed instructions.

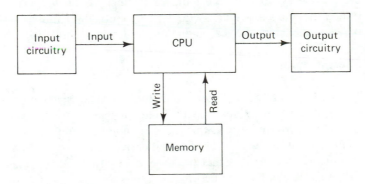

Figure 1.1   Block diagram of a computer system.

The ALU

The ALU performs arithmetic and logical functions. Addition, subtraction, and multiplication are typical arithmetic functions that an ALU performs, and AND, OR, XOR, and NOT are typical logic functions.

Registers

Registers are simply memory locations that reside within the CPU. CPUs contain 4 to 128 registers. These registers are classified by the type of information that they store. Some registers are used only to store addresses, others store specific kinds of data, and still others are general purpose in nature and can be used to store any type of information. The most important fact to remember about CPU registers is that they are used to store data and addresses only for a short period of time. They are not used like external RAM—loaded with programs or data that will be constant throughout a particular application. The information in these registers is dynamic, always changing to provide the current executing instruction with the data it needs to complete its task.

To access external RAM requires an appreciable length of time because the microprocessor has to place an address onto the address bus and signals on the control bus have to be asserted. In addition, the address decoders in external circuitry and those internal to the RAMs all have propagation delays. Because registers are internal to the CPU, none of the signals associated with a RAM access occur during a register read or write operation. This means that the access time of registers is extremely fast! A typical CPU register has a read/write access time of less than 50 ns in comparison to 120 ns for high-speed RAM.

Control and Timing

An important function of the CPU is to generate control and timing signals. All CPUs have a clock input; the clock is utilized as a time standard to generate the precise signals that are required to manipulate the system bus. Complex timing diagrams provided by the CPU manufacturer illustrate the relationships between the address, data, and control signals generated by the CPU.

Microprogram

The CPU is highly intelligent. It is the master of the system bus, generating timing and control signals; it has internal memory locations called registers; and it can perform basic arithmetic and logic functions. How can it perform all these tasks? From what source does it derive its innate intelligence? The answer is quite simple: An internal program is designed by the manufacturer of the CPU and cannot be modified by the user.

It is critical to distinguish between a microprogram and a program that is written by a systems or applications programmer. These latter programs are stored in external RAM or ROM. As CPU users you will write programs that reside in external RAM or ROM. All the while that your program is executing, another program is also executing—the program that resides in ROM within the CPU: *the microprogram*. It is this microprogram that knows how to generate the address and control signals to read the first step in your external program. It is the microprogram that actually adds two numbers together when your program requests an addition. It is also the microprogram that reads and writes information to or from the CPU registers.

The microprogram is the lowest possible level of programming. Each *microinstruction* talks directly to the thousands of transistors that constitute a CPU. The microprogram cannot be changed; it is an element of the electronic hardware. The technician or engineer does not have to understand how the microprogram functions. Each CPU has a set of instructions that it can perform. The fact that this instruction set is actually executed by the microprogram is completely transparent.

1.3 MEMORY

The second block in Figure 1.1 is memory. In addition to RAM and ROM, computer systems also have many forms of nonvolatile mass memory. This mass memory is used to store huge amounts of programs and data. The memory devices in computers are often the largest, most expensive, and most complex part of the system.

Main Memory

The main memory of a computer is used to store the programs and data that are currently being executed by the CPU. If CPUs are to run at full speed, the main memory must have a fast access time. The only modern type of memory that meets this requirement is *semiconductor memory*. Before semiconductor memory was invented or became cost-efficient, small ferrite doughnuts called *magnetic cores* were used to implement main memory. Thus the term *core memory* is still often used to refer to main memory, regardless of the fact that main memory is now constructed exclusively from semiconductor RAM.

Bootstrap Memory

When a computer is powered on, how does it know what to do? Every computer must have a low-level program in nonvolatile memory (ROM) called the *boot* or *bootstrap* program. (The term *bootstrap* is derived from the old saying about "pulling oneself up by one's own bootstraps.") When the CPU is first powered up, it automatically reads the memory location that contains the first instruction of the boot program. The boot program contains instructions that initialize the system hardware. The boot program then reads into main memory a complex program called an *operating system*, which then takes control of the computer. In Chapters 8 and 9 we study how the boot program housed in ROM loads the operating system from the floppy or hard disk drive on the IBM PC.

System ROM

Every computer contains system ROM. We have just seen that the boot program is contained in ROM. ROM is also used to hold computer languages (such as BASIC), tables for math functions, programs that interface the computer with input/output devices, and self-test programs. Process control computers that are dedicated to performing a single control function (such as monitoring a security system) hold their operating system and applications programs in ROM.

System RAM

System RAM is used for many different purposes. It holds the resident portion of the operating system that is loaded from the on-line mass storage device. RAM is also used to hold the currently executing applications program and the immediate data that it may require. It is also used for the important data storage function called a *stack*. The stack is a place in RAM where temporary data that can be effortlessly accessed by the CPU is stored. In Chapter 2 you will learn much more about the stack.

On microcomputers the image of the video display is kept in video-RAM. The contents of video-RAM are used to refresh and update the characters and graphics symbols on the microcomputer's display. Video-RAM is not considered a part of main memory because it is dedicated to refreshing the display and cannot be used for any other purpose.

Mass Memory

The preceding description of main memory had many references to mass memory. The capacity of a computer system is often judged in terms of the computer's mass memory devices. How fast are they? What is their total storage capacity? Can they be expanded?

Just like cassette and video tape, mass memories store data in the form of magnetized regions on an *oxide-coated medium*. Because data is stored in this form, mass memories are nonvolatile; they retain data without the requirement of an external voltage. The data bits are written onto and read from the magnetic media in the same manner that music is recorded and played back on cassette tape. That process uses a *magnetic read/write (R/W) head*.

Consider a simplified read operation. The head is placed (by some mechanical means) over the location where the data has been stored. Magnetic currents are induced into the head as it moves across the tape. These currents are then amplified, filtered, and decoded. This results in the retrieval of the original digital information.

Semiconductor memories have no moving parts; the only delays experienced in accessing a RAM or ROM are minor propagation delays. Mass memories, on the other hand, are hybrids of electronics and mechanics. Because of simple inertia, it takes an appreciable length of time to position a read/write head over the required location on the media. This means that mass memories have access times that are thousands of times slower than those of electronic memories.

We now see that mass memories are nonvolatile and can store enormous amounts of data, but they also have great speed limitations. RAMs are extremely fast but are relatively expensive per bit of storage and lose their contents when power is lost. Computer systems require the complementary attributes of both RAM and mass memory.

Floppy Disk

In microcomputer systems the most popular form of mass memory is the floppy disk. The floppy disk is a flat, circular piece of plastic coated with magnetic oxide. The floppy disk is placed into a protective square cardboardlike case. As the name ''floppy'' implies, it is flexible and is easily bent. For a computer to access a floppy disk for a read or write operation, the floppy must be inserted into an appropriate floppy disk drive. Floppy disk drives are analogous to cassette decks that play and record audio cassettes. An oval access hole is cut into the case that enables the R/W heads to touch the surface of the floppy disk.

Floppy disks are an extremely low-cost mass storage media. They are available in three standard diameters: 8-, 5¼-, and 3½-in. diameters. The *8-in. standard* is the oldest and is no longer used in new system design. It was originally used as low-cost mass storage for minicomputers. Floppy disk drives are often found in pairs. A pair of 8-in. floppy disk drives are installed in a large chassis that contains a +5-V and a +12-V power supply. Together the pair of drives, power supply, and chassis weigh almost 40 lb. Typically, 8-in. floppy disks use both sides for data storage, which gives them a capacity of 1.2 MB (megabytes). Data is transferred between a computer and an 8-in. floppy in a serial stream at the rate of 500 kilobits/s.

The *5¼-in. standard*, developed as a smaller, low-power alternative to the 8-in. floppy, is usually called a *minifloppy*. Until recently, 5¼-in. floppies were the exclusive mass memory storage device for microcomputers. A 5¼-in. floppy disk drive is about one-fourth the size and weight of an 8-in. floppy disk drive. Its power requirement is low enough to use the +5 V and +12 V from the microcomputer's power supply. The 5¼-in. floppy disk also uses both sides, typically has a storage capacity of 320 KB or 360 KB (kilobytes), and has a data transfer rate of only 250 kilobits/s. The newest generation of 5¼-in. floppies can store 1.2 MB and have a data transfer rate of 500 kilobits/s. They appear to be the electrical equivalent of the older 8-in. floppy.

After much competition, a new standard floppy has emerged: the *3½-in. floppy* developed as an alternative to the 5¼-in. floppy. Because of its small size, the 3½-in. floppy is called a *microfloppy*. Unlike the 8- and 5¼-in. floppies, the 3½-in. floppy is not really floppy at all. It is housed in a protective, hard plastic shell. When 8- and 5¼-in. floppies are not in a drive, they must be placed into paper envelopes to ensure that no foreign particles contaminate the oxide surface. The 3½-in. floppy does not require this protective envelope. The access hole on these floppies is covered by a thin piece of metal. The first 3½-in. floppies stored information on only one side and had a storage capacity of 400 KB. Newer 3½-in. floppies use both sides and have therefore doubled their storage capacity to 800 KB. It appears that the new 3½-in. floppy has been well received because of its small size and rugged package.

A new floppy disk is nothing more than a piece of oxide-coated plastic. Before it can hold any data, the floppy must be formatted with tracks and sectors. All operating systems contain a *formatting program* that initializes a floppy disk by writing special format information and creates tables that contain the names of files and their links and paths. This data defines concentric rings on the surface of the floppy. These rings are called *tracks*. Each track is then broken into sections called *sectors*. A sector is the smallest block of storage on a floppy disk. The actual formatting process and the formatting data that is written onto the floppy are extremely complex. Most companies follow precise formatting standards, which include information that identifies each track and sector, a *cyclic redundancy check (CRC)* byte, which is used to verify the validity of the data, and many different lengths of gaps and bytes of data used to synchronize the floppy disk drive and the computer.

Consider a typical 5¼-in. floppy disk. The format used is called a standard double-sided, double-density format. *Double sided* means that both sides of the floppy are used to store data. In earlier-technology drives, only one side of the floppy (the bottom side) was used to store data. *Double density* refers to how closely the tracks are squeezed together on the floppy. The double-density standard states that the *track density* is 48 *tracks per inch (tpi)*. The first 5¼-in. floppy disk drives employed a single-density format that allowed only 24 tpi. When a floppy is double-sided, the matching tracks on the top and bottom are called a *cylinder*. The first track on the bottom is track 0; the first track on the top is track 1. Tracks 0 and 1 constitute cylinder 0. This numbering scheme of even on the bottom and odd on the top is repeated for the entire floppy. Each track is divided further into eight sectors. Notice that it is a matter of tradition to refer to the first track as track 0 but the first sector as sector 1. Figure 1.2 describes the logical groups on the 5¼-in. floppy formatted for a capacity of 320 KB on an IBM PC.

Floppy disk drives have a switch that senses the state of the *R/W notch*.

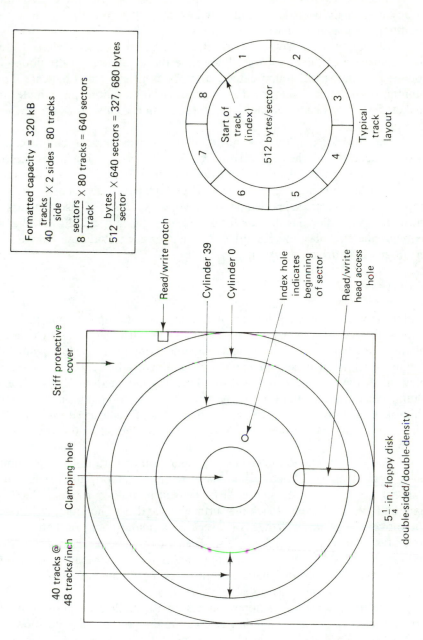

Formatted capacity = 320 kB

$40 \dfrac{\text{tracks}}{\text{side}} \times 2 \text{ sides} = 80 \text{ tracks}$

$8 \dfrac{\text{sectors}}{\text{track}} \times 80 \text{ tracks} = 640 \text{ sectors}$

$512 \dfrac{\text{bytes}}{\text{sector}} \times 640 \text{ sectors} = 327,680 \text{ bytes}$

Read/write notch

Cylinder 39

Cylinder 0

Index hole
indicates
beginning
of sector

Read/write
head access
hole

Start of
track
(index)

512 bytes/sector

Typical track
layout

Stiff protective
cover

Clamping hole

40 tracks @
48 tracks/inch

$5\frac{1}{4}$-in. floppy disk
double-sided/double-density

Figure 1.2 Structure of a 320KB floppy.

11

If the notch is covered with a piece of tape, the disk is write-protected, and the floppy essentially becomes a read-only device. If the notch is left uncovered, the floppy is enabled for write operations.

The floppy disk drive uses an infrared transmitter and receiver to sense the occurrence of the *index hole*. Each time the index hole in the floppy disk rotates past the small, round cutout, a strobe is generated to indicate the beginning of the track. A floppy disk rotating at 300 rotations per minute (rpm) makes 5 rotations each second. Therefore, an index pulse is generated every 200 ms.

The IBM PC employs 5¼-in. floppy disk drives that can be formatted to have a capacity of either 320 KB or 360 KB. Figure 1.2 illustrates the basic format of a 320 KB floppy as formatted on an IBM PC; the 360 KB format allows an additional sector per track. High-capacity (quad-density) 1.2 MB floppy disk drives are supported on the IBM PC/AT. The PC also supports 3½-in. double-sided floppies that are formatted for a capacity of 720 KB to appear as twice the size of a 360 KB drive. In Chapter 8 we study the IBM-PC 5¼-in. floppy disk drive subsystem.

Hard Disk

Mainframes and minis need much more mass storage capacity and speed than floppy-disk technology can possibly offer. A hard disk is created by coating or plating large platters of metal with a magnetic oxide material. Floppy disks are single units. Hard disks, on the other hand, are constructed from multiple platters. A typical hard disk has 3 to 10 platters mounted on a single spindle. Both sides of each platter (except the top side of the top platter and the bottom side of the bottom platter) are used to hold data. Thus a drive that uses an 8-platter hard disk pack requires 14 R/W heads, all precisely aligned to a known reference.

The easiest way to understand the operation of hard disks is to compare and contrast them with floppy disks. The R/W head on floppy disk drives actually touches the surface of the floppy disk. Typical hard disks rotate at 3600 rpm, and the R/W heads never touch the surface of the disk. The motors that control the movement of the R/W heads (to seek a particular track) on hard disks are much faster than those on a floppy disk. Because of these faster head-positioning motors, hard disks have access times that are much shorter than those of floppy disks. A typical floppy disk has a track-to-track access time of 75 ms, compared with 25 ms on a typical hard disk.

The track density of a floppy disk is greatly limited because floppy disk drives use an *open-loop system* for calculating the present track position of the R/W head. When the R/W head encounters track 0, a mechanical switch is closed. Each time the floppy disk drive steps the R/W head toward the center of the floppy disk, the track count is incremented. Each time the R/W head is stepped toward the edge of the disk, the track count is decremented. There is no information recorded on the floppy disk that can be used to give positioning feedback information to the R/W head-stepper mechanism.

Hard disks use a *closed-loop* head-positioning system. A hard disk is formatted not only with data tracks but also with extra tracks that contain servo information. These *servo tracks* supply feedback data to the head-positioning circuitry. The R/W head can be much more precisely positioned, which allows greater track density and also decreases the track-to-track seek time. Hard disk packs have a storage capacity of 80 MB to 10 GB (gigabytes).

As we have said, hard disks come in groups of 3 to 20 platters. A group of platters is called a *disk pack*. A disk pack is removed by inserting it into a protective heavy-gauge plastic case. A disk pack weighs 5 to 20 lb. A hard disk drive with associated circuitry is often the size of a small chest of drawers.

The R/W head in a hard disk drive never touches the surface of the hard disk. It flies over the surface at a height of less than 0.0001 in. If the R/W head touches the surface of a hard disk while the pack is spinning, the event is called a *head crash*. A head crash usually destroys both the R/W head and the hard disk platter.

Winchester Hard Disk

The hard disks that we have just discussed are used in the mainframe and mini environment. They are much too bulky and expensive to be used in microcomputer applications. The newest-technology disk drives, which were developed by IBM, are called Winchester drives. The first Winchester was a dual 30-MB drive called the 30/30. The name 30/30 was soon changed to Winchester after the famous Winchester 30/30 rifle. To ensure an ultraclean working environment, the hard disk platters in Winchester drives are not removable; a Winchester drive is a closed unit. For this reason Winchester drives are often called *fixed disk drives*. The equivalent of the nonremovable disk pack in the Winchester is called the *HDA (hard disk assembly).*

Winchesters used in mini and mainframe environments are about one-fifth the physical size of conventional hard disk drives. We focus our attention on the 5¼-in. Winchester drives used with microcomputers.

Winchesters used in micro systems are the same physical size as 5¼-in. floppy drives. They are available in capacities of 5 MB to 76 MB. Winchesters have a data-transfer rate of 5 MB/s, 20 times faster than a 5¼-in. floppy. This greatly enhances the performance of applications that require continual disk access. Because of their light weight, low cost, and small physical size, Winchester disk drives have become extremely popular. Most business-oriented microcomputers have both a floppy drive and a fixed disk drive. The floppy drive is used to install new programs onto the fixed drive and make backup copies of data in the event that the fixed drive experiences a failure.

Mass Memory Backup

If a hard disk crashes, the data stored on the disk pack is lost. To avoid this potentially disastrous situation, data from *on-line* mass storage devices are periodically recorded onto a secondary form of mass storage, which is usually magnetic tape. If you have 2 hours of music on a cassette tape and wish to find a song near the end of the tape, you must fast-forward the tape, constantly checking to see if you have reached the song—an extremely slow process. Magnetic tape is also a serial form of storage; the data bits are written one following another. Magnetic tape is inexpensive per bit of storage, but it is much too slow to be used as on-line mass storage. When a hard disk crashes, a spare disk drive is put into service and the contents of the last tape backup are transferred to the new drive. The data that was stored between the time of the last backup and the time that the drive crashed is lost. That is a good reason to make frequent tape backups of all on-line mass storage devices. A microcomputer that has one fixed disk and one floppy disk can use floppies to back up the fixed disk. A 5 MB fixed disk requires almost 20 floppies to back it up. For this reason microtape backup and removable disk cartridges are now available for microcomputer systems.

1.4 INPUT/OUTPUT DEVICES

The CPU controls the internal operation of the computer system. But computer systems must also communicate with the "outside" world. *Input/output (I/O) ports* interface the CPU with the outside world. Some I/O devices are designed to interface with human beings; others connect the CPU with remote computer systems, transducers and sensors, or other electronic devices.

The Keyboard and Video Display

The keyboard is the most familiar computer input device. With a typewriterlike keyboard, users can enter programs, commands, and data quickly and efficiently. Paired with each keyboard is a visual output device. The most common output device is the CRT display. These video displays usually have a screen of 24 lines by 80 columns. Video displays can output characters with many different *attributes*: high intensity, blinking, underlined, and reverse video (dark characters on a light background). Many video displays can also display colors. These display attributes and colors are used to enhance communication between the computer and the human user. Some inexpensive computers use home television sets as their video displays. Commercial-grade TV sets have very poor *resolution*. (Resolution is the distance between dots on a video display. The closer and smaller the dots, the better the resolution.) Because of this poor resolution, TV sets can usually display a screen of only 16 lines by 40 columns.

Mainframe and minicomputers use keyboard/video display devices called *terminals*. Terminals are usually connected to computers via a serial communications link. Most computers interface with terminals using a standard form of serial communications called RS-232. Hundreds of manufacturers supply terminals that support the RS-232 communications interface, which makes it possible for one terminal to be used with any kind of mainframe or minicomputer. (This is a great asset that you will more fully appreciate after our discussion of modems later in this chapter.) All terminals have internal memory that is used to refresh the video display. It is the job of the terminal, not the host computer, to execute this periodic refresh operation. Some terminals are called *smart terminals*. Smart terminals have an on-board CPU that enables the terminal to accomplish local processing and formatting of data. Smart terminals relieve the host computer of many time-consuming housekeeping chores. *Dumb terminals* have no local intelligence. They are basically nothing more than a video display, control electronics, and circuitry used to transmit and receive data on the serial link.

Microcomputers do not use terminals as their keyboard/video display device. A detachable keyboard communicates with the input circuitry of the microcomputer via a serial cable. The video display (called a monitor) usually sits on top of the computer. Unlike the terminal, the video display in a microcomputer does not contain memory or communications electronics; it contains only the basic CRT drive circuitry. The video memory and CRT control circuitry are housed within the computer unit. This integral keyboard/video display is designed to be a cost-efficient alternative to the terminal and enables micros to support many different video displays and special-purpose keyboards.

The greatest limitation of conventional CRTs is that they are bulky and heavy. In the quest to develop truly portable computers, the flat screen display was invented. Unlike CRTs, which require long electron guns, flat screens are solid-state devices that use LCDs or *EL (electroluminescent)* displays. During transportation, the flat screen is folded down on top of the computer, creating an extremely light, (12- to 14-lb) low-profile package. When the computer is to be used, the flat screen is unfolded to a comfortable viewing angle. Although flat-screen technology still has many technical problems to overcome (including the lack of color), it is sure to be the dominant video display in the very near future.

I/O devices other than the required keyboard and video display are called computer *peripherals*. Typical peripherals are printers and modems.

Printers

With the exception of the video display, the most common computer output device is the *printer*. A printer provides a hard copy of the computer data, program runs, or program listings. The printer, like the disk drive, is constructed from a combination of electronic and mechanical components. Printers suffer a much higher percentage of mechanical, rather than electronic, failures.

Large computer facilities have expensive printers called *line printers*. As the name implies, line printers appear to print a whole line of characters simultaneously. Line printers use many different methods to accomplish high-speed printing. Some have a chain that rotates horizontally that is embedded with multiple sets of print hammers. Other designs use rotating drums or vertical bars containing a set of hammers for each print column. Using high-speed mechanics, these printers can output 400 to 3600 lines per minute. Line printers are used in high production environments where massive amounts of data must be quickly printed.

In the microcomputer world there are two major types of printers: *daisy wheel* and *dot matrix*. They are called *serial printers* because each character is printed successively, one after the other. The three major considerations used in judging printers are print quality, speed, and price.

Daisy wheel printers employ a circular printer element with 96 spokes. At the end of each spoke is a print block embossed with a letter or symbol. The printer derives its name from the print wheel's resemblance to a daisy, with its many petals. The daisy wheel is easily removed, which allows the use of many print types and character sets. To print a letter or character, the appropriate petal is rotated into position and struck by a hammer, impacting the ink ribbon and paper. The print head is then moved horizontally to the next column and the process repeats.

Like a good-quality typewriter, a daisy wheel printer produces *letter-quality* print. Letter-quality print is the easiest type or print to read and is preferred in office environments. Because of the rotating petals, daisy wheel printers are extremely slow. Low-cost daisy wheel printers print 8 to 16 characters per second (cps), while the more expensive daisy wheel printers print 60 to 80 cps. You will find daisy wheel printers wherever letter-quality printer output is required.

The most popular printer used in the microcomputer environment is the dot-matrix printer. Dot-matrix printers do not print a solid character. Instead each character is constructed from many small dots. Usually, a 7 by 5 matrix of overlapping dots is used to create a character. The print head contains a vertical column of pins. These pins are used to strike the appropriate dots to create the required character. The pins of the print head can quickly bang out a pattern of dots; unlike the daisy wheel printer, no rotating head is required. This greatly increases the print rate, to 140 to 160 cps. But because the representation of each letter is composed of many small dots, the print quality of most dot-matrix printers is considered quite low. A method used to greatly improve the appearance of dot-matrix characters is to print each character twice, offset by a minute distance. This improves the appearance of the characters but at the sacrifice of print speed.

Another advantage of dot-matrix printers is that they are not limited to standard letters and numbers. Unlike the daisy wheel printer, which must have multiple print wheels to create different sets of characters, an infinite number of patterns can be created with a dot-matrix printer. Therefore, dot-matrix printers can output letters, numerals, standard symbols, and graphics characters. The same dot-matrix printer can print in many different languages. The final advantage of dot-matrix printers is price. A top-of-the-line dot-matrix printer costs less than half the price of a comparable daisy wheel printer.

The printers that we have just examined are called *impact printers* because the character is created by impacting a head or pin against an ink ribbon and onto paper. There are many different methods of nonimpact printing. The *laser printer* is used in environments where letter quality and speed are required. A complex process uses a laser to produce high-quality characters up to the rate of 200 ppm (pages per minute).

In the micro world, laser printers are becoming extremely popular to support a new activity called *desktop publishing*. Instead of sending user's manuals and company bulletins to a printer to be *typeset*, a person can use a laser printer and appropriate page composition software to produce typeset-quality documents. The laser printers employed in the micro world cost between $1800 and $4000. They have the appearance of desktop photocopy machines and typically produce 8 to 12 ppm.

Thermographic Printing

Thermographic printing is an older technology that uses a head implanted with a heating element and special heat-sensitive paper. A character is essentially burned onto the paper. *Ink-jet printing* is a new technology that is in competition with conventional dot-matrix printers. Charged drops of ink are fired at the paper, creating a dot-matrix character. Ink-jet printers are extremely quick and quiet, and the print quality is consistent because there is no ribbon wear out.

The Mouse and Digitizer Pad

The mouse and digitizer pad are popular forms of computer input devices. A *mouse* is a small box the size of a deck of cards that is used to control the movement of a cursor. The mouse sits on the desk top next to the micro. The physical movement of the mouse is translated into an electronic signal that moves the cursor on the computer's display. The mouse is equipped with one or more buttons that can be used to issue commands to the computer. Mice are useful in word processing, selecting options from computer menus, and for using computers as electronic paint screens. Mice come in many different forms, but *mechanical mice* are the most popular. On the bottom of the mechanical mouse is a round ball that rests on the table top. As the mouse is moved, the ball also moves. This mechanical movement is used to drive vertical and horizontal gears. The output of these gears is converted into horizontal and vertical electronics signals that move the cursor.

Mice are too clumsy to produce high-quality artwork. *Digitizer pads* are used to enter detailed, high-resolution graphics images into a computer. These pads appear to resemble a normal pen and tablet. A typical digitizing pad is constructed with a grid of hundreds of wires. A *stylus* with a magnetic coil in its tip is used. As the stylus is pulled across the pad, the motion is sensed and converted into an electronic signal that positions the cursor.

1.5 COMPUTERS AND COMMUNICATIONS

Computers do not exist as isolated entities. It is important for computers to be able to communicate with terminals and other computers. Consider the following example. A salesperson for a small company is on a sales trip. The current inventory, which is stored in mass memory of the computer in the home office, must be checked and an order must be placed.

The odds are that wherever this salesperson is, there is also a telephone. Communicating directly with a computer can not be done over an ordinary telephone line. Telephone lines have too much capacitance and resistance to send high-speed digital signals for any appreciable distance. A device called a modem is used to solve this problem. The *modem (MODulator-DEModulator)* takes the digital signal from the terminal's communications I/O part and modulates it onto a carrier. The newly created analog signal can easily be sent over the telephone line. At the other end of the phone line, another modem is used to demodulate the analog signal and recapture the original digital information. In this manner terminals and computers can communicate over great distances. The modem transmits data from the terminal to the computer and receives data from the remote computer, so it is both an input and an output device. With a modem and a two-wire telephone line one can have inventories checked, orders placed, applications programs written and run, remote devices controlled, and information exchanged.

Communication programs are available that enable a microcomputer to emulate an RS-232 terminal. With a microcomputer or terminal and a modem, one can access information networks that have stock reports, news stories from hundreds of sources, on-line research libraries, technical computer users' groups, and general-purpose communications bulletin boards, all of which are available at a reasonable hourly rate. Teleprocessing is one of the most exciting and fastest growing of all computer fields.

IMPORTANT CONCEPTS OF CHAPTER 1

- Computers are usually classified into three groups: mainframe, mini, or micro.
- Mainframe computers are employed in environments where tremendous amounts of data must be stored and manipulated.
- Minicomputers are used to process moderate amounts of data in environments where a powerful computer must be dedicated to one purpose or process control.
- Microcomputers usually support only one user. They are employed as personal workstations and support a wide variety of applications
- A Workstation is a new class of supermicro that supports traditional minicomputer operating systems and performance yet it is inexpensive enough to devote to a single user.
- The four major blocks in a computer system are the CPU, memory, input ports, and output ports.
- A microprocessor is a CPU on a chip.
- The CPU contains an ALU, registers, control and timing circuitry, and a microprogrammed instruction set.
- If a memory loses its contents when power is lost, it can be described as volatile. Semiconductor RAM is an example of volatile memory.
- The term *on-line* describes a memory device that is fast enough not to diminish severely CPU performance. Floppy and hard disk drives are on-line mass storage devices, whereas magnetic tape is off-line or mass storage backup.
- Microcomputers usually contain RAM, ROM, floppy disk, and often hard disk memory subsystems.
- Bootstrap memory refers to programs in ROM that are executed each time a computer is powered on. After intelligent devices in the system are tested and initialized, the program in bootstrap ROM loads the operating system from the floppy or hard disk drive.
- System RAM is used to hold the resident portion of the operating system, the applications program and data, the system stack, and other system pointers and information.
- Video-RAM holds the image of the video display. Its contents are used to periodically refresh the display.
- Because all mass storage devices are electromechanical, they are much slower than semiconductor RAM.
- Floppy and hard disk drives employ one set of R/W heads for each surface used to store data.

- Floppy disk storage uses flexible, removable floppy disks, typically called *diskettes*.
- The 5¼-in. double-density floppy disk drives on the IBM PC system can hold 320 KB or 360 KB of data.
- The 5¼-in. quad-density floppy disk drive employed on the IBM PC/AT stores 1.2 MB of data.
- The new 3½-in. drive supported on the IBM PC holds 720 KB of data.
- Winchester hard disk drives (called fixed disk drives in IBM nomenclature) have access times of 65 ms to 30 ms. Floppy disk drives are considerably slower; they have access times above 75 ms.
- In theory a hard disk drive can transfer data 20 times faster than a double-density floppy disk drive. In reality, this factor is usually 3 to 8 times the floppy disk transfer rate.
- The R/W heads on floppy disk drives actually touch the surface of the diskette, whereas the heads on a hard disk drive "fly" extremely close but never touch the hard disk platter.
- Because of their limited capacities, floppy disks are not a viable form of mass storage back-up for large Winchester disk drives. Magnetic tape and removable hard disk cartridges are used for that purpose.
- The keyboard and video display are the two most common I/O devices.
- Typical peripherals for microcomputers are a printer and modem. They are connected to the computer system via standard interface ports.
- Daisy wheel and dot-matrix printers are the two most popular printers employed with microcomputers.
- Laser printers are extremely fast and quiet and have high resolution. They are used in the desktop publishing field.
- A microcomputer with a terminal emulation program can be used with a modem to dial up remote computers and access vast data bases throughout the world.

2

THE MICROPROCESSOR AND THREE-BUS ARCHITECTURE

Chapter 1 provided a brief orientation to the major elements of a computer system. In this chapter we study the architecture and instruction set of a "generic" microprocessor. This lays the ground work required to support the detailed analysis of the IBM PC processor system that we undertake in Chapter 4.

2.1 THE GENERIC MICROPROCESSOR

Microprocessor systems are based on the simple, yet powerful, concept of *three-bus architecture*.

Power Requirements

Figure 2.1 depicts a block diagram of a generic microprocessor. Like all electronic devices that contain transistors and other active components, the microprocessor requires DC power and ground. To be compatible with TTL logic, the power requirements of microprocessors are simply +5 V and ground.

Clock Input

A flip-flop is an example of a simple digital device whose operation is synchronized to a clock signal. We can expand this concept of an absolute time reference to a microprocessor system. A microprocessor requires an extremely accurate and stable clock. The clock is the timing reference that synchronizes

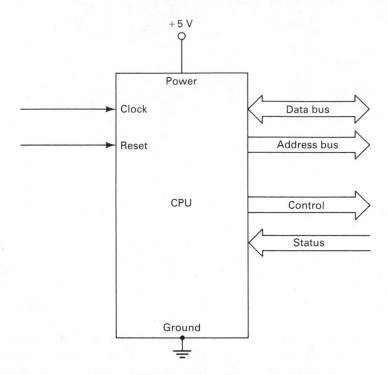

Figure 2.1   A generic microprocessor.

the address and data buses and the control signals. Some microprocessors have an internal oscillator and require only the connection of an external crystal. Other microprocessors require that the clock input be generated with external logic. The clock must meet precise rise- and fall-time specifications. All internal activity within the microprocessor and external memory and I/O accesses are synchronized to the clock.

The clock for the 8088 microprocessor used in the IBM PC is generated by a crystal connected to the 8284 clock generator IC. In Chapter 4 we study the numerous system clock signals generated by the 8284.

To a certain extent, the processing speed of a microprocessor is directly proportional to the frequency of its clock. Thus a particular microprocessor with a 12-MHz clock may appear to run twice as fast as an identical microprocessor with a 6-MHz clock. This may not always be true. Main memory access speed (both RAM and ROM), I/O access, and floppy and hard disk access are other factors that can greatly reduce the overall throughput of a system. If an applications program spends a high percentage of time accessing an extremely slow electromechanical device (floppy disk drive), the system may be described as *I/O bound* because the microprocessor spends most of its time waiting for data to be read from or written to floppy disk. RAM is purely electronic in nature and has no mechanical elements, so its access time is thousands of times faster than those of floppy and hard disks. A system with an abundance of RAM can hold more data in electronic storage, and disk access is minimized, appreciably increasing overall system throughput.

Reset Input

When a system is energized, the microprocessor automatically outputs a specified address and fetches an instruction. This begins the process of *booting* the system. From the moment that power is applied, it takes a finite length of time before all the components are "awake" and ready to function. How does the microprocessor know when all the components in the system are ready and that the first memory access and instruction fetch can occur? Every microprocessor has a reset input. When this input is at an active level, the microprocessor is held in a *reset state* and will not perform any internal or external functions. Figure 2.2 illustrates a simple reset circuit.

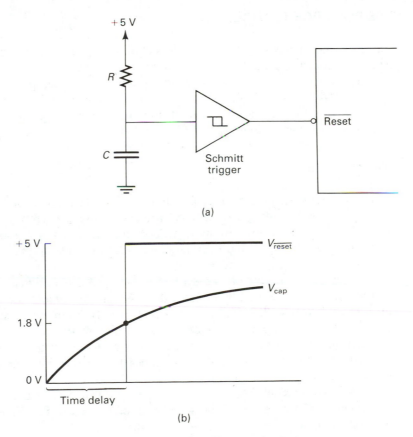

Figure 2.2   R/C reset circuit.

Figure 2.2(a) shows an R/C voltage divider that drives a Schmitt trigger noninverting buffer. As you remember from basic DC theory, when power is first applied to the circuit in Figure 2.2, the capacitor will appear to be a short to ground and the entire 5 V will be dropped across the resistor. After a short period the voltage on the capacitor will increase to 1.8 V—the upper threshold voltage on a TTL Schmitt trigger. This will cause the reset input to go to an inactive logic 1 level.

Figure 2.2(b) is a graph of the voltage across the capacitor plotted against the output of the Schmitt trigger. Typically, the reset delay on microprocessor systems is 100 to 500 ms. This ensures that all devices will be up and running when the microprocessor is taken out of a reset state and attempts its first memory access. If the reset power-on delay is too short, the microprocessor will fetch an incorrect instruction from memory and the system will behave in a random manner.

2.2 THREE-BUS ARCHITECTURE

In electronics a *bus* is defined as a collection of signals that are grouped by similar function. Figure 2.1 indicates that the microprocessor has three distinct busses: data bus, address bus, and control/status bus. A microprocessor can be described as *the master of the bus system*. It coordinates and synchronizes the circuit action for the entire system. It uses the system busses to retrieve and execute stored instructions.

The Data Bus

Microprocessors spend a great deal of time reading instructions and data from memory and writing data into memory. The data bus on a microprocessor must be bidirectional; data flows from the memory into the microprocessor during a read operation and from the microprocessor into memory during a write operation.

Microprocessors are often described as *n-bit*, where *n* designates the width of the data bus. The Intel 8085 and Zilog Z80 are examples of 8-bit microprocessors. The Intel 8086 and Motorola 68000 are 16-bit microprocessors, and the Intel 80386 and Motorola 68020 are 32-bit microprocessors. Because a 16-bit microprocessor fetches twice as much data each time it accesses memory as does its 8-bit counterpart, it makes sense that the 16-bit microprocessor processes data at a much higher rate.

We have now discovered two important hardware factors that govern the performance of a microprocessor—the width of its data bus and the speed of the system clock.

The Address Bus

The address bus is output only. The microprocessor is the master of the bus system. It outputs the address of the next instruction or the memory location where a particular byte of data resides. Like the data bus, address buses also vary in width. The 8085 and Z-80 that we have described as 8-bit micro-processors both have address buses that are 16 bits wide. Thus they can address 2^{16}, or 65,536, unique memory locations.

To avoid suffering under such ungainly numbers, the concept of a *K of memory* was developed. 1K of memory is equal to 2^{10}, or 1024 bytes of memory. Therefore, 65,536 is described as 64K. With a 20-bit address bus, the 8088 microprocessor used in the IBM PC can address 1 MB ($2^{20} = 1,048,576$) of memory.

Because of the desire to limit the number of pins on IC packages, many microprocessors multiplex the address and data buses, which means at the beginning of a memory access cycle, an address appears on the address/data bus. External TTL flip-flops latch the memory address; for the remainder of the memory-access cycle, the address/data bus will be used to input or output data.

In Chapter 4 we examine how the 8088's multiplexed address/data bus is demultiplexed with the aid of a special control signal and transparent TTL latches to create a 20-bit address bus and an 8-bit data bus.

Control/Status Bus

A control line governs the interaction between the microprocessor and external devices such as memory or I/O ports. Control lines are output only. Status lines are input only. The microprocessor uses status lines to monitor the state of devices and sense the occurrence of important events. Microprocessors typically have a control/status bus that is 6 to 12 bits wide.

To understand fully the concepts of three-bus architecture, let's examine the timing diagrams of simple read and write operations. Figure 2.3(a) describes three typical control lines that are used to coordinate the memory subsystem with the operation of the microprocessor. The overbars on $\overline{RD}$, $\overline{WR}$, and $\overline{MEMRQ}$ indicate that these signals are active when they are at logic 0 levels. Two negative-logic OR gates are used to decode the read ($\overline{RD}$), write ($\overline{WR}$), and memory request ($\overline{MEMRQ}$) into memory-read ($\overline{MEMRD}$) and memory-write ($\overline{MEMWR}$) commands.

Figure 2.3(b) describes a memory-read operation. The data output of the memory device is a three-state output structure. This structure stays in a *high-impedance state* until the microprocessor initiates a memory-read or memory-write operation.

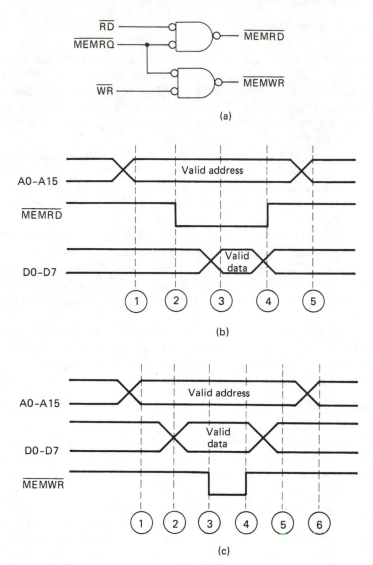

Figure 2.3   Operation of control lines in memory access.

Event 1. The microprocessor outputs the address of the memory location that it wishes to read.

Event 2. The $\overline{\text{MEMRD}}$ signal goes to an active-low level. This indicates to the memory IC that it should place the byte of data residing at the specified location onto the data bus.

Event 3. After a short delay (due to the operation of address decoder ICs and internal delays within the memory IC) the data is valid on the data bus. The microprocessor stores this byte in a register.

Event 4. The microprocessor returns $\overline{RD}$ and $\overline{MEMRQ}$ to inactive logic 1 levels. This results in $\overline{MEMRD}$ returning to an inactive level, and the memory will return its output lines to a high-impedance level.

Event 5. The microprocessor removes the address from the address bus. This completes the memory-read operation.

You may not be thoroughly familiar with the concept of the high-impedance output. Most digital devices output either a logic 0 or logic 1 level. When the outputs of conventional digital devices are tied together, they will battle each other, resulting in an undefined voltage level. The three-state output was developed to support bus systems where many outputs must be connected together. Figure 2.4 illustrates a small bus system that allows a decoder to select one of four digits to be displayed on a seven-segment LED.

U1 through U4 are called *three-state buffers*. Notice that their outputs are tied together and are driving the inputs of a seven-segment decoder/driver IC. From the discussion in the previous paragraph, we must assume that U1 through U4 have three-state outputs. At the bottom of each of these ICs is an input labeled $\overline{G}$. G stands for *gate* but is most often called the *enable*.

From your knowledge of digital electronics you should know that U5 is a 1-of-4 decoder. The 2-bit address placed on inputs A and B will select which of the four outputs will go active-low while the other three outputs are held at logic 1 levels. This logic 0 will be applied to one of the enable inputs of U1 through U4. This will cause the selected device to pass the four signals on its inputs to its outputs and drive the *BCD* (*binary coded decimal*) inputs of the seven-segment decoder/driver.

The *truth table* of a three-state noninverting buffer is illustrated at the bottom of Figure 2.4. When the enable input is active, the logic level on the input of each buffer will pass to the output. When the enable goes to an inactive-high level, the four outputs will go a high impedance state (usually termed *high-z*, where z stands for impedance.) The high-z output is symbolized by an open switch.

In a microprocessor system the data inputs and outputs of the RAMs are tied together to form the data bus. As you can now appreciate, the data outputs of these RAM chips must be capable of going to a high-z output level. In fact, high-z is the level that the outputs of the memory ICs will maintain unless explicitly selected for a read or write operation by the microprocessor. In a later section we examine a RAM subsystem and how each chip is selected by the microprocessor.

In Figure 2.3(c) we see the timing diagram for a memory write operation.

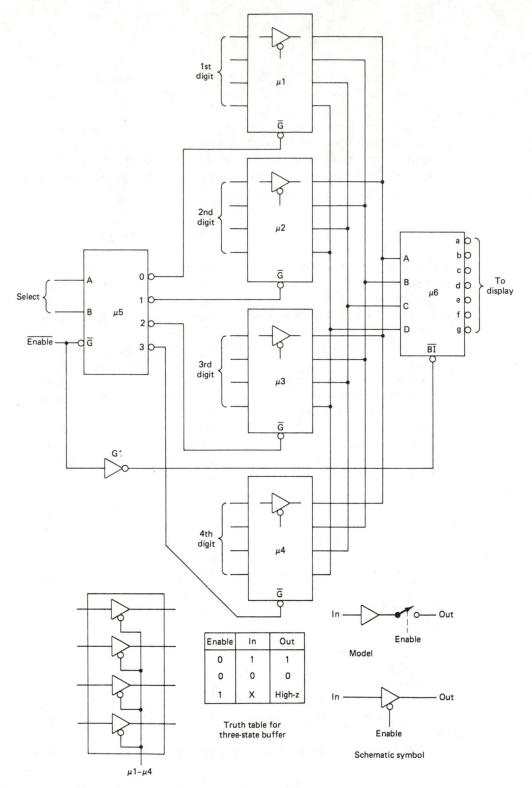

Figure 2.4 Three-state bus system.

Event 1. The microprocessor outputs the address of the memory location where the data byte is to be stored.

Event 2. The microprocessor then places the byte of data onto the data bus.

Event 3. The $\overline{\text{MEMWR}}$ signal is brought to an active-low level. The memory device now transfers the byte of information residing on the data bus into the storage location pointed at by the contents of the address bus.

Event 4. $\overline{\text{MEMWR}}$ must be held active for a minimum specified interval. It is then returned to an inactive level.

Event 5. The microprocessor removes the byte of data from the data bus.

Event 6. The microprocessor finally removes the address from the address bus.

Although these examples of memory read and write operations have been greatly simplified, they give extremely valuable insight of the operation of three-bus architecture.

2.3 A SIMPLE 8K RAM SYSTEM

The previous section illustrated how the bus systems of the microprocessor are used in simple memory-read and-write operations. Figure 2.5 is the block diagram of an elementary 8K memory system. The 6116 RAM has 2K unique storage locations, each capable of holding 1 byte of data. The 8 data input and output pins are labeled I/O1 through I/O8. To address the 2K unique locations requires 11 address lines ($2^{11} = 2K$). The pin labeled $\overline{OE}$ is the *output enable*. It is taken to a logic 0 level to enable the RAM to be read. $\overline{WE}$ (*write enable*) must be taken active-low to write data into the RAM.

Although it may not be entirely clear from the figure, all 8 data lines and the first 11 address lines of the microprocessor are in parallel with the I/O and address lines of the four RAMs. At the bottom of each RAM is a pin labeled $\overline{CS}$. $\overline{CS}$ stands for *chip select*; a RAM will not respond to R/W control signals from the microprocessor unless its $\overline{CS}$ is taken to an active-low level. In Figure 2.5 this is accomplished by the 74LS138 1-of-8 decoder, which is actually functioning as a 1-of-4 decoder because the C input is grounded.

How does the system function? Remember that in initiating a memory access the first action of the microprocessor is to output an address. The lower 11 bits of the address bus are connected to the address inputs of the four RAMs. The upper five address bits and $\overline{\text{MEMRQ}}$ are used in conjunction with the three switches (Sw.1 through Sw.3) and the 74LS85 magnitude comparator to place the 8K RAM subsystem into one of eight locations within the 64K addressing space of the microprocessor.

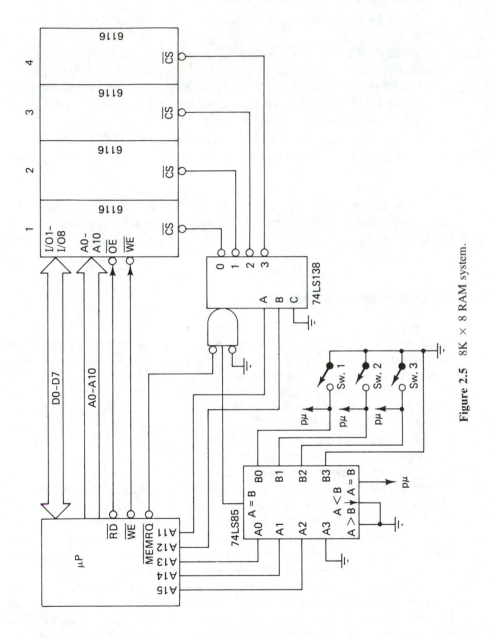

Figure 2.5 8K × 8 RAM system.

2.4 FUNCTIONS OF THE CONTROL/STATUS BUS

In addition to memory access, the control/status bus provides many other important functions. Figure 2.6 illustrates an expanded version of the control/status bus on the generic microprocessor.

Memory and I/O Control

The basic block diagram of a computer system indicates that the CPU must communicate with I/O ports and memory. Microprocessors reference I/O ports in one of two ways. The most natural method is to treat I/O ports as if they were no different than memory locations. A block of memory addresses are simply set aside and reserved for I/O ports. This is called *memory-mapped I/O*. The Motorola family of microprocessors employs memory-mapped I/O.

The second method clears the clutter and possible confusion that results in mixing memory and I/O ports. A control line on the microprocessor is used to distinguish between memory and I/O operations. Figure 2.7 shows how the IO/$\overline{\text{M}}$, $\overline{\text{WR}}$, and $\overline{\text{RD}}$ control lines are decoded to provide memory and I/O command outputs. Compare this with Figure 2.3(a), which has only memory-read and memory-write decoded outputs.

When the microprocessor accesses a memory or I/O device that is too slow to respond within the period of the normal read or write cycle, external

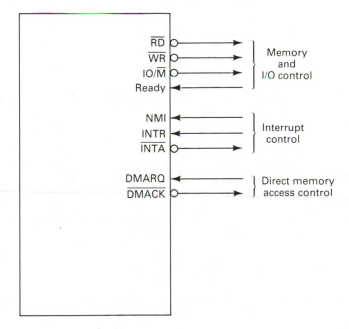

Figure 2.6   Typical control/status functions.

IO/$\overline{\text{M}}$	$\overline{\text{WR}}$	$\overline{\text{RD}}$	Action
0	1	0	Memory read
0	0	1	Memory write
1	1	0	I/O read
1	0	1	I/O write
X	0	0	Illegal
X	1	1	No memory or I/O access

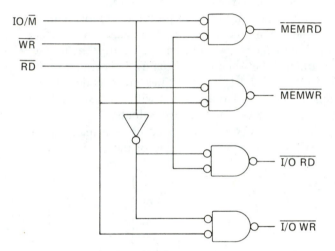

Figure 2.7   Decoding memory and I/O control outputs.

circuitry will take the *ready input* of the microprocessor to an inactive level. The microprocessor marks time by holding the signals on the address, data, and control buses stable until the ready line returns to an active level. The memory or I/O access can then be completed. In Chapter 4 we see how the ready input on the 8088 microprocessor system functions.

Interrupts and Direct Memory Access

Notice that the two remaining groups of control/status lines are labeled *interrupt control* and *direct memory access control*. Later in this chapter we discuss how these important functions are utilized by the microprocessor.

2.5 THE GENERALIZED INTERNAL ARCHITECTURE OF THE MICROPROCESSOR

We know that a CPU contains an ALU, registers, and control and timing circuitry. Let's examine these groups as they appear within a microprocessor.

The Accumulator

Every CPU contains a special register called an accumulator. The accumulator is the location where the result of arithmetic and logical operations are automatically stored. The accumulator is always the center of action. Some microprocessors have two accumulators. With these microprocessors it is the programmer's responsibility to designate which accumulator will be used.

General-Purpose Registers

General-purposes registers are not dedicated to a specific function (as is the accumulator). They are used temporarily to hold operands and other data that the CPU currently requires. Some microprocessors have many general-purposes registers, whereas others do not have any and must rely on RAM to hold temporary operands and data. The major advantage of having onboard general-purpose registers is that they have a much faster access time than external RAM.

Dedicated CPU Registers

CPUs also have many registers that are not used to hold temporary operands or general-purpose data. These registers are dedicated to store specific types of information that the microprocessor may require during the execution of an instruction. Consider the following dedicated registers that appear in every microprocessor.

Flag register.   The flag register is really a collection of independent flip-flops. Each flip-flop is a flag that reflects the current state of an operational parameter of the microprocessor. A typical flag is the *carry flag*. Assume that all the registers in a microprocessor are byte-wide (8 bits). If the addition of two 8-bit binary numbers results in a sum that is greater than 8 bits, the sum placed into the accumulator will be 256 less than the true value.

$$
\begin{array}{ll}
1111\ 0000 & (240) \\
+\ 0001\ 0011 & (19) \\
\hline
(1)0000\ 0011 & (259)
\end{array}
$$

The carry generated in this addition cannot fit into the accumulator. The accumulator indicates that the result of the addition is 3 when the actual sum is really 259. The carry flag is set to indicate an operation that results in a carry and is reset to indicate an operation that does not generate a carry. The status of the carry flag can be tested in a program; in the case of this simple addition example, if the carry flag is set, the program may branch to an error routine.

That is an example of how the flip-flops in the flag register are used to indicate the operational status of the microprocessor after the completion of each instruction. For that reason, flag registers are often called *status* or *condition code* registers. It is important to remember that the microprocessor automatically sets or clears the flags, giving the program a means of making intelligent decisions.

Other typical flags indicate whether the result of an operation is 0 (the *zero flag*), the arithmetic sign of the number in the accumulator (*sign flag*), and if the number of logical 1s in the accumulator is an odd or even number (the *parity flag*).

Stack pointer.   Often, microprocessors are in the middle of performing one job when they are suddenly required to suspend execution to service a second, higher-priority task. At that time the CPU registers will contain information that is important to the first task. This information must be saved in RAM before the microprocessor can began servicing the second task. After execution of the second task is complete, the microprocessor will read the information from RAM back into the proper CPU registers, and execution of the first task can continue. A dedicated register is used to simplify the operation of *preserving the CPU environment*. It is called the *stack pointer*.

A portion of RAM is always reserved to store CPU registers temporarily. This area of memory is called *the stack*. The stack register holds the address of the next available memory location in the stack. Using the current contents of the stack pointer as an address, the microprocessor can easily access the stack. The address stored in the stack pointer is automatically updated each time the stack is accessed for a read or write operation. One of the first steps in any program is to load the stack pointer with the first address in the RAM stack. We will learn more about the stack later in this chapter.

Program counter.   The program counter, like the stack pointer, is used to hold an address. The contents of the program counter always point to the memory location of the next instruction or data byte. The program counter is automatically incremented after each instruction or data byte is *fetched* from memory.

Instruction register.   When a microprocessor fetches a byte of data from memory that is to be interpreted as an instruction, it places this *op-code* (short for operation code) into the instruction register.

Temporary registers.   The CPU also contains many registers that are used by the microprocessor to store data, addresses, and operands for short periods of time. These registers are not available to the programmer.

Address and Data Buffers

The microprocessor also contains a unidirectional address bus buffer and a bidirectional data bus buffer. These buffers isolate the internal bus system of the microprocessor from the external computer system bus and provide enough current gain to drive a few LS TTL inputs. Almost all microprocessor systems also use external TTL buffers. As you are aware, TTL buffers are designed to drive the large number of inputs that are connected to the system bus.

2.6 SERVICING I/O DEVICES: POLLING AND INTERRUPTS

In Figure 2.6 we saw a group of control/status lines called interrupt control. Consider a microprocessor system that is used to monitor many important parameters in an automobile: oil pressure, radiator temperature, and brake and clutch fluid levels. A pressure sensor is used to monitor the oil pressure; if the oil pressure falls below a certain level, the output of the pressure sensor goes to an active logic 0 level. The temperature sensor monitoring the radiator and the float sensors monitoring the brake and clutch fluid levels operate in a similar manner. Devices in the "outside" world are interfaced to the CPU via I/O ports. Assume that the output of each sensor drives an input port connected to the CPU.

How is the CPU going to know when the output of a particular sensor has switched to an active level? There are two methods that a microprocessor can use to monitor input ports. The first method uses a program that periodically checks the value on each of the four input ports. If the microprocessor detects an active level, it sets the appropriate alarm LED on the car's dashboard. Periodically, this program may first check the value on the pressure sensor input and determine if the oil sensor LED should be illuminated. It then checks the status of the remaining input ports in a similar manner. Notice that the program does all the work; the input ports do not indicate to the microprocessor that a sensor output has gone to an active level. The method of using a program to periodic interrogate the status of input devices is called *polling*. The term *poll* is taken from its common usage as the process of questioning people to obtain information. Therefore, a program that periodically queries the status of input devices is called a *polling program.*

The action of polling input devices is like that of a telephone with no bell; every minute or so, you have to lift the receiver and ask if there is anyone on the line. To ask a person to poll the status of a telephone is unreasonable. But if a computer is not otherwise occupied and the device requiring service can afford to wait, polling is a good, simple method of monitoring the status of input devices.

If polling is like having a telephone with no bell, is there a method of monitoring input devices analogous to having a bell on a telephone? The answer is yes; the method is called an *interrupt*. Let's continue with the telephone analogy. You are busy performing an important task, such as reading a book or doing your math homework, when the telephone rings. The first thing you must decide is whether you want to bother answering the telephone. (You could always ignore it and risk missing an important call.) If you decide to answer the phone, you must stop what you are doing and mark your place in the book or write down the intermediate result of a math problem. After you have finished the conversation, you must hang up the phone and resume your reading or math homework. (Remember that you placed a bookmark or wrote down an intermediate answer so that you can continue at the place where you were interrupted.)

The major difference between a telephone without a bell (polling) and one with a bell (interrupts) is that the telephone with a bell indicates to you when a caller is on the line. In the same manner, if an input device signals to the microprocessor whenever it has an active input level, it is "ringing a bell" that will gain the microprocessor's attention. Like a person, the microprocessor can choose to ignore the input device or stop what it is currently doing (and, of course, place bookmarks and record intermediate results) and service the input device.

Microprocessor systems use both polling and interrupts to interface with input devices. The most important input devices are connected to interrupt inputs on the microprocessor. They immediately gain the microprocessor's attention. Other devices that are less critical wait their turns to be polled by the microprocessor.

Sometimes a combination of polling and interrupts is used. The interrupt request outputs of many devices can be ORed together and drive a single interrupt request input on a microprocessor. When the microprocessor senses the interrupt, it can then poll each device to establish which one requested service.

The interrupt input labeled *NMI* in Figure 2.6 is the *nonmaskable interrupt*. The NMI cannot be ignored (i.e., masked) by the microprocessor. It is used to signal critical or catastrophic events such as the pressure on a boiler going critical or an AC power failure. After receiving an active NMI, the microprocessor will finish its currently executing instruction and branch to a special location in memory that contains the program to manage the critical interrupt, which in the case of the boiler should disable the heating unit and set off an alarm.

The *INTR* interrupt pin is the standard maskable interrupt. Under program control the microprocessor can be commanded to either acknowledge active levels on this input or ignore (i.e., mask) them. A program will mask interrupts when it is entering a time-critical routine and must not be interrupted by any but the most urgent interrupt requests.

When the INTR input goes active, the microprocessor finishes executing its current instruction and brings the $\overline{INTA}$ (*interrupt acknowledge*) output to an active-low level. This indicates to the interrupting device that it must identify itself so that the microprocessor will execute the appropriate *service routine*. Some microprocessors expect the interrupting device to provide the op-code of a special 1-byte instruction that indirectly points to the address of the appropriate service routine. Other microprocessors may require that the interrupting device provide the actual address of the interrupt routine. In Chapter 5 we examine the sophisticated manner in which the IBM PC manages interrupts.

2.7 DIRECT MEMORY ACCESS

Microprocessors are optimized to access system RAM on a byte-by-byte basis. Because of this byte orientation, they are intolerably slow at moving large blocks of data between RAM and mass storage. Most microprocessors have two pins that are used to enable a *direct memory access controller* (DMAC) to take command of the bus system. An input typically called *hold* or *bus request* is driven by the DMAC to indicate its intention to take control of the bus system. The microprocessor will finish executing its current instruction, take its data, address, and control buses to high-z output levels, and then acknowledge the DMA request by taking an output called *hold acknowledge* or *bus acknowledge* to an active level.

Because the microprocessor has taken its bus outputs to a high impedance state, the external bus master (the DMAC) can now take control of the data, address, and control/status bus to perform highly efficient block transfers (memory read and write operations) directly between RAM and mass storage.

When the DMAC has completed the block move, it will take the hold or bus request input to an inactive level. The microprocessor will respond by taking the DMA acknowledge output to an inactive level, recover control of the bus system, and resume normal processing activities.

The most important aspect to understand about DMA is that it is a process designed to move large blocks of data at a very high rate. Because the microprocessor is not capable of such high-speed block performance, a DMAC must gain control of the bus system, quickly execute its chore, and then pass control back to the microprocessor. In Chapter 5 we examine the DMAC employed by the IBM PC and the different system functions supported by this block-processing capability.

2.8 GENERALIZED INSTRUCTION SET

Digital circuitry "thinks" in binary at logic 0 and logic 1 levels. When a CPU fetches an instruction from memory, the instruction is in the form of binary data. After the CPU decodes the byte in its internal microinstruction ROM, the instruction can be executed. It is extremely difficult for human beings to memorize and recognize the patterns of 1s and 0s that constitute an instruction.

For that reason, each instruction is available in two forms. The first form is the sequence of 1s and 0s that the microprocessor can understand. It is called *machine language*. The second form is a three- to five-letter *instruction mnemonic*. A mnemonic is a symbolic name that is assigned to each microprocessor instruction. It helps us understand what the instruction actually does. Mnemonics make much more sense than do a string of 1s and 0s. This mnemonic form of instructions is called *assembly language*.

All microprocessors have the same basic instruction set, but each uses a different set of mnemonics. Once you understand one instruction set, others are easy to learn. This section describes basic instructions that are common to all microprocessors.

Data Transfer Instructions

The most basic group of microprocessor instructions contains *data transfer instructions*. Data is stored in both CPU registers and RAM. Data transfer instructions accommodate the movement of data from register to register, register to memory, or memory to register. The mnemonics for these instructions are often *MOV* (move) or *LD* (load). The MOV or LD instruction copies the contents of one register or memory location (called the *source*) to another register or memory location (called the *destination*).

There are MOV and LD operations that involve *immediate data*, as opposed to data already stored in a register or memory. If you want to load a register with an explicit byte of data (for example, load the accumulator with C4H), the data is called immediate because the source of the data is not another register or memory location; rather, it immediately follows the instruction in memory. An instruction that uses immediate data must specify the actual data and the destination of the data.

Arithmetic Instructions

You have learned that the ALU in a CPU can perform basic arithmetic and logic functions. All microprocessors can perform simple binary addition and subtraction. If an addition results in a carry or a subtraction in a borrow, the carry flag is set to indicate a potential program error. There are special addition and subtraction instructions that are used to add or subtract strings of numbers that must manipulate carries or borrows. The result of an addition or subtraction is stored automatically in the accumulator.

The operation of adding or subtracting 1 is so common that *increment* and *decrement* instructions are included in every instruction set. This enables registers to be used as event counters.

Only advanced microprocessors have explicit multiplication and division instructions. Simple microprocessors perform multiplication and division in-directly. What does it mean to multiply a binary number by 2? Consider the following example:

$$(a) \ 0001 \ 0000 \rightarrow (b) \ 0010 \ 0000 \rightarrow (c) \ 0100 \ 0000$$
$$(16) \qquad\qquad (32) \qquad\qquad (64)$$

The byte in (a) is equivalent to decimal 16. If we shift the byte once to the left and fill in the least significant bit (LSB) with 0, the result is decimal 32. If we shift the byte in (b) once to the left and fill the LSB with 0, the result is 64. We can now derive the simple rule that links *logical shifts* with multiplication:

To multiply a binary number by 2, shift it once to the left, inserting a 0 into the LSB. This operation is called an *arithmetic-shift-left*.

Because division is the inverse of multiplication we can state:

To divide a binary number by 2, shift of once to the right, inserting a 0 into the most significant bit (MSB). This operation is called an *arithmetic-shift-right*.

What is the process of multiplying a number by 6? Two consecutive arithmetic-shift-left operations multiply the number by 4. Another arithmetic-shift-left would multiply the number by 8. The question is, How do we handle multiplications that are not powers of 2? Consecutive addition is the basic definition of multiplication. Applying that thought to the problem of multiplying a number by 6, we can see that after two arithmetic-shift-left operations, we should perform two consecutive additions. This results in a times-6 operation.

For example, multiply the number 8 (0000 1000) by 6 (0000 0110).

(a) Arithmetic-shift-left: 0000 1000 → 0001 0000 (16)
(b) Arithmetic-shift-left: 0001 0000 → 0010 0000 (32)
(c) Add 8: 0010 0000 + 0010 1000 → 0010 1000 (40)
(d) Add 8: 0010 1000 + 0000 1000 → 0011 0000 (48)

$$0000 \ 1000 \times 0000 \ 0110 = 0011 \ 0000$$

Of course, the actual assembly language program would be much more com-plicated than in the preceding example. The product would have to be checked after each operation to ensure that the accumulator does not overflow to create a carry. Also, the problem of negative numbers has to addressed. What is important now is that you understand the concept of arithmetic-shift-left and arithmetic-shift-right operations.

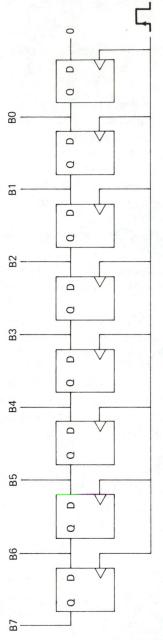

Figure 2.8 Hardware equivalent of arithmetic shift-left instruction.

Shift and Rotate Operations

The preceding example illustrated the arithmetic-shift-left and shift-right instructions. Notice that in an arithmetic-shift-left instruction, the MSB is lost; it is essentially shifted off the end of the register. The same is true for the LSB in an arithmetic-shift-right operation. The hardware analogy of an arithmetic-shift-left instruction is illustrated in Figure 2.8 as an 8-bit serial-in/parallel-out shift register. The data input of the LSB is tied to a logic 0 level. After the clock pulse, all the data have shifted to the left by 1 bit. The data that was in the MSB is lost.

Microprocessor instruction sets also contain *rotate instructions*. The difference between shift and rotate instructions is quite simple: If the output of the MSB flip-flop (data bit 7) is tied to the D input of the LSB flip-flop, the hardware configuration will execute a rotate-left instruction on each positive edge of the clock. No bits are lost as a result of a rotate instruction. They are merely moved to a different flip-flop in the storage register. Rotate instructions are used in programs for two major purposes: as a method of moving a data bit to affect a flag in the status register and to control hardware devices, such as the four-phase digital *stepper motors* that control the position of the R/W heads in a floppy disk drive.

Logical Instructions

The Boolean functions AND, OR, XOR, and NOT can also be performed under program control. Consider an instruction that tells the ALU to AND the contents of two registers: the accumulator and a register that we will call register B. The result will be placed in the accumulator, overwriting the original operand, and the contents of the B register will not be affected. Each bit in the accumulator is ANDed with the same data bit in the B register. This instruction is the software equivalent of the eight two-input AND gates pictured in Figure 2.9. The same method is used to perform the OR and XOR functions. The invert function requires only a single operand. Suppose that we wanted to NAND together the contents of the accumulator and B register in Figure 2.8. After the result of the AND operation is placed into the accumulator, the contents of the accumulator can then be complemented, and the NAND function is complete.

The Boolean operations in microprocessor instruction sets are used in the same manner as hardware AND, OR, and XOR gates and inverters. A microprocessor can be made to accomplish any function with a program that can be performed with digital hardware.

Jump and Branch Instructions

Consider the general flowchart of a microprocessor system that is used to control the heating and air-conditioning units in a house (Figure 2.10). The control

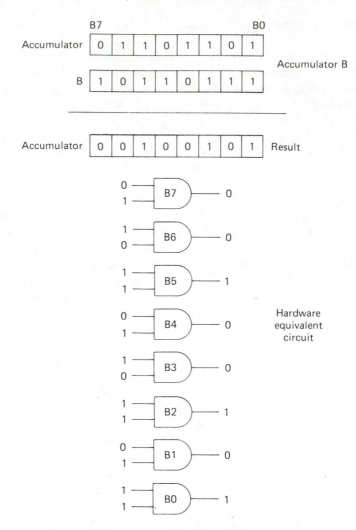

Figure 2.9 Hardware equivalent of AND instruction.

sequence is initiated when the microprocessor reads the output of the temperature *analog-to-digital (A/D) converter* and stores this value in a CPU register. If the temperature is greater than 78°, the microprocessor jumps to a subroutine that engages the air conditioner. If the temperature is less than or equal to 78°, the microprocessor executes the next sequential instruction. This instruction checks to see if the temperature is less than 65°. If the condition is true, the micro-processor jumps to a subroutine that engages the heater.

The different paths of the flowchart intersect at the box labeled as a 3-min delay. After 3 min, enough time has passed for the heater or air conditioner

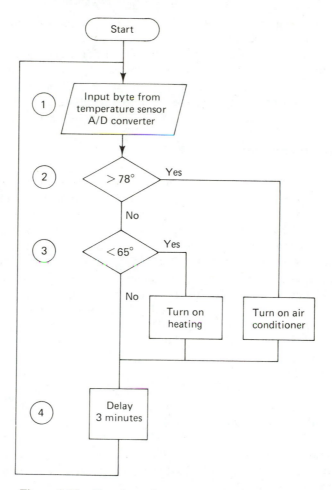

Figure 2.10 Flowchart of heater/air conditioner program.

to affect the temperature. The program execution resumes with another temperature sample.

The microprocessor is considered to be an intelligent device because it can respond to as many different conditions as the program allows. Normally, a microprocessor executes a program in a sequential manner. Figure 2.10 demonstrates a situation where the execution of a program is based on the condition of certain parameters. The variable parameter in this example is temperature.

Jump and branch instructions are used to change the normal sequential execution of a program. They are often used in conjunction with the flag register to test for certain conditions. *Jump instructions* place the address of the next instruction to be executed into the program counter of the microprocessor. Jump instructions are said to use *absolute addressing*, because they provide a completely new address.

Branch instructions are similar to jump instructions except that they add a value to the contents of the program counter. This value, called an *offset*, also changes the sequence of a program's execution. Because a positive or negative offset is added to the current contents of the program counter, the operation is said to be *relative* to the program counter.

Calls and Returns

Microprocessor programs are usually constructed from many small subprograms that are called *subroutines*. Each subroutine accomplishes a small, discrete task. Programs written as a collection of subroutines are much easier to debug and modify. Subroutines can be tested as individual units. After each subroutine is debugged and running correctly, the subroutines can be strung together to perform a complex operation. This method of programming is called *structured*, or *modular*, programming. Each subroutine is a separate module (a building block) that is used to construct a whole program.

The call instruction is used to invoke a subroutine. When a microprocessor executes a call instruction, two important events occur: (1) The current contents of the program counter are automatically saved (remember that this is the address of the next instruction that would be normally executed), and (2) the address of the subroutine is placed into the program counter. The microprocessor jumps to the first instruction of the subroutine, but unlike the jump instruction, a *return address* has been saved.

The *return* instruction is the last instruction in a subroutine. When the microprocessor sees a return instruction, it places the return address into the program counter. The program then effectively jumps back to the instruction following the original call. For every call instruction, there must be a matching return instruction.

Breaking large programs into many simple subroutines not only eases program writing and testing but also saves memory, because once a subroutine is part of a program, it can be called an unlimited number of times. Figure 2.11 illustrates a block diagram of a program that calls three subroutines. Each subroutine ends with a return statement. Notice that the second subroutine calls yet another subroutine. This practice is called *nesting* subroutines. When the second-level subroutine reaches the return statement, it returns to the subroutine that called it. It is a common practice to have many levels of nested subroutines.

To experienced programmers who have built large libraries of subroutines, creating a new program is little more than tying together the required subroutines.

In Chapter 1 we mentioned the concept of an operating system. An operating system is a large program that is used to help the programmer efficiently interface with the computer hardware. An operating system is really a large collection of subroutines. Each subroutine accomplishes a small task, such as

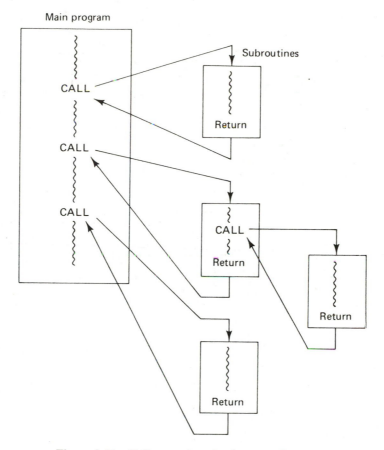

Figure 2.11   Calling a subroutine from a main program.

writing a character to the video display or inputting a character from the key-board. The programmer is allowed to use any of the operating system's sub-routines. It is like having a built-in library of I/O routines that one can use at will.

Maintaining the CPU Working Environment: Stack Operations

We have just stated that microprocessor programs are constructed from many subroutines. If the main program is using the registers to hold important in-formation and a subroutine is called, it may also require the use of the registers. This would result in important data being overwritten and destroyed.

   To ensure that subroutines can have free use of the CPU registers and not destroy important information, a portion of RAM is set aside to store data

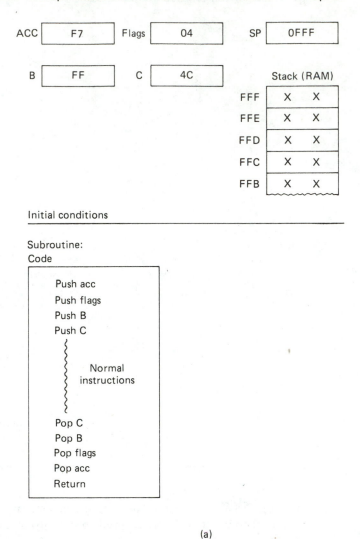

(a)

Figure 2.12 Stack operations.

temporarily. This block of RAM is called the *stack*. You already know that every CPU has a register called the stack pointer. The stack pointer holds an address that points to the next free location in the stack. When data is read from the stack it is said to be *popped off* the stack.

The easiest way to understand the stack is to follow an example that *pushes* data onto the stack and then pops it off, restoring the original CPU environment. Figure 2.12(a) illustrates the initial contents of the accumulator (Acc), flag

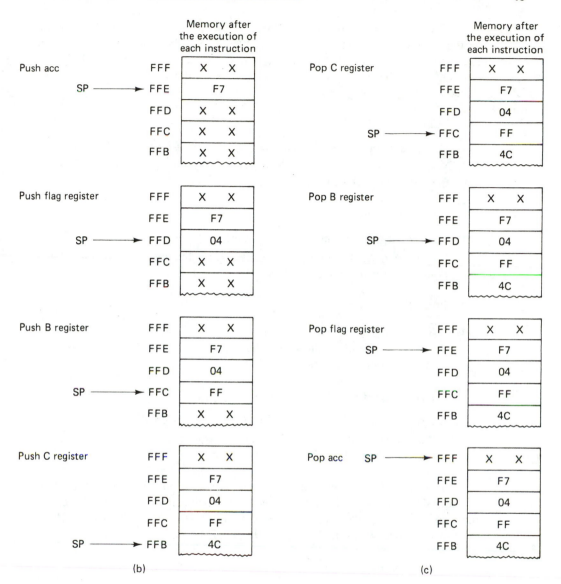

Figure 2.12   Continued.

register, B register, C register, and SP (stack pointer). The B and C registers can be thought of as general-purpose CPU registers. The SP is initialized to OFFFH. The memory location OFFFH is said to be the *top of the stack*. It is the highest memory location in the RAM stack. We are interested in the first five bytes of the stack. The XX denotes an unknown value in a memory.

The subroutine segment in Figure 2.12(a) illustrates saving the contents of the four registers on the stack and then proceeding with the subroutine execution. The last instructions before the return must restore the CPU environment, previous to the subroutine call. That is the function of the pop instructions. Refer to Figure 2.12(b).

Push Acc

1. Decrement the contents of the SP, OFFF-1 = OFFE.
2. Write the contents of ACC (F7) into the memory location pointed to by the contents of the SP:F7 → OFFE.

Push flag register

1. Decrement the contents of the SP, OFFE-1 = OFFD.
2. Write the contents of the flag register into the memory location being pointed to by the contents of the SP: 04 → OFFD.

Push B register

1. Decrement the contents of the SP, OFFD-1 = OFFC.
2. Write the contents of the B register into the memory location pointed to by the contents of the SP, FF → OFFC.

Push C register

1. Decrement the contents of the SP, OFFC-1 = OFFB.
2. Write the contents of the C register into the memory location pointed to by the contents of the SP,4C → OFFB.

The subroutine can now execute normal instructions. The original contents of the ACC, flags, and B and C registers are being held in the stack. Before the return instruction is executed, the contents of the ACC, flags, and B and C registers must be restored. Refer to Figure 2.12(c).

Pop C register

1. Read the contents of the memory location (4C) pointed to by the stack pointer (OFFB), and place it in the C register.
2. Increment the contents of the SP, OFFB + 1 = OFFC.

Pob B register

1. Read the contents of memory location (FF) pointed to by the stack pointer (OFFC), and place it in the B register.
2. Increment the contents of the SP, OFFC + 1 = OFFD.

Pop flag register

1. Read the contents of the memory location (04) pointed to by the stack pointer (OFFD), and place it in the flag register.
2. Increment the contents of the SP, OFFD + 1 + OFFE.

Pop Acc

1. Read the contents of the memory location (F7) pointed to by the stack pointer (OFFE), and place it in the ACC.
2. Increment the contents of the SP, OFFE + 1 = OFFF.

There are many important observations that we can make from the push/pop example. Notice that the stack grows downward in memory. Each byte that is pushed onto the stack resides at a lower address than the previous byte. Also notice that the registers must be popped off the stack in the opposite order from that in which they were pushed onto the stack. The stack pointer always points to the last byte that was pushed onto the stack. Even after a byte is popped off the stack, it still resides in the stack—a pop instruction is a normal nondestructive memory-read operation. The contents of the stack will not change until a new push instruction overwrites a previous byte or power is lost.

The push instruction decremented the SP pointer first and then wrote the register to memory. The pop instruction did exactly the opposite; it read the byte from memory first and then it incremented the SP. The most powerful aspect of the push and pop instructions are that the programmer need not keep track of the stack addresses where the registers are stored. This is done automatically by the microprocessor. After the SP is loaded with the address of the top of stack, all further stack operations are referenced to the contents of the SP. This makes saving and restoring register data a simple and painless operation.

Although push and pop instruction are not complex, the concept of the stack is still widely misunderstood. Carefully follow the sequence of operations in Figure 2.12 until you thoroughly understand the basic operation of the stack.

Input and Output Instructions

We learned earlier in this chapter that microprocessors can treat I/O devices in one of two ways. An I/O device can be addressed using an I/O read or I/O write instruction. The I/O read and I/O write instructions are analogous to memory-read and memory-write instructions. The I/O read or write control signal can be used to enable an I/O decoder, just as we have seen memory-read and memory-write signals enable memory address decoders.

Both I/O-mapped and memory-mapped I/O have advantages. Some microprocessors do not have I/O control signals, and all I/O must be memory-mapped.

Other microprocessors have I/O control signals. This gives the circuit designer the option to choose I/O-mapped or memory-mapped I/O.

2.9 OPERAND ADDRESSING MODES

We have just studied the general types of instructions that are found in every microprocessor instruction set. We now consider the general methods used to provide the required data for each instruction. For example: If we want to add two numbers together, an address or location must be provided to help the microprocessor locate each operand. Understanding addressing modes is as important as understanding the actual microprocessor instructions.

Implied Addressing

Implied addressing is the simplest form of addressing an operand. Some instructions have the address of the operand implied as part of the instruction. Consider an instruction whose only purpose is to reset the carry flag. This instruction need not call out an explicit address, because the carry flag is the address and is implied in the instruction.

Register Addressing

Many times, the operands of an instruction will be in the CPU registers. If this is the case, an instruction need call out only the register(s) that are involved in the instruction. A typical instruction to copy the contents of the B register into the C register is

LD C,B

where LD is the mnemonic that represents the load or copy instruction, B is the source register (the place where the data will be found), and C is the destination register (the location to place the copy of the B register).

Immediate Addressing

This addressing mode provides the data as part of the instruction. Reconsider the LD instruction. We may want to load the C register with the byte of data 7FH. The *H* tells the microprocessor that the byte 7F is in hex.

LD C,7FH

Direct Addressing

Many instructions need to supply the address of memory location or I/O port. The jump instruction is used to force a new value into the program counter.

As you remember, the contents of the program counter are used as an address to find the next instruction to execute.

JMP FFOOH

This instruction loads the program counter with the address FFOO. The microprocessor will then fetch its next instruction from memory location FFOO. This is called *direct addressing* (or *absolute addressing*) because the instruction provides two bytes of data, which represent the address where the microprocessor will jump.

Register Indirect Addressing

The push and pop instructions use the contents of the stack pointer as an address to access the stack.

PUSH B

This instruction says: Write the contents of the B register into the memory location pointed to by the SP. This is an example of register indirect addressing. Unlike the jump instruction that provided the address, the push instruction uses an indirect method of finding the address—the contents of the SP. You will find that register indirect addressing is one of the most useful addressing modes.

There are many more advanced addressing modes that are available on sophisticated microprocessors such as the one employed in the IBM PC. But once you understand these basic addressing modes, the others will be much easier to understand.

IMPORTANT CONCEPTS OF CHAPTER 2

- Microprocessors operate on standard $+5V$ TTL compatible power supplies.
- Every microprocessor has a clock input. This clock is the absolute timing reference to which all system R/W accesses are synchronized.
- The speed of the clock and the width of the data bus are the two most important factors regarding the raw processing power of a microprocessor.
- Holding the reset input on the microprocessor at an active level for 100 ms to 500 ms allows time for the circuitry in the system to be powered up and ready to perform the initial op-code fetch of the boot program.
- The microprocessor is best functionally described as the master of the bus system.
- All devices connected to the address and data bus must be capable of taking their outputs to high-z.

- The data bus is bidirectional, enabling data to flow in and out of the microprocessor.
- The address bus is output only. The microprocessor always designates the address of the memory or I/O access. An exception to this is when a DMAC seizes control of the bus system. It will then perform memory and I/O accesses in a manner similar to the microprocessor.
- The control bus consists of outputs that are used to coordinate memory and I/O accesses and interrupt and DMA acknowledges.
- The status bus is the complement to the control bus. It is used to provide the microprocessor with status information, including the reset status, memory and I/O status (via the ready input), and interrupt and DMA requests.
- RAMs are chip selected by employing the high bits of the address bus and the memory-control outputs of the microprocessor to drive the select and enable inputs on TTL decoders.
- I/O devices can be mapped in a manner similar to memory. This process is called memory-mapped I/O. Some microprocessors provide a separate I/O command output. In these systems the I/O devices can be mapped entirely independent of the memory system.
- The microprocessor contains many dedicated and general-purpose registers.
- The flag register, program counter, instruction register, and stack pointer are examples of dedicated registers that store very specific data and address information.
- The flags in the flag register and conditional jump and call instructions enable the microprocessor to display intelligent behavior.
- The stack is used with push and pop instructions to save the contents of CPU registers during the execution of subroutines and interrupt service routines.
- The model of polling devices to gain their statuses is equivalent to the model of a telephone without a ringer.
- The NMI and Intr inputs are used by I/O devices to interrupt the normal processing cycle of the microprocessor to request service.
- The model of interrupt-driven systems is equivalent to the model of a telephone with a ringer.
- DMACs are designed to move blocks of data between RAM and mass storage devices. DMACs request the use of the system bus by asserting the DMA request input of the microprocessor and waiting for the DMA acknowledge. After the microprocessor acknowledges the DMA request, the DMAC becomes the master of the bus system.
- Machine language consists of the logic 0s and 1s that constitute the actual op-code of each instruction.

- Assembly language is a symbolic form of specifying microprocessor instructions by the use of mnemonics that sound like the function of the instruction.
- All microprocessors share the same basic instruction set and addressing modes.
- The microprocessor is capable of executing the logical instructions of AND, OR, XOR, and NOT in the same manner as hardware gates.
- The stack is a portion of RAM dedicated to saving and restoring registers. The stack pointer is initially loaded with the location of the top of the stack and always points to the last valid entry on the stack.

3

OVERVIEW
OF THE
IBM PC

For the sake of brevity and bowing to popular usage, the IBM PC is simply called the PC for the remainder of this book. Unless otherwise indicated, any reference to the PC applies to the 64K and 256K versions of the original PC and the 256K model of the IBM PC/XT.

The primary reason for the unprecedented success of the PC is the concept of *open architecture*. IBM has published volumes of technical information describing in minute detail the PC hardware, firmware, and *disk operating system (DOS)*. Developers at all levels, from the weekend hobbyist to professional hardware and software developers, have easy and inexpensive access to all the documentation and technical specifications required to design any enhancement product.

This information is also extremely valuable to technicians who wish to perform maintenance service and hardware support on PCs. The *IBM Technical Reference Manual* provides the description and schematics of all PC hardware designed and manufactured by IBM. Other hardware-enhancement manufacturers are also often willing to provide documentation and schematics of their products to maintenance organizations.

3.1 HARDWARE/SOFTWARE RELATIONSHIPS

We know that the hardware level of microprocessor-based systems is extremely complex. To program a microprocessor at a machine language level, the appropriate combination of 1s and 0s must be entered for each instructon. The goal of the microcomputer revolution is to place powerful personal workstations in the hands of nontechnical users—people who have no understanding of computer hardware.

Before we examine the actual hardware that constitutes the PC, we must take a moment to understand the relationship of the PC hardware, firmware, operating system, and applications programs. An *applications program* is a program that is created to solve a specific problem or perform a particular task. Examples of applications programs are anything from a simple checkbook-balancing program to complex word processing, spreadsheet, and data base–management systems.

Figure 3.1 shows that the applications program level is isolated from the microcomputer hardware by the operating system and *basic input/output system* (BIOS) levels. When an applications program is loaded from a disk drive, the user is placed into an environment where high-level, easy-to-understand English-like commands are executed. The applications program provides a hardware-independent interface to a microcomputer. Application programs running on different computer systems should look exactly the same to the user—the actual hardware that performs the computations is completely transparent.

The PC utilizes a DOS called *PC-DOS*. PC compatibles use MS-DOS. Both PC-DOS and MS-DOS were developed by MicroSoft Corp. For the purposes of this book we consider PC-DOS and MS-DOS as identical operating systems. When a PC is powered up, it runs a firmware-based power-up self-test and then boots the operating system from a floppy or hard disk. If a PC boots from drive A (the first disk drive on a PC), the user is taken to the *command line* level of the operating system, usually denoted by A>. This indicates that the system is ready to take DOS commands or execute applications programs. Unlike applications programs, which are often designed to run on computers of extremely different architectures, PC-DOS can run only on microcomputers that are architecturally compatible with the Intel 8086/8088 series of microprocessors.

The DOS command level is used to perform system housekeeping chores such as formatting floppy diskettes, copying files from drive to drive, copying programs from floppy disks onto hard disks, displaying the contents of files and the directories of disk drives, and—most important—loading and executing applications programs. Unlike the applications level, to enter and execute DOS commands requires a moderate level of technical knowledge and training.

| Applications program |
| PC-DOS |
| BIOS |
| Hardware |

Figure 3.1   Hardware/software relationships.

It is important to realize that the actual computer hardware and memory and I/O allocation between microcomputers running PC-DOS need not be identical because the PC-DOS layer is buffered from the actual computer hardware by the BIOS. The BIOS is housed in *firmware* on the system board of the PC. Remember that firmware describes programs (software) that are stored in ROMs (hardware).

The BIOS level for each make and model of computer is a custom creation. It is the BIOS that translates the high-level applications program and PC-DOS system commands into low-level machine language programs that can be directly executed by the hardware. The BIOS is really a collection of dozens of simple programs, each of which performs a specific hardware dependent task.

Imagine an applications program that is waiting for the user to respond to a prompt or input data. The application calls a particular BIOS routine that waits for the user to press a key and then translates the key-scan code into ASCII and returns this value. Notice how a hardware-independent program relies on the BIOS to know the actual physical address of the keyboard-input buffer and the keyboard-input status register. To achieve an even greater level of hardware independence, the applications program can call a routine in DOS, which in turn calls a routine in BIOS that finally executes a low-level program on the hardware. The problem with such an approach is that the response time of the applications program would slow considerably due to the time delay induced by passing the request through three layers. Most applications programs call the BIOS directly.

If speed is a major concern, an applications program can contain its own low-level programs and completely bypass the BIOS! This creates an extremely fast program that is dependent on an exact PC hardware design.

3.2 PC COMPATIBILITY

Many companies, both foreign and domestic, manufacture IBM PC compatible computers. To be truly compatible with all software designed to run on a PC, both the hardware and BIOS levels of Figure 3.1 must be functionally equivalent to a true PC. The PC circuitry and BIOS are protected by copyrights and patents. True PC compatibles must have equivalent hardware circuitry and also a BIOS that contains the identical system calls of the PC BIOS.

If a microcomputer is described as being MS-DOS compatible, an applications program designed for the PC will run on such a computer only if all system requests are filtered through MS-DOS function calls and if they do not have any direct BIOS or hardware-dependent routines. The majority of applications programs will not execute correctly on MS-DOS compatibles unless the software manufacturer rewrites the programs to run in the different BIOS and hardware environment.

3.3 KEYBOARD AND VIDEO DISPLAY INTERFACE

One of the great attractions of the PC is the availability of dozens of expansion boards, video displays, keyboards, peripherals, add-ons, and software to optimize the PC for a particular application. The PC is truly a computer that can be all things to all people. In addition, IBM guarantees that all future improved and enhanced versions of the PC will be compatible with its present line of PCs.

The complete PC system resides in three separate units: the system unit, video display, and keyboard. Figure 3.2 illustrates the block diagram of a typical microcomputer system. The input device is the keyboard, and the output devices are the video display and a printer. The modem enables the PC to communicate with other computers from great distances via standard public telephone lines.

The large rectangle in Figure 3.2 represents the major blocks of circuitry that reside in the system unit of the PC. Notice that each I/O device is connected to the system unit by means of a special interface.

Let's examine how the keyboard functions. When a key is pressed, a microcomputer chip in the keyboard enclosure transmits a unique scan code (representing the position of the depressed key) in a serial bit stream to the system unit to be processed. The keyboard interface circuitry translates this serial bit stream into a parallel byte of data; the BIOS keyboard input routine translates the scan code into the standard ASCII code that applications programs will recognize.

The number and types of keys on computer keyboards differ widely between microcomputer systems. This results in a unique keyboard interface circuitry for each microcomputer and terminal. Dozens of manufacturers provide keyboards that are compatible with the PC.

The original PC keyboard manufactured by IBM had a nonstandard layout and poor tactile response. This created a market for keyboards that were designed be used by a skilled typist employing word-processing programs.

Another limitation of the IBM keyboard was that the *numeric keypad* used for high-speed numeric data entry was shared by the *cursor-control* keys. A key labeled Num Lock toggles the function of the keypad between cursor control and numeric entry. A *spreadsheat* program is used to support row and column mathematics and is widely employed in accounting and financial analysis. These programs are much easier to use when the keyboard has a separate numeric keypad and cursor-control keys. Many manufacturers provide such a keyboard. IBM now manufacturers an enhanced keyboard that has an extra set of cursor-control keys.

The video display is connected to the system unit with a circuit board called a *display adapter*. The display adapter card is plugged into one of the expansion slots on the system board. The PC supports many different types of displays and display adapter cards. The standard IBM *monochrome display adapter* drives a high-resolution green phosphor video display. This display is

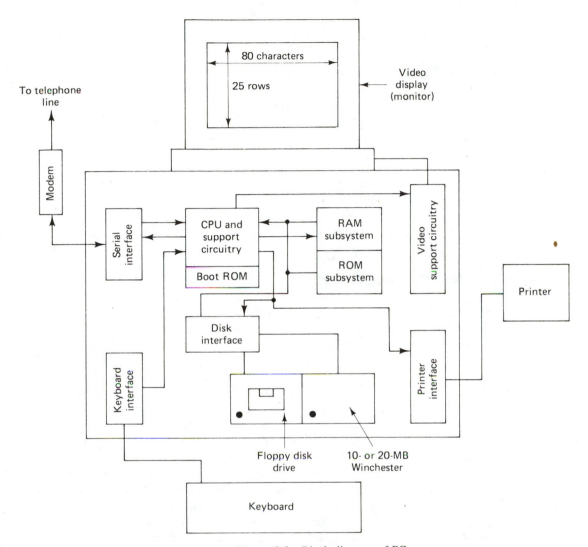

Figure 3.2 Block diagram of PC.

optimized for exceptionally readable alphanumerics. Other monochrome display adapters available from third-party manufacturers are capable of displaying *all points addressable* (APA) graphics on the standard IBM monochrome display.

IBM and third-party sources also manufacture display adapters that are capable of driving medium- and high-resolution color displays. The many different display adapters and video displays available for the PC are a strong indication of the PC's ability to be customized for a specific application. We investigate the technical aspects of video adapter cards and video displays in Chapter 7.

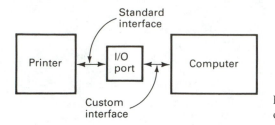

Figure 3.3   Block diagram
of computer/printer interface.

An important point to understand is that, like the keyboard, the video
display requires an interface circuit (video adapter) that is specifically designed
to operate with the PC. Contrast this concept of PC hardware dependence with
the printer interface and serial interface illustrated in Figure 3.3.

3.4 STANDARD INTERFACE CIRCUITS

Most peripherals (with the exception of the keyboard and video display) are
designed to be connected to a *standard interface circuit*. Figure 3.3 illustrates
a computer and printer that are interfaced via an I/O port. The function of a
standard interface I/O port is quite simple. On the peripheral device's side of
the interface, the I/O port must conform to a widely established and accepted
standard. The computer's side of the I/O port conforms to the individually
designed circuitry that is unique to every make and model of computer. In the
case of the PC, specific port addresses are allocated for the printer and communications ports. The adapter board that contains the I/O port is plugged into
an expansion slot on the system board in the same manner as the display adapter.

Manufacturers of I/O devices must appeal to the widest possible market,
and every computer manufacturer wants its customers to have the greatest
selection of peripherals. Consequently, peripheral manufacturers design their
products to meet an accepted communications interface standard, and computer
manufacturers provide I/O ports that also conform to accepted standards. In this
way any peripheral device can be connected to any computer, provided that
they both support the same interface standard.

3.5 PARALLEL AND SERIAL INTERFACES

As illustrated in Appendix B, a byte of digital data can represent a letter,
numeral, punctuation mark, standard symbol, or equipment-control code. I/O
ports are designed to transfer the byte of data on a bit-by-bit basis in a *serial
stream* over a single wire or simply send the byte in a single *parallel* operation
employing eight lines, one for each bit of data. The model of the *serial interface*

in Figure 3.4(b) is constructed from two digital devices called *shift registers*. The *parallel-in serial-out (PISO)* shift register serializes a byte of data into a stream of bits. On each rising edge of the clock, the next data bit is transmitted. The *serial-in parallel-out (SIPO)* shift register provides the complementary function; on each falling edge of the clock, the data bit on the serial input is transferred into a storage cell (a flip-flop). After eight clock pulses the byte

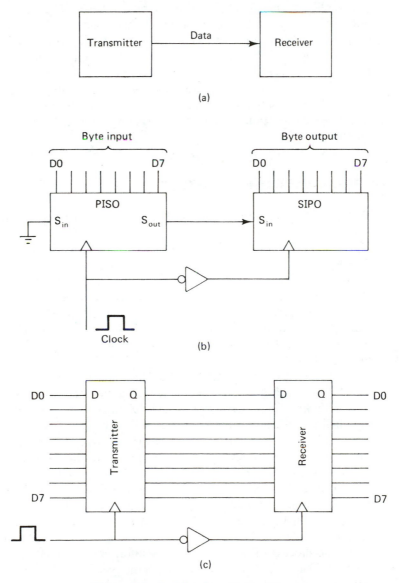

Figure 3.4 Serial and parallel interfaces.

residing on the inputs of the PISO shift register is also stored on the outputs of the SIPO shift register.

Notice that the data in the serial interface is sent on a single line. Contrast that with the model of the parallel interface illustrated in Figure 3.4(c). Each bit of data is sent on a separate line.

The natural attraction of the serial interface is that it takes only one wire to communicate between devices. A pair of wires can be employed to enable both devices to transmit and receive simultaneously. The significance of communications via a stream of data bits is that standard two-wire phone circuits can be used to carry on a full two-way conversation between a computer and a peripheral. It is this simple feature that is responsible for the popularity of the serial interface.

The beauty of the parallel interface is its sheer simplicity. A byte of data is placed on the output of the transmitter, and a single clock pulse transfers the data. The data-stream method of exchanging data lends itself to many complexities.

3.6 THE PARALLEL PRINTER ADAPTER

The industry standard parallel port is called the *Centronics Parallel Interface*. Although the Centronics Standard defines a total of 34 pins, the parallel port on the PC is terminated (connected to the outside world) on a 25-pin *D-type* female connector that is accessible on the back panel of the system unit. The circuitry that comprises the parallel port is so simple that it is usually included on more complex boards, such as the monochrome display adapter and most memory-expansion boards. The PC is capable of supporting a maximum of two parallel ports, which are called *LPT1:* and *LPT2:*, where LPT stands for line printer. Figure 3.5 describes the actual pinout of the parallel printer port on the PC.

Notice that the direction of the data flow is from the PC to the printer. The LPT port on the PC is output only. Parallel ports are also available that provide *bidirectional operation*. In addition to supporting standard printers, the output lines on parallel ports can be used to control devices such as motors, relays, LEDs, or *digital-to-analog converters* (DACs). The input lines are used to sense the status of devices such as switches, contacts, or input data from an *A/D converter*.

The status lines from the printer enable the PC to respond to conditions when the printer is busy printing and cannot accept further data (pin-11), out of paper (pin-12), selected (also called *on-line* (pin-13)), or suffers a fault condition (pin-32).

The process of monitoring status information while two devices are exchanging data is called *handshaking*. In the previous paragraph we discovered how the printer provides status information to the PC via four input pins.

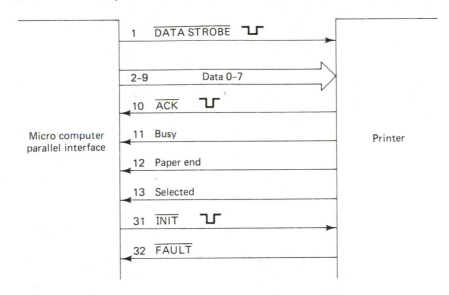

Figure 3.5   Pinout of printer port on PC.

Typically, DOS or an applications program call a BIOS routine that outputs data to LPT1: or LPT2:. The BIOS routine makes the status information on these four pins available to the calling program. If the BIOS routine indicates a printer malfunction, the applications program will transform the error code returned by the BIOS call into an error message in simple English. This enables the user to easily rectify the problem. This process makes complete sense given the relationship of the hardware, BIOS, DOS, and applications program illustrated in Figure 3.1.

3.7 THE ASYNCHRONOUS COMMUNICATIONS ADAPTER

Figure 3.2 shows a modem that is connected to the PC via a serial interface. The serial interface in the PC is called the *asynchronous communications adapter*. The most common method of serial communications is called *asynchronous* because the data stream is sent without regard to an absolute timing source or common clock. The majority of RS-232 devices operate in an asynchronous mode and are compatible with the asynchronous communications adapter.

The PC can support a maximum of two serial adapters, which are called *COM1:* and *COM2:*. In this case COM means communications port. This indicates that IBM has assumed that the majority of applications employing the serial adapter connect the PC to a communication device such as a modem. The serial adapter connects to a modem via a 25-pin D-type male connector on the back of the system unit. Notice that the parallel and serial ports both use

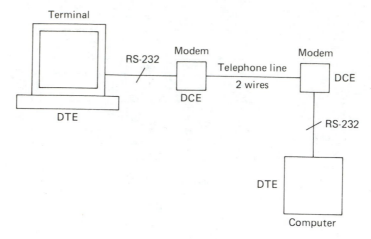

Figure 3.6   Remote terminal/computer connection.

25-pin connectors. The difference is that the parallel port has a female connector, and the serial port has a male connector.

We have established the need for a widely followed and accepted I/O interface standard. The *RS-232 standard* (RS stands for recommended standard) was established by the *Electronics Industries Association* (EIA) in the 1960s to facilitate compatibility and interchangeability between computers and peripheral devices that were connected via serial ports. Most literature refers to RS-232 as RS-232C, which is the latest revision. We will drop the ''C'' and simply use RS-232 as the name of the interface standard.

RS-232 defines the electrical signal characteristics, mechanical interface, and the functional description of the interchange circuits in a large technical document available from the EIA.*

We now take a moment to examine RS-232 in an intuitive and practical light. It is easiest to understand the RS-232 connection by describing the application for which it was originally designed. Most terminals are connected to computers via an RS-232 serial interface port. Consider the situation where an individual needs to access a computer from a distant location. How can the remote terminal be physically connected to the computer? Wherever one travels throughout the world the two utilities that are inevitability available are AC power and telephone service.

Figure 3.6 depicts the connection of a remote terminal and a computer via a standard telephone line. The terminal and computer are not directly connected; they are separated modems. Digital waveforms can not be transmitted

*Electronic Industries Association, 1430 Broadway New York, NY 10018

over long lengths of wire. Every wire has an associated amount of capacitance and resistance.

Figure 3.7(a) illustrates the resistance and capacitance as it is distributed along the length of a wire. You may recall from basic DC theory that

1. Resistances in series are accumulative.
2. Capacitances in parallel are also accumulative.

Figure 3.7(b) indicates that the resistance and capacitance in a wire can be symbolized as a total value of R_T and C_T. If a square wave is input into the circuit in Figure 3.7(b), it will be distorted on the output, as depicted in Figure 3.7(C). This is because R_T and C_T form a circuit called an *integrator*. It is the basic nature of capacitors to oppose any change in voltage. At the first moment

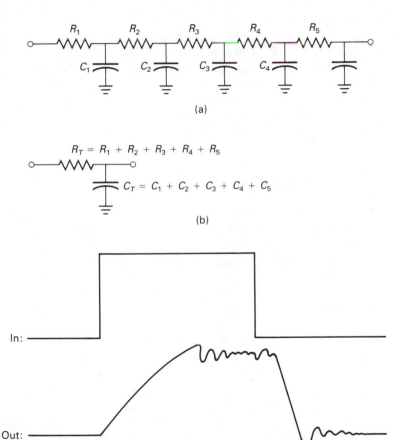

(a)

(b)

(c)

Figure 3.7   The effects of capacitance and resistance on a long wire.

that the input changes to a logic 1 level, the capacitor will appear to be a short circuit to ground and the entire input voltage will be dropped across R_T. It will take a total of five RC time constants before V_{out} is equal to V_{in}. The output is no longer a digital signal! For an appreciable length of time it exists between a logic 0 and a logic 1.

Figure 3.7 leads us to believe that digital communications cannot occur directly between a terminal and a computer employing standard telephone lines. Telephone lines were designed to carry signals in the audible (voice) range of frequencies. The modems in Figure 3.6 are devices that convert the two levels of a digital signal into two different tones. These audible tones can propagate along commercial phone lines with little degradation. The modem is a *transceiver*. That means it transmits and also receives data. The process of impressing a digital signal onto an *analog carrier* frequency is called *modulation*. The reverse process of recovering a digital signal from an analog carrier is called *demodulation*.

Because the RS-232 standard is so widely followed and accepted, the serial port on the IBM is used to interface not only with modems and printers (with serial instead of parallel interfaces) but also with dozens of serial devices such as mice, voice synthesizers, bar code readers, optical scanners, and data acquisition and control modules.

In a later chapter we examine the internal and external loop-back tests used to validate the operation of the parallel and serial ports on the PC.

3.8 INSIDE THE SYSTEM UNIT

We have examined all the I/O devices connected to the system unit. We know that in addition to I/O ports, a computer system contains a CPU and memory. These two subsystems are housed within the system unit. The system unit is a rectangular metal box measuring approximately 18 in. wide, 14 in. deep, and 8 in. high.

Power Supply

All electronic components require precisely filtered and regulated DC voltages. The system unit contains a power supply that outputs $+5$ V, $+12$ V, -12 V, and -5 V. These voltages are used to power the TTL circuitry in the CPU and memory subsystems, the floppy and hard disk drives, and the adapter boards that are inserted into the expansion slots on the system board. The original version of the PC had a 63.5-W power supply. In 1981 main memory (semiconductor memory) was very expensive and Winchester disk drives for microcomputers were not yet commercially available. The original PC was typically ordered with 64 KB of RAM and two single-sided floppy disk drives.

Today PCs are typically ordered with 640 KB of RAM, one 360-KB double-sided floppy disk drive, and one 20-MB hard disk drive. Starting in 1983 the PC power supply was upgraded to a 135-W model to reflect the additional current load consumed by the additional main memory and mass memory systems.

The System Board

The system board measures approximately 8½ in. by 12 in. and is mounted on the base of the system unit. It contains many important blocks of circuitry.

The CPU subsystem.   The PC employs the Intel 8088 microprocessor, which requires system controller and clock-generator ICs. In addition to the main CPU, there is also a 40-pin socket for an optional 8087 *Numeric Co-Processor*. This device performs high-speed floating point arithmetic. An Intel 8259 *programmable interrupt controller* (*PIC*) is used to coordinate the many I/O and housekeeping tasks in this complex computer system.

ROM subsystem.   As we discussed in the beginning of this chapter, the BIOS translates high-level DOS and applications calls into machine-executable subroutines. The ROM subsystem on the original PC was contained in five 8KB ROMS.

Note that there is often confusion regarding the designations that describe ROMs and EPROMs. The ROMs on the original system board can be correctly described in two different ways:

1. 64K ROM means the ROM has a total of 64K storage locations. One bit of data can be stored in each location.
2. 8KB ROM means that the ROM has 8K storage locations, each having a capacity of 8 bits or 1 byte of data.

Because most computers are byte-oriented, the 8KB designation means much more than the 64K (bit) designation. However, manufacturers of ROMs describe their devices in total capacity of bits. The point here is be extremely cautious when discussing the capacity of ROMs.

A sixth ROM socket was available for custom devices. One 8KB ROM contained the BIOS, *power-on self-test* (*POST*), dot patterns of the graphics characters for the monochrome display adapter, and the *boot loader*. The other four ROMs (a total of 32 KB) contained the BASIC computer programming language. The BIOS in the XT version of the system board is still housed in one 8 KB ROM, but the BASIC interpreter is now contained in one 32KB (256K) ROM.

LSI support circuitry.   Three powerful system-support ICs are used to assist the microprocessor. These 40-pin devices provide three programmable timers, three programmable parallel ports (not to be confused with the Centronics parallel printer port, which is contained on a separate adapter board), and four DMA channels. These are extremely complex devices and functions that we discuss at length in a later chapter.

Main memory.   The original PC had a system board that could house a maximum of 64KB of RAM employing four banks of 16K RAM chips. The next-generation system board could house a maximum of 256K of RAM employing 4 banks of 64K RAM chips. The latest system board houses 640K of RAM employing two banks of 256K memory chips and two banks of 64K memory chips. Notice that all three system boards had space for four banks of RAM chips. It is the advances in memory IC technology that have provided the increased RAM capacity on the system board.

Although the 8088 microprocessor can address 1 MB of memory, PC-DOS has reserved only 640 kB of this memory space for RAM. The other 360K is used to address the ROM BIOS subsystem and display memory on display adapter boards.

Expansion slots.   The PC's open architecture encourages third-party manufacturers to design enhancement products that plug into the internal expansion slots on the system board. The original PC had five expansion slots. The newest PC has a total of eight expansion slots. The expansion slots are standard dual-sided 62-pin edge connectors. All the expansion slots are identical. The important signals on the system board are bused to the expansion slots; these include the data bus, address bus, interrupt lines, DMA control lines, and memory and I/O request signals. In Chapter 6 we examine all the signals that are bused to the expansion slots.

Setup DIP switches.   The PC can support both monochrome and color display adapters. Because of the different ways that these adapters store characters to be displayed, they occupy different areas in the *DOS memory allocation map*. When the PC is powered on, how does it know which type of display adapter is currently installed in the system? This problem is solved by DIP switches that reside on the system board. The main switch block consists of eight SPST (single-pole single-throw) switches enclosed in a 16-pin DIP package. When the PC is energized, it reads the contents of these switches to establish a default equipment environment. The functions of the switches are described in Figure 3.8.

On the original system board a second block of switches was employed to indicate how much memory was installed on adapter boards. The newer system boards do not employ this second block of switches. RAM is added to a PC in a sequential order. The starting address of the new RAM must be set to the next available address. The total amount of system memory is established in the power-up program by writing/reading specific bit patterns to memory

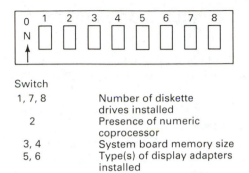

Switch
1, 7, 8	Number of diskette drives installed
2	Presence of numeric coprocessor
3, 4	System board memory size
5, 6	Type(s) of display adapters installed

Figure 3.8   Main switch block.

every 16 KB until an incorrect pattern is read. This process is called *auto-memory sizing*.

Mass Storage

Also enclosed in the system unit are the mass storage devices. These take the form of floppy and hard disk drives. The original version of DOS (1.0) supported a single-sided 160 KB 5¼-in. floppy disk drive. The next version of DOS (1.1) supported the new double-sided floppy disk drives with a capacity of 320 KB. The next version of DOS (2.0) supported 5¼-in. hard disk drives with a capacity of 10 MB and a new floppy disk format that enabled a double-sided drive to increase its capacity to 360 KB. As new mass storage devices are developed, DOS is updated to support the interface to the new hardware.

Originally 5¼-in. disk drives were 6 in. tall. The newest disk drives are described as *half-height* because they are only 3 in. tall. This means that two half-height disk drives can fit in the same space as a full-height drive. This enables more than two disk drives to be housed in the system unit. Half-height disk drives also have a lower power consumption. The latest version of the PC employs half-height drives.

Small Speaker

How does an applications program get the user's attention to indicate an incorrect entry or operation? A small speaker is mounted in the system unit. It is driven by one channel of the programmable timer and parallel port IC. The BASIC programming language supports commands that enable the user to write programs to play music, but the most common use of the speaker is to get the user's attention to flag special events and indicate incorrect entries and operations.

IMPORTANT CONCEPTS OF CHAPTER 3

- It is extremely important to understand the relationship of the hardware, BIOS, operating system, and applications program, as illustrated in Figure 3.1.
- The great majority of PC users employ the PC-DOS operating system, developed by Microsoft Corp.
- The DOS command level enables the user to execute DOS utilities and load and execute applications programs. On termination, applications programs return the user to the DOS command level.
- In an ideal situation DOS is independent of a particular hardware environment of the computer system. However, PC-DOS and MS-DOS run only on microcomputers based on the Intel 8086/8088 microprocessor architecture.
- The BIOS is a group of low-level hardware-dependent routines that enable the application program and DOS to interact with the system hardware.
- True PC-compatibles must employ a BIOS that is functionally identical to the copyrighted IBM BIOS.
- The BIOS links logic devices with physical memory and I/O locations.
- Many companies manufacture keyboards that are compatible with the PC's keyboard port and BIOS.
- A video display is connected to the PC via a display adapter inserted into one of the PC's expansion slots.
- The PC supports many different types of monochrome and color display adapters and displays.
- Printers are usually connected to the PC via a Centronics compatible parallel port called LPT1: or LPT2:.
- Modems, printers (with serial interfaces), mice, bar code readers, and a host of other RS-232 asynchronous serial devices are connected to the PC via an asynchronous communications adapter. These serial RS-232 ports are designated as COM1: or COM2:.
- The only difference between the 25-pin D-type connectors on the parallel and serial ports is their gender: The parallel port has a female connector and the serial port has a male connector.
- The modem enables the PC to communicate with physically distant computers via unconditioned public telephone lines.
- The modem overcomes the problem associated with transmitting digital signals along highly capacitive lines by converting a digital level into an analog signal.
- The power supply, system board, mass storage devices, and system speaker are contained within the system unit.

- The performance of the 8088 microprocessor is enhanced by many intelligent special-purpose LSI devices mounted on the system board and in the video and floppy disk drive adapters.
- PC-DOS supports a maximum of 640K of main memory.
- The remainder of the 1 MB memory space of the 8088 is used to support ROM and video-RAM.
- The system board contains one or two sets of DIP switches that are read by the microprocessor to define a default hardware configuration.

4

ANALYSIS OF THE 8088 PROCESSOR SUBSYSTEM

In Chapter 3 we learned that the system board contains the CPU and RAM/ROM memory subsystems as well as expansion slots designed to accommodate I/O ports, video adapter boards, additional RAM, and controllers for mass storage devices. In this chapter we apply our general knowledge of microprocessor architecture to the study of the the Intel 8088.

4.1 THE 8088 MICROPROCESSOR

The 8088 is a complex microprocessor that can best be described as *pseudo-16-bit*. It has an 8-bit external data bus and thus is technically an 8-bit microprocessor; however, internally the 8088 has a 16-bit data bus and 16-bit registers. Intel describes it as a "high performance 8-bit microprocessor," whereas IBM touts it as a 16-bit microprocessor.

The 8088 has two distinct modes of operation: minimum mode and maximum mode. In *minimum mode* it functions as an enhanced version of its predecessor, the 8085. The PC implements the 8088 in *maximum mode*. This enables the system to support the addition of a coprocessor, the 8087 *numeric data processor* (NDP).

In most microcomputer systems, trigonometric, logarithmic, and floating-point math are performed by software routines in the applications program. This results in extremely poor performance from numeric-intensive programs. The 8087 adds 69 instructions to the 8088 assembly language set and performs arithmetic functions up to 300 times faster than the equivalent program simulation.

A switch on setup switch bank 1 informs the 8088 that an 8087 is resident and also enables the interrupt request from the 8087 to be passed onto the 8088. Applications programs must be written to exploit the instruction set of the 8087, or its presence will be ignored. 8087 support is a feature that is important to spreadsheet and data base programs and to language compilers.

When operating in maximum mode, the 8088 requires two additional support ICs to form the *basic CPU subsystem*: the 8284 Clock Generator and the 8288 System Controller. Figure 4.1 illustrates the general configuration of the CPU subsystem that is employed on the PC. The 8284 is the 8088 system clock generator/driver. It generates several clock signals and also manages the reset and ready inputs. The 14.3-MHz crystal functions with an oscillator within the 8284 to create three clock outputs.

CLK is the output that drives the 8088 microprocessor and 8288 system-controller clock inputs. Its frequency is approximately 4.77 MHz, one-third of the crystal frequency.

OSC is the TTL-level output of the internal oscillator. It is routed to pin B30 on the expansion slot connectors. This signal is used as a *dot-clock*, the timing source for the color graphics adapter.

PCLK is the peripheral clock. Its frequency is approximately 2.38 MHz. Because the original crystal frequency is divided by six to derive the PCLK, it is an extremely stable signal. PCLK is further divided by a factor of 2 to form a 1.19-MHz signal that is used as the timing reference for the 8253 PIT (programmable interval timer), a three-channel counter/timer that we study in the next chapter. PCLK is also used to synchronize the keyboard clock.

The 8284 is also capable of controlling two ready inputs. RDY1 is an active-high input and $\overline{AEN1}$ is the active-low qualifier for RDY1. When RDY1 is high and $\overline{AEN1}$ is low, the ready output of the 8284 will be an active-high level. DMA request circuitry drives the RDY1 input. We discuss the need for DMA later in this section.

All electronic devices have a *propagation delay*. What happens if a particular memory or I/O device has a long read or write access time compared to the system processor? Each time a slow memory or I/O device is accessed, external circuity (called a *wait state generator*) brings the $\overline{AEN1}$ to an inactive level. The 8088 adds wait states to the memory or I/O access—that is, the address, data, and control lines are held stable for an additional tick of the 4.77 processor clock cycle. The 8088 will continue to generate wait states until the wait state generator brings $\overline{AEN1}$ to an active-low level, indicating that the memory or I/O access can proceed. At 4.77 MHz the 8088 is running slow enough that neither system RAM (rated at 250 ns access time) or ROM needs additional time. However, all I/O accesses on the PC have one wait state automatically inserted. Two other inputs, RDY2 and $\overline{AEN2}$, are not illustrated in Figure 4.1. You should assume that they are tied to active levels.

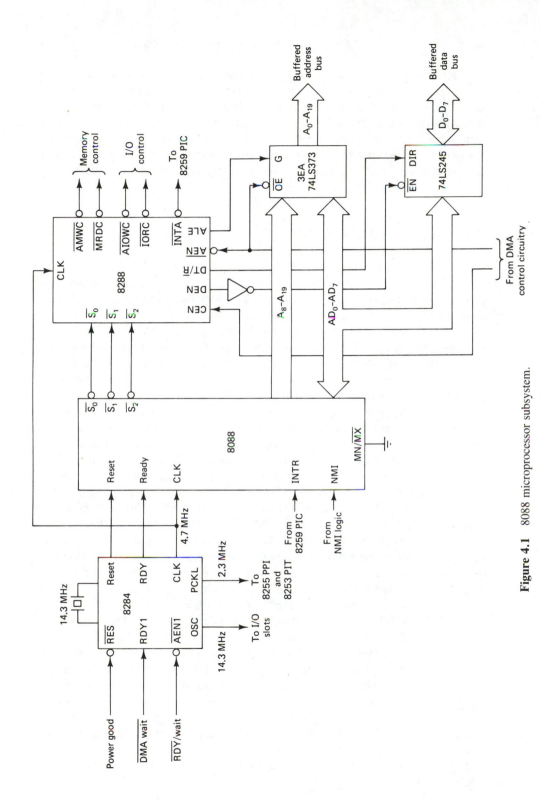

Figure 4.1 8088 microprocessor subsystem.

$\overline{\text{RES}}$ is the system reset input. It is driven by a signal from the power supply called *power good*. When power good goes inactive-high (after a 100-ms to 500-ms delay), the system circuitry has had sufficient time to be prepared to receive commands from the 8088. The 8284 responds to a logic 1 on its $\overline{\text{RES}}$ input by bringing reset on the 8088 to an inactive-low level. The reset output of the 8284 is also routed to important circuits on the system board. The power good output of the PC's switching power supply replaces the RC reset delay circuit that we studied in Chapter 2.

4.2 THE 8288 SYSTEM CONTROLLER

Let's examine the function of the 8288 *System Controller*. The 8088 provides 3 bits of encoded *status information* on pins $\overline{\text{S}_0}$ through $\overline{\text{S}_2}$. The 8288 decodes these inputs to create memory and I/O control signals, interrupt acknowledgement, and bus-control outputs.

The 8088 has a 20-bit address bus. Like its predecessor, the 8085, it has a multiplexed address/data bus—AD_0 through AD_7. The first 8 bits of the address bus (A_0 through A_7) share the same pins as the 8-bit data bus. Figure 4.2 illustrates how the address/data bus of the 8085 and 8088 (running in minimum mode) is demultiplexed.

The 74LS373 is an *octal (8-bit wide) transparent latch*. Its gate input is driven by a control signal from the microprocessor called the *address latch enable* (ALE). Every memory or I/O access is initiated by placing the appropriate address onto the address bus. When the address is stable the output of ALE will be a short logic 1 pulse. This pulse latches the lower 8 bits of the address bus onto the outputs of the 74LS373. For the remainder of the memory or I/O cycle the lower 8 bits of the address/data bus are used exclusively as a data bus. The octal latch essentially expands the address/data bus by 8 bits.

As illustrated in Figure 4.1, when the 8088 is operating in maximum mode, ALE is derived from the status outputs of the 8088 and is generated by the 8288 system controller. ALE drives the enable inputs of three 74LS373; all 20 bits on the address bus are latched on the falling edge of ALE.

Notice the two interrupt request inputs on the 8088—INTR and NMI. The standard *INTR sequence* is initiated when a device takes INTR to an active-high level. After the 8088 finishes its current instruction, the value of the program counter (called the instruction pointer in the 8088) is automatically saved on the stack. The interrupt acknowledge ($\overline{\text{INTA}}$) output consists of two active-low pulses. The first acknowledges the interrupt request and the second commands the interrupting device to place an 8-bit *interrupt number* onto the data bus. An *interrupt vector table* is set up in the beginning of RAM that translates the interrupt number (0–255) into the address of the appropriate service routine.

The interrupt request and interrupt acknowledge are both associated with

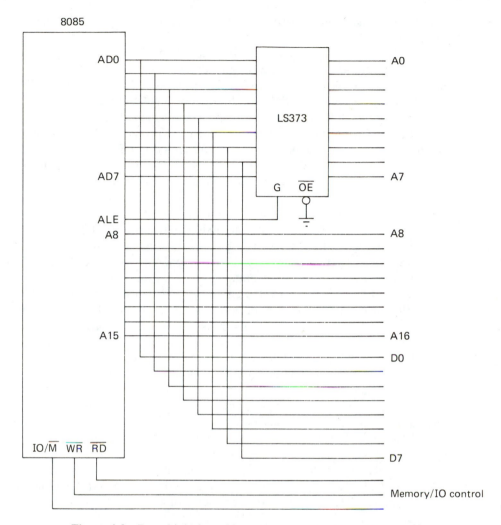

Figure 4.2   Demultiplexing address/data bus with address latch enable signal.

the 8259 *Programmable Interrupt Controller* (PIC). This device is employed to help manage the complex interrupt structure in the PC. In the next chapter we examine the 8259 and the how interrupt addresses are actually derived.

As you learned in Chapter 2, the 8088 can be instructed to disregard interrupt requests that occur on the INTR input. However, the event of an active-high level on NMI cannot be ignored by the microprocessor. When NMI goes active, the 8088 automatically vectors to a reserved location in memory that contains the address of the NMI service routine. The NMI is used in the PC system to display an error message and halt the system when the contents of a RAM location contains corrupted data. This is called a *RAM parity error*.

The NMI is also used by the 8087 NDP to request service from the 8088 processor.

Let's examine the remaining functions of the 8288. *Advanced memory write command* ($\overline{\text{AMWC}}$) and *advanced I/O write command* ($\overline{\text{AIOWC}}$) are the active-low memory and I/O write control signals; *memory read command* ($\overline{\text{MRDC}}$) and *I/O read command* ($\overline{\text{IORC}}$) are the memory and I/O read signals. These four lines are identical in function to the control signals derived in Figure 2.7.

The following inputs and outputs are used to enable the PC processor system to support DMA operation, as we discussed in Chapter 2.

Command enable (CEN) is a status signal that is controlled by external circuitry to enable or disable the memory and I/O command outputs. When CEN is at an inactive-low level, all memory and I/O command outputs and *data enable* (DEN) go to their inactive levels.

Address enable ($\overline{\text{AEN}}$) is used in a similar manner to CEN. When $\overline{\text{AEN}}$ goes inactive-high, all the command outputs go to high-z. In the PC, CEN and $\overline{\text{AEN}}$ are driven by DMA circuitry. When a DMA request occurs, the DMA wait input to the 8284 clock generator goes to an inactive level, forcing the 8088 to generate wait states and the CEN and $\overline{\text{AEN}}$ lines to go inactive, which causes the memory and I/O control lines and the data and address bus buffers to float their outputs to high-z. Thus the system is ready for an external bus master to take charge.

Notice that CEN and $\overline{\text{AEN}}$ are active at complementary logic levels. These inputs are actually driven by the Q and $\overline{\text{Q}}$ outputs of a DMA enable flip-flop.

In addition to the standard memory and I/O R/W control signals, the 8288 provides three outputs that simplify interfacing the 8088 with address and data bus buffers. Figure 4.1 indicates that the 20-bit address bus is buffered by three 74LS373 octal, three-state transparent latches. When $\overline{\text{AEN}}$ is active low, the Q outputs of the latches are enabled. ALE from the 8288 functions as a timing signal to demultiplex the address/data bus, as illustrated in Figure 4.2. On the falling edge of ALE, the 20-bit address is latched onto the outputs of the three 74LS373s. The 74LS373s provide five useful functions:

1. Increase the drive capabilities of the 8088 address output lines.
2. Demultiplex the address/data bus.
3. Latch the 20-bit address.
4. Accommodate DMA accesses by using an inactive level on $\overline{\text{AEN}}$ to bring the outputs of the 74LS373 to high-z, enabling a DMAC to drive the address bus.
5. Help to isolate bus faults to the unbuffered 8088 address bus, which simplifies the location of open or shorted address lines.

The 74LS245 is an octal, three-state bidirectional buffer. It accomplishes functions for the data bus similar to those the 74LS373 accomplishes for the address bus. Although bidirectional buffers do not need the ALE signal, they must be driven by a signal that indicates the direction of data flow. When the 8088 is reading memory or I/O devices, the 74LS245 must pass data from the buffered data bus into the microprocessor; when the 8088 is writing data to memory or I/O, the 74LS245 must pass data from the microprocessor onto the buffered data bus. The direction control input of the 74LS245 is driven by *data transmit/receive* (DT/$\overline{\text{R}}$) of the 8288. As the name of the output implies, when the 8088 is performing a read operation, DT/$\overline{\text{R}}$ is low; a write operation takes DT/$\overline{\text{R}}$ high.

Data enable (DEN) from the 8288 is used to enable data bus drivers. When DEN is active-high, its inverted level enables the 74LS245. To accommodate the data bus for DMA operation, when CEN is taken inactive-low the 8288 brings DEN inactive-low, causing the outputs of the 74LS245 to go to high-z.

We have now covered the major aspects of the 8088, 8284, and 8288 three-chip CPU system. Like all microprocessor systems, the PC revolves around the simple concept of three-bus architecture providing memory and I/O access, wait states, interrupt structures, and DMA operation. No matter how complex a microprocessor systems appears to be, those four elementary hardware functions must be implemented.

In addition to the three-chip CPU system, the system board employs four other LSI support devices. In Chapter 5 we examine those devices and the functions that they contribute to the PC system architecture.

4.3 THE REGISTER SET OF THE 8088

In Chapter 2 we examined the internal registers of a generic microprocessor. The purpose of this section is to gain an understanding of the internal register structure of the 8088. Each register is described in terms of the function that it contributes to the internal operation of the 8088. Each of the registers illustrated in Figure 4.3 is 16 bits. The 14 user-accessible registers in the 8088 can be grouped according to function: data registers, pointer and index registers, segment registers, instruction pointer, and status flags. We will discover that the letters used to describe each register form a mnemonic that represents the typical function that the register performs.

Data Registers

The data registers in the 8088 are natural extensions of the registers in the 8085. Each of these registers can be used as a single 16-bit register or two independent 8-bit registers. In Intel microprocessor terminology, the letter *L* indicates the low byte and the letter *H*, the high byte of a 16-bit register. Logically, the letter *X* stands for a register pair, or 16-bit register. Thus AX stands for the 16-bit

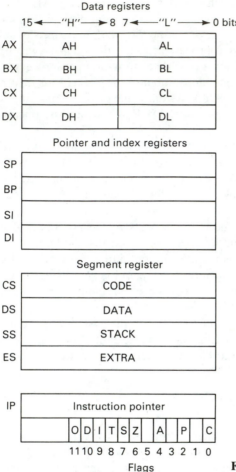

Figure 4.3　8088 register set.

accumulator, AH stands for the high byte of the accumulator, and AL stands for the low byte of the accumulator. The data registers provide general-purpose operand storage for simple arithmetic and logical instructions. AX is the *accumulator* for 16-bit multiplication and division, whereas AL and AH perform the same function for 8-bit arithmetic.

On the PC, the AH register is used to hold the function number for a BIOS or MS-DOS function call; AL is used as the data register when the routine requires a byte of data (such as sending a character to a printer) or returns a byte of data (such as read the keyboard input buffer). AL corresponds to the accumulator of the 8085.

BX is used as a *base register*. A base register holds the starting address of a table of data. An *offset* or *displacement* is added to the value of a base register to form the *physical* or *effective address* of a specific byte of data. For those familiar with the 8085, BX is equivalent of the HL register pair. We will soon discover that BX is not the principal base register of the 8088.

CX is the *count register*. It is used as an automatic counter for string and loop instructions. The 8088 assembly language contains many instructions that perform a function, decrement the contents of CX, and then test for a value of zero as an indication that the current program loop should be terminated. CX roughly corresponds to the BC register pair of the 8085.

DX is a *data register*. It is used to hold a 16-bit operand for multiplication and division instructions. It can also be used to hold the address of an I/O port.

In PC-DOS the DL register is used to hold the time and date. DL plays the same role as a data register for MS-DOS functions as AL performed for BIOS calls. DX corresponds to the DE register pair of the 8085.

It is important to note (with the exception of AH) that the data registers of the 8088 are duplicated from its predecessor, the 8085. Also remember that when the 8088 operates in minimum mode (without the 8288 system controller), it functions as an enhanced 8085 microprocessor. You can now begin to understand how microprocessors evolve by augmenting existing architectures. The remaining registers are unique to the 8088 family of microprocessors and do not correspond to 8085 registers. Furthermore, they are used only as 16-bit registers and can not be broken into individual 8-bit registers.

Pointer and Index Registers

SP is the *stack pointer* register that we studied in Chapter 2. Remember that the SP holds the address of the next available location in the RAM stack. We have indicated that when the 8088 receives an interrupt request, it finishes executing its current instruction and then saves the contents of the program counter onto the stack. The SP is the default reference for all stack operations.

It is often advantageous for programmers to have an additional stack— not to be used when servicing interrupts or calling subroutines but as a convenient location to temporary store data that is exchanged between subroutines. This programming technique is called *passing data* or *parameters* via the stack. The *base pointer* (BP) is used as the stack pointer to implement a data stack.

We saw that the BX register is the base register and is used to hold the base address of a group of data in memory. It is a common programming task to move blocks of data between locations in memory. To facilitate this operation, the 8088 has the *source index* (SI) and the *destination index* (DI) registers. The 8088 *string instructions* employ the SI, DI, CX registers: SI contains the starting address of the data, DI contains the beginning destination address, and CX contains the number of bytes to be copied. After each byte is copied, the contents of the index registers are incremented (or decremented) and the contents of the count register is decremented. This continues until the contents of CX is equal to zero.

Segment Registers

The segment registers of the 8088 are its most mystifying characteristic. Fully grasping the segmented structure of the 8088 is crucial to understanding the PC architecture. Each time the 8085 performs an op-code fetch, the address bus is driven with the contents of the program counter and a memory-read operation occurs.

You have probably noticed that the 8088 does not have a program counter. To add confusion to this apparent oversight, all the registers in the 8088 are 16-bits wide, but the address bus is 20 bits wide. How are the extra 4 bits of the address derived?

During the execution of a program, the contents of RAM hold three specific types of information: the machine language code of the program, a data area where constants and variables are stored, and the contents of the system stack. Intel elected to design the architecture of the 8088 to reflect these different types of information.

The *segment registers* hold the base address of the designated segment. The *code segment register* (CS) holds the base address of the memory segment that contains the currently executing *program code*. Because CS is 16 bits wide, a code segment is a maximum of 64K in length.

The *instruction pointer* (IP) is the 8088's equivalent of the program counter that we examined in Chapter 2. It is a 16-bit offset into the 64-kB addressing space of the code segment. Figure 4.4 illustrates how the contents of the CS and IP are combined to produce the actual 20-bit address that identifies an individual memory location within the 1-MB addressing range of the 8088.

The 16-bit segment address must be expanded to 20 bits. This is accomplished by multiplying the contents of the CS register by 16. As you remember from Chapter 2, this operation consists of placing a 16-bit value into a 20-bit register and performing four consecutive arithmetic shift-left operations. This

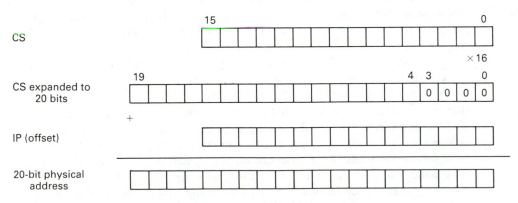

Figure 4.4 Segmented memory conversion.

established a 20-bit base address that starts on a *paragraph boundary* (i.e., an address divisible by 16).

The contents of the IP register are used as an offset to address any of the 64K unique memory locations within the code segment. The contents of the expanded CS register summed with the contents of the IP register yield the actual 20-bit physical address of the next instruction. This physical address is called the *effective address*. Figure 4.5 is a symbolic description of the derivation of the effective address.

We have now seen how the CS and IP work together to form the physical address of the next instruction to be executed by the 8088. The *data segment register* (DS) performs the same function for the data area as the CS performs for the program area. All addresses associated with data transfers are taken relative to the DS.

The stack segment is the third type of information that we find in the computer's memory. Although the CS and DS can both reside in RAM and ROM, the stack segment must be placed in RAM. The *stack segment register* (SS) defines the base of the 64K stack segment. The SP register is used with the SS register to determine the effective address of the next available location on the system stack. The BP and SS registers define the effective address of the data stack.

The *extra segment register* (ES) contains the value of an additional segment, which is used as a secondary data segment. The contents of the ES and DI register are used to calculate the effective address during string operations.

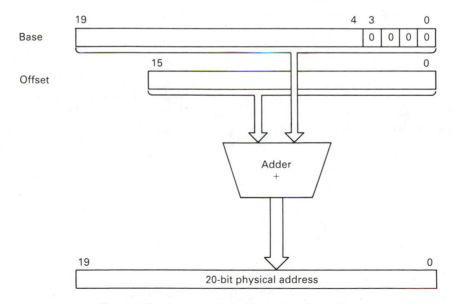

Figure 4.5   Symbolic derivation of effective address.

4.4 THE 8088 FLAGS REGISTER

It is important to comprehend fully that each of the flags is an independent entity, a simple 1-bit location that contains a logic 0 (flag reset) or logic 1 (flag set). Figure 4.6 illustrates the flags register of the 8088.

Seven bits of the flags register are not currently implemented; their contents should be ignored. Of the remaining 9 bits, six are used to reflect the status of the latest arithmetic or logical operation. Five of the six status flags are simply taken from the 8085 microprocessor. The other three flags indicate internal 8088 controls.

Carry Flag (CF)

The carry flag is set when the result of an operation produces a number that will not fit into the 8-bit or 16-bit accumulator. This happens when either a carry or a borrow occurs. Arithmetic and logical instructions affect the state of the CF. Shift and rotate instructions can be used to move a bit into the CF position to be tested by a conditional jump instruction.

Parity Flag (PF)

The parity flag reflects the combined number of bits set in the accumulator. The PF flag is set if the number of logic 1s in the accumulator is even and reset when it is odd. The PF was originally designed to test for transmission errors and is the least used of all the flags.

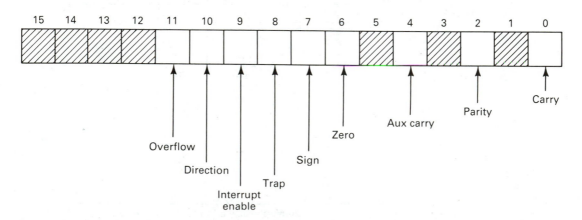

Figure 4.6   8088 status flags.

Auxiliary Carry (AC)

The AC flag is used to simplify the processing of *binary-coded decimal* (BCD) math. In BCD math a single decimal digit is stored in the upper of lower *nibble* (4 bits) of a register. The AC flag is set to indicate a BCD carry or an illegal BCD digit residing in the accumulator. The status of AC and the standard carry flag are used with the *decimal adjust after addition* (DAA) and *decimal adjust after subtraction* (DAS) instructions.

Zero Flag (ZF)

The ZF is one of the most useful flags. When an operation returns a value of zero, the ZF will be set; otherwise, the ZF will be reset. The ZF is used as an indication of equality during the comparison of two quantities. Consider the simple example where a register is used as a counter. It is initialized to the number of times a particular operation should be performed. After each iteration, the contents of the counter register are decremented and the condition of the ZF is checked. When the ZF is set, the loop should be exited.

The CX register on the 8088 is used as a counter for most operations. It is automatically decremented and the ZF tested after each loop iteration.

Sign Flag (SF)

Microprocessors perform subtraction utilizing 2*s complement math*. In signed arithmetic, if the MSB of a byte is 0, the number is positive; if the MSB is a logic 1, then the number is negative and is encoded in 2s complement notation. The SF flag is a copy of the MSB of the accumulator. In the 8085 microprocessor, bits in the accumulator were often rotated into the MSB position to be tested using a conditional jump instruction. The 8088 has an instruction called *test*, which enables any bit to be tested directly.

Overflow Flag (OF)

The OF is not derived from the 8085 microprocessor. It reflects an overflow condition that is the result of signed arithmetic. It is the signed arithmetic equivalent of the carry flag.

The remaining three carry flags indicate internal processor controls.

Trap Flag (TF)

Setting the TF under program control places the processor in *single-step mode*, which is used to debug programs. After each instruction is executed, an internal interrupt causes the processor to execute a user-defined routine where the contents of registers and memory can be examined and changed.

Interrupt Flag (IF)

Setting the IF enables the 8088 to recognize an active level on the INTR input. Resetting the IF results in the 8088 ignoring all INTR requests. Remember that the NMI can not be ignored or internally masked by the 8088.

Direction Flag (DF)

You have just learned that the SI and DI are index registers used in conjunction with CX to move blocks of data between memory locations. Resetting the DF causes the contents of SI and DI to be incremented after each instruction. Setting the DF causes the contents of SI and DI to be decremented after each instruction. As you can see, the setting of the direction flag determines the direction (low to high, DF = 0, or high to low DF = 1) in which block moves are processed.

IMPORTANT CONCEPTS OF CHAPTER 4

- In the PC the 8088 operates in maximum mode.
- The 8088 is an 8-bit microprocessor with a 20-bit address bus. The address/data bus must be demultiplexed by external TTL latches.
- The NMI on the 8088 is driven by circuitry that detects RAM parity errors and 8087 NDP service requests.
- The maskable interrupt input on the 8088 is driven by a complex programmable interrupt controller that manages the entire system's interrupt structure.
- The 8284 is the system clock generator for the 8086/8088 microprocessor. It generates three system clock signals and manages the system reset and ready status lines.
- The 8288 system controller effectively expands the control/status bus of the 8088. It provides memory and I/O access commands, interrupt acknowledgement, the ALE signal to demultiplex the address/data bus, and several bus buffer enable control signals.
- The address enable ($\overline{\text{AEN}}$) and data enable (DEN) signals are used to bring the 8088's address and data bus buffers to high-z. In that manner the system can accomodate bus requests from a DMAC.
- The register set of the 8088 is a natural extension of the 8085's register set.

- The register set is broken into data registers, pointer and index registers, segment registers, and an instruction pointer and flag register.
- The data registers can be employed as single 16-bit registers or dual 8-bit registers.
- The location of the next instruction is derived by performing four consecutive arithmetic-shift-left instructions on the CS register and adding this 20-bit value to the 16-bit offset of the IP.
- The three types of information associated with any program are the code, data, and stack.
- All addresses pertaining to data are taken relative to the expanded 20-bit address of the DS. The same relationship is true for the SS and SP.
- The extra segment is used as an additional data segment.
- All 20-bit addresses in the 8088 are derived from a 20-bit base address and a 16-bit displacement.
- Five of the six status flags function identically to the flags in the 8085.
- The trap flag is used in debugging routines to single-step the microprocessor through each instruction.
- The interrupt flag is used to enable or disable maskable interrupts.
- The direction flag is used to set the direction of block transfers employing the SI and DI registers as memory pointers and the CX as a counter.

5

LSI SUPPORT DEVICES ON THE SYSTEM BOARD

In Chapter 4 we studied the three-chip 8088 microprocessor subsystem. We now turn our attention to the LSI support devices that provide important system services. This is a long and detailed chapter that will enable you to fully understand how the resources provided by these support devices are employed to create a powerful and easily expandable computer system.

5.1 THE 8255 PROGRAMMABLE PERIPHERAL INTERFACE

The system board employs the 8255 *programmable peripheral interface* (PPI) that manages many important system functions. We perform a detailed analysis of the 8255's role in the PC, which will help you appreciate the overhead associated with all microcomputer systems. Figure 5.1 is a block diagram of the 8255.

The 8255 used in the PC is the 8255-5. The 8255 is available in two versions: the standard 8255 and the 8255-5. The difference in the two devices is the maximum speed at which they can be accessed. In high-speed systems, such as the PC, the 8255-5 is employed. It is important to verify that the correct part number (including suffix) is used to replace a malfunctioning IC.

Let's examine how the 8255 connects with the address, data, and control/status bus of the microprocessor system.

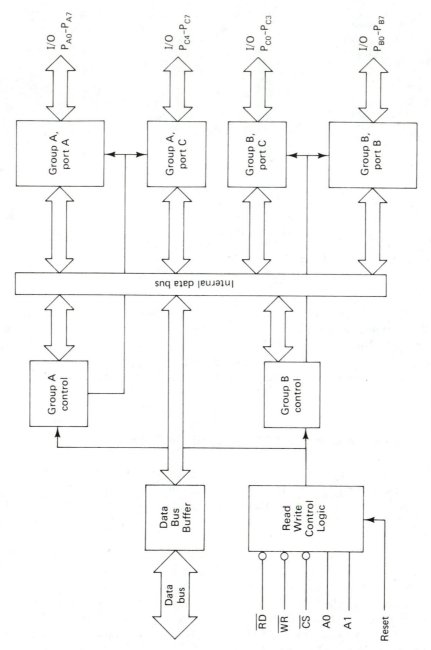

Figure 5.1 8255 programmable peripheral interface IC.

Data Bus Buffer

Internal buffers are used in complex ICs to minimize the load factor that the system buffers must drive.

R/W Control Logic

The I/O control lines of the 8288 are $\overline{\text{AIOWC}}$ and $\overline{\text{IORC}}$. These two outputs drive the $\overline{\text{WR}}$ and $\overline{\text{RD}}$ inputs of the 8255. When the *reset input* is at an active logic 1 level, the 8255 automatically assumes a set of default parameters.

Chip Select ($\overline{\text{CS}}$)

$\overline{\text{CS}}$ is an active-low enable input. When $\overline{\text{CS}}$ is at an inactive-high level, the 8255 is disabled and ignores all activity on the buses. When the microprocessor wants to communicate with the 8255, it outputs a specific address. The upper bits of the address drive the inputs of an address decoder, which generates the active-low $\overline{\text{CS}}$ signal. The lower two bits of the address bus (A_0 and A_1) are connected to the 8255. They are used to select one of four unique I/O address locations within the 8255.

Although the 8088 microprocessor uses 20 bits to address memory locations, only the lower 16 bits of the address bus are used to address I/O devices. This enables the 8088 to generate 64K unique I/O addresses. Figure 5.2 illustrates how the address bus is decoded in the PC to access I/O devices.

One megabyte of system memory is quickly and easily consumed in the PC. There is always need for more RAM and ROM address space. I/O devices, on the other hand, are not required in nearly such large numbers. For this reason, the upper 5 bits of the I/O address (A_{15} through A_{10}) are not decoded on the PC system board. Address bits A_9 and A_8 are both taken to a logic 0 level to indicate that the I/O device being accessed physically resides on the system board. The lower 8 bits of the address bus (A_7 through A_0) are used to select 1 of 256 possible I/O addresses of devices on the system board.

We have noted that the 8255 has two address inputs; this permits the microprocessor to select one of four locations that are internal to the 8255.

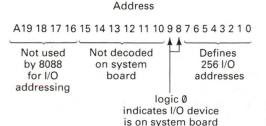

Address

A19 18 17 16 15 14 13 12 11 10 9 8 7 6 5 4 3 2 1 0

| Not used by 8088 for I/O addressing | Not decoded on system board | Defines 256 I/O addresses |

logic 0 indicates I/O device is on system board

Figure 5.2   8088 I/O addressing in PC system.

Sophisticated I/O devices have many internal registers. The number of internal addresses varies in direct proportion to the complexity of programming an I/O device. For convenience, the 256 possible addresses of I/O devices that reside on the system board are broken into 8 groups of 32 addresses each. This enables the PC's circuit designers to place a maximum of eight I/O devices on the system board, with the limitation that none of these devices have more than 32 internal addresses. It is important to realize that an I/O device is not required to use all 32 unique addresses to which it is assigned.

The 8255 is a perfect example of this concept. It needs only four unique addresses. If the fifth address in the 32-address block assigned to 8255 is accessed, it actually "wraps around" and addresses the first unique location in the 8255. This phenomenon is called *shadow* or *foldback* addressing. This apparently obscure terminology is mentioned to help you understand similar references in manufacturer's documents.

Let's refocus our attention on the characteristics of the 8255. The group A and B blocks in Figure 5.1 contain control and status registers. The 8088 issues commands to be stored in the control registers and interrogates the 8255 by reading the status registers. Once again, we see that the idea of control and status is a recurring theme in three-bus architecture.

The block diagram indicates that the 8255 has three 8-bit bidirectional parallel ports. Ports A and B are always used as 8-bit ports; Port C can be used as an 8-bit port or programmed to function as two independent 4-bit ports.

Because the 8255 is programmable, it provides many modes of operation. A control word is written to configure the 8255's operational parameters. The 8255 has three operational modes.

Mode 0. In mode 0 the 8255 functions with three independent 8-bit I/O ports. Each port is programmed as either an input port or an output port. The two 4-bit parts of Port C can be independently programmed as 4-bit input or output ports. Mode 0 is called the *basic I/O mode*; in mode 0 operation the 8255 is not capable of hardware handshaking. An output byte is simply latched on the 8 output lines, and an input byte is internally latched and accessible to be read by the system processor.

Mode 1. Mode 1 is used to support the full hardware handshaking requirements for the Centronics Parallel Interface. In mode 1 operation Ports A and B function as input or output ports; Port C is broken into two 4-bit handshaking ports to coordinate the orderly transfer of data between the parallel port and peripheral device.

Mode 2. Mode 2 supports a bidirectional I/O port. This is used in applications where a parallel port must transmit and receive data simultaneously. Mode 2 is rarely used in general-purpose microcomputers.

The startup program in system ROM initializes the 8255 to operate in mode 0. Port A is programed as an 8-bit input port. The outputs of the system setup switch 1 are connected to the inputs of Port A. One of the first operations performed by the startup program is to program the 8255 and then read the contents of Port A. In this manner the system configuration is established.

However, it may seem a waste to dedicate an entire 8-bit port to an operation that occurs only once each time the PC is powered up. Consider an event that occurs frequency in regular operation. A key on the keyboard is pressed and the serial data is sent through the keyboard cable to the system board. The data is then converted into a parallel 8-bit byte and an INTR request is issued. The 8088 responds by calling a service routine to read the byte of keyboard data. Port A of the 8255 is also used to read the output of the keyboard SIPO three-state shift register.

How can two output devices (the setup switches and the keyboard SIPO shift-register) share the same input port? Figure 5.3 illustrates how this problem is solved. The outputs of the setup switch block drive a three-state noninverting buffer. (This concept was originally illustrated in Figure 2.4.) The byte of keyboard data is held in an 8-bit SIPO shift register with three-state outputs. Notice the signal called keyboard/switch (KB/$\overline{\text{SW}}$). When this signal is high, the switch buffer is disabled and the outputs of the keyboard SIPO shift register drive the inputs of Port A. When KB/$\overline{\text{SW}}$ is low, the switch buffer is enabled and the keyboard SIPO shift register is disabled. This signal selects which device will drive the inputs of Port A of the 8255.

Port B on the 8255 is programmed as an output port. Each bit in Port B is used for a special purpose. A programmer will want to set or reset a particular bit in Port B without affecting the logic levels on the other 7 bits. Even when a port in the PPI is programmed as an output port, the contents of that port may be read and the bit of interest modified without changing the logic levels

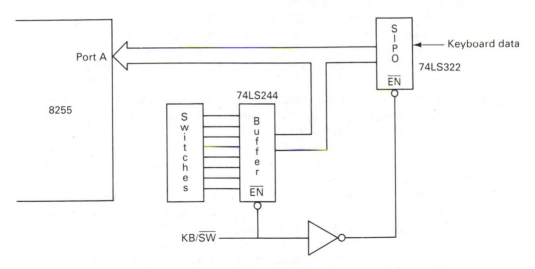

Figure 5.3   Sharing port-A on the 8255.

on the other bits. However, in the design of the PC, BIOS and PC-DOS calls provide all the low-level bit tinkering. The physical characteristics of I/O devices are transparent to the applications programmer.

PB_0 and PB_1 are used to control the audio-tone-generating system of the PC. We examine their usage later in this chapter. PB_2 has a very interesting use that is similar to the multiplexing example of Port A. Remember that the early versions of the system board had an additional system setup switch that was used to indicate how much RAM resided on expansion boards. This required that an additional eight SPST switches be read. As you may be beginning to sense, the 24 I/O lines of the 8255 are quickly consumed. The lower half of Port C (PC_0 through PC_3) is used to read the eight switches in switch bank 2. With the use of three-state devices, when PB_2 is at a logic 0 level the outputs of the last four switches in switch bank 2 are placed onto the inputs of PC_0 through PC_3; when the signal on PB_{23} goes high, the outputs of the first four switches in switch bank 2 drive the inputs of PC_0 through PC_3.

When the PC was first introduced in 1981, floppy disk storage was moderately expensive. In a misguided attempt to capture the lower portion of the personal computer market, IBM included a cassette interface port on the system board that was intended to enable the use of a low-cost audio cassette drive as the primary form of mass storage. Because cassette storage was intolerably slow and each cassette could hold only a small amount of data, it was never widely supported. Nonetheless, the legacy of cassette-control circuitry existed for the first two versions of the system board. On those system units you will see a cassette connector (which is identical to the keyboard connector). PB_3 of the 8255 was used to enable (logic 0) or disable (logic 1) the cassette-drive motor relay on the system board.

PB_4 is used to enable RAM parity checking on the system board, and PB_5 enables parity checking in expansion RAM. PB_6 enables/disables the keyboard clock. This clock is used to transfer the serial bit stream that describes the scan code of the depressed key into the SIPO shift register, whose contents are read by Port A.

Figure 5.3 illustrates a signal called $KB/\overline{SW}$ that was used to select whether the keyboard shift register or switch bank 1 drives the inputs of Port A. That signal is actually the output of PB_7.

We have already described how the low nibble of Port C is utilized. The high nibble of Port C is programmed as an input port. PC_4 was originally the cassette data input. In later models of the system board it is used to test the speaker drive circuitry. PC_5 was originally intended to support two functions: cassette data output and the output of a special timer/counter IC that is part of the audible tone subsystem. During the power-on self-test, the system reads this bit to establish that the system timer/counter is functioning properly. PC_6 and PC_7 are used to read the status of the expansion RAM and system board RAM parity errors.

Figure 5.4 summarizes the functions of the 8255 on the first two versions

8255 Programmable Peripheral Interface

```
060 - 060  PPI
  sense sw 1: r ffxxxxxx ff=1 to 4 floppy disk drives
              r xxddxxxx dd=0 no display
                            =1 40 x 25 color display
                            =2 80 x 25 color display
                            =3 monchrome or two displays
              r xxxxrrxx rr=0 16/64K RAM (system board)
                            =1 32/128K RAM
                            =2 48/196K RAM
                            =3 64/256K RAM
              r xxxxxxnx n=1 if 8087 is present
              r xxxxxxxr r=1 if any floppy drives
  keyboard:   r bsssssss b=0 make code, =1 break code
                         sssssss is the keyboard scan code
061 - 061  PPI
              w xxxxxxx0 disable timer 2
              w xxxxxxx1 timer 2 drives speaker
              w xxxxxx0x direct speaker drive
              w xxxxxx1x use timer 2, if active
              w xxxxx0xx gate sense switch 5
              w xxxxx1xx gate sense switches 1-4
              w xxxxcxxx cassette motor: =0 on, =1 off
              w xxxpxxxx RAM parity chk: =0 enab, =1 disab
              w xx0xxxxx enable expansion memory parity chk
              w xx1xxxxx disable    "        "     "    "
              w xkxxxxxx keyboard clock: =0 disable, =1 enab
              w 0xxxxxxx enable sense sw1, disable keyboard
              w 1xxxxxxx disable sense sw1, enable keyboard
062 - 062  PPI
              r xxxxssss ss=sense sw2 positon 4-1 or 5
              r xxxcxxxx c=cassette data in
              r xxcxxxxx c=cassette data out/timer 2
              r xpxxxxxx p=1 expansion memory board parity error
              r pxxxxxxx p=1 system board parity error
063 - 063  PPI
              w 0xxxcccs s=1 set port c bit code ccc
                         s=0 reset port c bit code ccc
              w 1mmxxxxx mm mode select a, upper c
              w 1xxaxxxx a=1 port a input, =0 output
              w 1xxxuxxx u=1 upper c input, =0 output
              w 1xxxxmxx m mode select b, lower c
              w 1xxxxxbx b=1 port b input, =0 output
              w 1xxxxxxl l=1 lower c input, =0 output
064 - 07F                shadow 060 - 063
```

Figure 5.4 Summary of the 8255 functions on the original system board.

of the PC system board. The left column indicates the I/O address of Ports A, B, and C, and the control register. A lowercase *r* indicates a read operation (input port), and a lowercase *w* indicates a write operation (output port). If you are not familiar with the hexadecimal number system, please refer to Appendix A.

The new versions of the system board have excluded all references to cassette circuitry and have dropped the additional expansion RAM setup switch. This has resulted in many I/O reassignments for the 8255. The setup switch and the keyboard SIPO shift register no longer share Port A of the 8255.

You may wonder how these I/O address reassignments affect the compatibility of the old and new system boards. Remember that the applications program should not directly access the hardware. It is proper programming technique to pass all system requests through PC-DOS or BIOS calls. When address reassignments occur, the BIOS firmware is merely updated to reflect the new physical address. The applications program still makes the same call, and the BIOS simply guides the request to appropriate device.

5.2 THE 8253 PROGRAMMABLE INTERVAL TIMER

Computer systems often have time-dependent functions that must be performed at precise intervals. The 8284 clock generator illustrated in Figure 4.1 has three clock outputs—all derived from the same 14.3-MHz crystal. The third output of the 8284 is PCKL. The PCKL is the highly stable *peripheral clock*. This 2.3-MHz clock is divided by a factor of 2 to create a an extremely reliable 1.119-MHz timing reference for the 8253-5 *programmable interval timer* (PIT). PITs are also called *timer/counters* (T/Cs). The -5 suffix of the 8253 indicates that is slightly faster than the standard 8253.

A PIT can be used to perform many useful tasks: generate precise timing delays, count external asynchronous events, generate custom clock signals, and provide variable-width "one-shot" output pulses.

Before we examine how the 8253 is utilized in the PC system, let's study its inputs and outputs. Figure 5.5 illustrates the block diagram of the 8253 PIT. You should expect to see the familiar data bus connection and control inputs. A_0 and A_1 are used to select one of four internal programmable mode, control, status, and count registers. The 8253 contains three identical 16-bit negative edge–triggered down counters. Each counter is associated with three pins. The clock input is a standard TTL signal with a maximum frequency of approximately 2.63 MHz. On the falling edge of each clock pulse the programmed contents of the counter are decremented. All the clock inputs are tied together and driven by the 1.119-MHz signal.

The gate input acts as a counter-enable signal. When the signal on the gate is active-high, the counter is enabled; when it is taken low, the counter is disabled and ignores all falling edges on the clock input. Finally, there is one

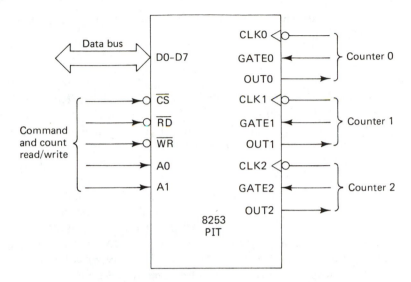

Figure 5.5   8253 programmable interval timer.

output for each counter. Like the ports on the 8255, each counter in the 8253 can be programmed to operate in many different modes. These modes define each counter's output characteristics. The 8253 is initialized by the power-up program so that each channel performs an important system task.

Timer 0

The Timer 0 channel is always enabled because its gate input is tied to $+5$ V. Timer 0 is used to provide a *time-of-day* (TOD) clock—also known as a *watchdog timer*. This channel of the 8253 is programmed to operation in mode 0; when the programmed contents of the counter are decremented to zero; the output goes to a logic 1 level, which causes the interrupt input of the 8088 to go active. This happens 18.2 times each second (every 54.936 ms). The main function of the TOD interrupt is to do exactly what one would think—update a memory location that contains the current time and date. This time and date is used by DOS and applications programs to time-stamp files.

The Timer 0 interrupt routine is also used as a reference to provide a motor-off delay for the floppy drive spindle motor. This allows the spindle motor to rotate for a short period after a read or write operation is complete. If another operation occurs before the time-out interval, the spindle motor need not be restarted and the system will not have to wait for the floppy disk drive spindle motor to come up to speed.

A unique function that the TOD interrupt provides is to generate a user-defined interrupt service routine (INT 1CH). This routine can be used by an application program to check the status of a particular input device or perform a periodic task, such as a software print spooling program or updating a digital display of the current time.

Timer 1

The simplest memory ICs are called *static RAMs* (SRAMs). They use the equivalent of a flip-flop to store each bit of data. The word *static* implies that once a bit of data is written into a SRAM, it will remain unchanged until another write operation occurs or power is lost. As you might expect, SRAMs have an extremely limited storage capacity because each memory cell takes up a large area of real estate on an IC die. SRAMs also consume a great deal of power.

The type of main memory employed in most computers are called *dynamic RAM* (DRAM). The storage cells of a DRAM are constructed from *metal-oxide semiconductor* (MOS) transistors that function like simple capacitors. A capacitor can be charged to a particular voltage to represent a logic 1 and discharged to 0 V to represent a logic 0. The problem is that capacitors are not perfect voltage reservoirs; they suffer from a phenomena called *leakage*. After a few milliseconds a logic 1 voltage level stored in a DRAM memory cell will discharge to a logic 0 level.

Thus the contents of each memory cell in a DRAM must be periodically *refreshed*. The refresh process essentially entails reading and then rewriting the contents of each DRAM cell. Refresh operation is fairly simple because the memory cells in DRAMs are organized in a rectangular matrix of rows and columns.

> When any cell in a particular row is read, all cells in that row are automatically refreshed.

We can now understand the requirements of the refresh procedure in a DRAM system; at least once every 2 ms one cell in each row of DRAM must be accessed for a refresh operation. We learn much more about the DRAM subsystem in Chapter 5. The information provided in the previous paragraphs serves as a foundation for helping you understand the function of Timer 1 of the PIT.

The output of Timer 1 is used to generate a periodic *dummy DMA cycle*. Recall that the conventional use of DMA is to move blocks of data between memory and mass storage. This dummy DMA cycle is used to simultaneously refresh a particular row of memory in every DRAM in main memory.

The original PC system board used 16K DRAMs. The next two versions of the system board employed 64K DRAMs. The latest system board employs both 256K and 64K DRAMs. All these DRAMs are internally constructed so that they have 128 rows. Timer 1 is programmed to produce an output every 15.2 µs. If a dummy refresh cycle occurs every 15.2 µs and 128 rows of DRAM must be refreshed, then the entire refresh operation takes 128×15.2 µs $= 1.94$ ms—just under the 2-ms specification!

In a later section in this chapter we discuss how a channel in the DMAC is used as a *row counter* in the refresh operation.

Timer 2

We should note that originally this channel of the PIT was intended to fulfill a dual role. It was to be the output of serial data for cassette storage and also drive the system speaker. We have discovered that none of the cassette functions were actually implemented.

Timer 2 is used in conjunction with 2 bits of the PPI to create a wide range of tones for the audible speaker. Figure 5.6 illustrates a block diagram of the speaker-drive circuit. Programmed in the 8253 mode 3, this timer outputs a symmetrical square wave whose pitch is inversely proportional to the 16-bit value loaded into the count register of Timer 2. The output remains high until the contents of the count register are decremented to half of the original value. The output then goes to a logic 0 level and remains low until the *terminal count* is reached (i.e., the contents of the count register are decremented to zero). The original count value is then automatically reloaded and the process repeats. Once loaded with a 16-bit value, the square wave output will continue without processor intervention.

Notice that PB_0 of the PPI drives the gate of Timer 2. When PB_0 is reset the timer is disabled; when it is set the timer is enabled and the contents of the count register are decremented after each falling edge on the clock input.

The output of Timer 2 is modulated by ANDing it with PB_1 of the PPI.

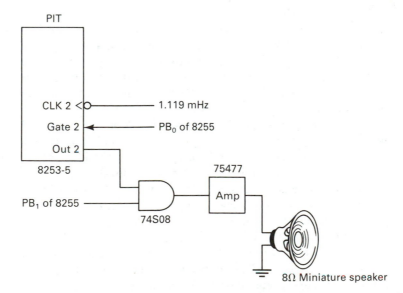

Figure 5.6   Speaker tone generator system.

8253 Programmable Interval Timer

```
040 - 040   TMR rw  dddddddd   counter 0 (1/2 byte sequence)
041 - 041   TMR rw  dddddddd      "     1   "   "        "
042 - 042   TMR rw  dddddddd      "     2   "   "        "
043 - 043   TMR w   ssxxxxxx   ss=0,1,2 select counter
            w       xxbbxxxx   bb=0 latch counter for stable read
                               =1 rd/wt most sig byte
                               =2 rd/wt least sig byte
                               =3 rd/wt least sig, most sig
                    xxxxmmmx   mmm=0 interrupt on term count
                               =1 programmable one shot
                               =2 rate generator
                               =3 square wave rate generator
                               =4 software triggered strobe
                               =5 hardware    "           "
                    xxxxxxxb   b=1 bcd, =0 binary
044 - 05F                      shadow of address 040 - 043
```

Figure 5.7   Summary of the 8253 PIT I/O addresses and functions.

This results in complex and interesting sound effects. Figure 5.7 summarizes the functions of the 8253 PIT within the PC.

5.3 THE PC INTERRUPT SYSTEM

In previous chapters we discussed the concept of interrupts and how they are employed to alert the microprocessor that a device is requesting service. We also touched on the fact that interrupt-driven systems make much more efficient use of the processor's time than do systems that require the processor to poll the status of each I/O device periodically. Figure 5.8 illustrates the management of the PC interrupt processing system.

Let's first focus on the NMI system. You know that NMIs cannot be ignored (i.e., masked) by the system processor. It is common practice in microprocessor system design to use a latch and AND gate to enable/disable a particular system function. The latch (D-type flip-flop) and AND gate in Figure 5.8 are used to enable/disable NMIs. Setting the NMI-enable flip-flop permits the AND gate to pass an active NMI request to the NMI input of the 8088. Resetting the flip-flop causes the output of the AND gate to be an inactive logic 0, regardless of the state of NMI requests.

The active-low input/active-high output OR gate (physically realized as a NAND gate) in Figure 5.8 allows three sources to initiate a NMI request: the 8087 NDP, parity generation logic on the system board, or parity generation

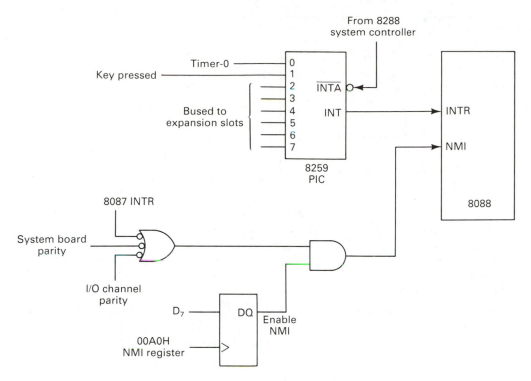

Figure 5.8   The PC interrupt system.

logic on expansion memory boards. After the 8088 receives the NMI, it reads bits PC_6 and PC_7 of the PPI to establish the source of the particular NMI request.

The INTR input of the 8088 is driven by the output of an 8259 *Programmable Interrupt Controller* (PIC). The PIC is a sophisticated device that allows a maximum of eight sources to request interrupt service. When two devices place simultaneous interrupt requests, the PIC will pass the request of the device that has been assigned the highest priority and hold the request of the second device until service of the higher priority device has been completed. In the PC, the PIC is programmed to give interrupt request 0 the highest priority and interrupt request 7 the lowest.

Timer 0, which updates the TOD clock, has the highest priority of the maskable interrupt requests. When the keyboard SIPO shift register has a byte of data, interrupt request 1 of the PIC goes active. The remaining six interrupt inputs of the PIC are routed to the expansion slots. Figure 5.9 indicates how the six expansion interrupts are typically (but not exclusively) employed. Most adapter boards (other than memory boards) usually have an interrupt select jumper. You must ensure that you do not assign an interrupt that is already in

Interrupt	Typical useage	
NMI 0 1	Parity, 8087 Timer-0 TOD Keyboard	Dedicated
2 3 4 5 6 7	Reserved Com2: Com1: Hard disk controller Floppy disk controller LPT1:	Selectable

Figure 5.9   PC system interrupt table.

use. This will not result in hardware damage, but the boards attempting to use the same interrupt will not function correctly.

5.4 THE 8259 PIC

Figure 5.8 illustrates a PIC that enables eight devices to share the INTR input of the 8088. Figure 5.10 illustrates the actual LSI IC that provides that function in the PC system—the 8259 PIC. On the left side of the PIC we note all the

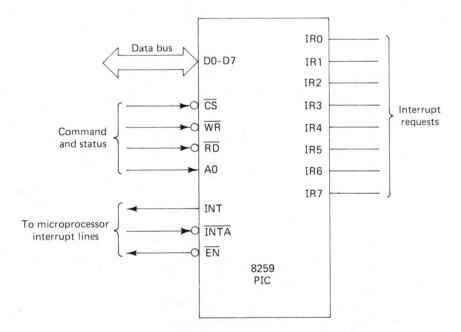

Figure 5.10   8259 programmable interrupt controller.

standard bus interface signals: 8 bits to the data bus, command inputs, and one address bit. As noted in Figure 5.8, the INT output of the PIC drives the INTR input of the 8088, and the $\overline{\text{INTA}}$ output of the 8288 drives the $\overline{\text{INTA}}$ input of the PIC. $\overline{\text{EN}}$ is an output that is used in some systems to enable data bus buffers so the microprocessor can read an interrupt vector from the PIC. The PC does not utilize this pin. The eight interrupt requests are employed as indicated in Figure 5.9.

The important question here is, How does the PC turn an 8-bit interrupt vector provided by the PIC into the 20-bit physical address of an interrupt service routine? The first 1K of RAM in an 8088 microprocessor system is dedicated to hold 256 interrupt vectors. Each interrupt vector consists of 4 bytes: a 2-byte code segment base address and 2-byte instruction pointer offset. Figure 5.11(a) describes the location in low RAM where the eight interrupt vectors to service PIC requests are stored. Those fluent in hexadecimal arithmetic will

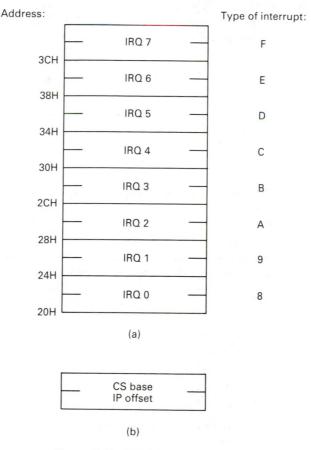

(a)

(b)

Figure 5.11 PIC interrupt vector table.

immediately notice that the address of the appropriate interrupt vector is *type of interrupt* multiplied by 4. Thus the vector address of INT 0 is 00H, and the vector address of INT 8 is 20H.

Figure 5.11(b) shows how the 4-byte interrupt vector is arranged in the table. The first 2 bytes are the IP offset and the second 2 bytes are the CS base. Using the method described in Chapter 4, the 8088 derives the physical address of the interrupt service routine. It is extremely important to realize that the 4 bytes dedicated to each interrupt type are only a pointer to the actual service routine, which may exist in system RAM or ROM.

To complicate matters the Intel family of microprocessors assume that 16-bit quantities of data in RAM or ROM are stored in *Intel format*. Intel format maintains that a 16-bit quantity is stored in memory with the LSB at the low address and the MSB at the high address. Figure 5.12 illustrates the contents of four bytes of RAM starting at location 20H. These four bytes of memory happen to be the address vector for IRQ-0 of the PIC. The 2 bytes stored at memory locations 20H and 21H hold the IP offset and the next 2 bytes hold the CS base. Together these 4 bytes form a 20-bit physical address that usually takes the symbolic format

BASE:OFFSET

In Figure 5.12 the interrupt vector can be described as having a symbolic address of F000:FEA5, which has the physical address equivalent of FFEA5H. Notice that the symbolic form shows the contents of the base and offset elements from which the 20-bit physical address can easily be derived. However, given a 20-bit physical address it is impossible to derive the original base and offset elements.

The 8259 is an extremely complex device to program. The following description of the PIC initialization is intended to help you understand how the 8259 operates in the PC system.

The PC's power-up program initializes the PIC by writing several *initialization control words* (ICWs). The 8259 is designed to be used in cascade mode. A maximum of eight 8259s may be connected in cascade to increase the number of system interrupts to 64. Also, the IRQ inputs of the PIC can react

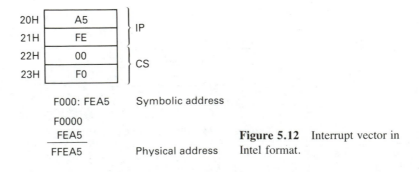

Figure 5.12   Interrupt vector in Intel format.

to a rising edge or an active-high level. ICW1 indicates to the PIC that it is the only 8259 in the system and that the IRQ inputs should react to the rising edge of an interrupt request.

Figure 5.11 indicates that the PIC will produce an interrupt type 8 when IRQ-0 goes active; IRQ-1 will produce an interrupt type 9, IRQ-2, an interrupt type of A, and so on. ICW2 tells the PIC to equate IRQ-0 to interrupt type 8. The PIC then assigns a sequential relationship to the remaining seven interrupts. ICW3 is used only in systems that have multiple 8259s.

ICW4 is used to set many options. One bit is used to select the 8085 or 8088 mode of interrupts. Another bit is used to define how an interrupt input will react to multiple requests. Consider the situation where an active edge occurs on IRQ-3 and the 8088 reacts by executing the service routine. If another active edge occurs on IRQ-3 during the execution of the service routine, should this interrupt be recognized? A bit in ICW4 is used to indicate whether an interrupt input should automatically be reenabled after the occurrence of an interrupt or wait until the system processor sends an *end of interrupt* (EOI) command to the PIC. This bit is reset, indicating that the 8088 must issue an EOI command to the PIC before another interrupt of the same type will be recognized.

Now that you understand the 8088 interrupt system, let's examine the actual events that occur when an IRQ input on the PIC gets an active edge.

Event 1. An interrupt cycle is initiated by a rising edge on an IRQ input of the 8259.

Event 2. The PIC examines the priority of the incoming interrupt request and places it in an interrupts-pending queue.

Event 3. The INT output of the PIC goes active-high, driving the INTR input of the 8088.

Event 4. The 8088 acknowledges the interrupt request by pulsing the $\overline{\text{INTA}}$ output of the 8288 active-low. This freezes the priority queue of the PIC.

Event 5. The 8288 pulses $\overline{\text{INTA}}$ active-low a second time. This commands the PIC to place the 8-bit interrupt type onto the data bus.

Event 6. The 8088 reads the interrupt type and calculates the address of the interrupt vector.

Event 7. The 8088 reads the four bytes in low RAM that contain the address of the service routine.

Event 8. The 8088 pushes the current contents of the CS and IP onto the stack and loads the CS and IP with the values read in event 7.

Event 9. The 8088 executes the service routine.

Figure 5.13 illustrates how the PC employs the 256 possible interrupt types. Nine of the BIOS interrupts (NMI and the eight IRQs from the PIC) are initiated by hardware. The other interrupts are invoked using the 8088 instruction

INT (type)

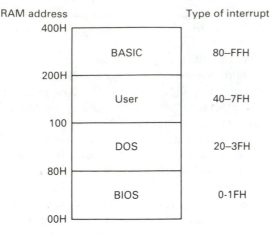

RAM address   Type of interrupt

400H

BASIC   80–FFH

200H

User   40–7FH

100

DOS   20–3FH

80H

BIOS   0-1FH

00H

Figure 5.13 Interrupt-type usage overview.

where type is 0 through 255 decimal or 00H through FFH. This instruction is called a *software interrupt*. DOS and BIOS service routines are called from an applications program by executing an 8088 INT instruction.

Figure 5.14 summarizes the two I/O addresses and functions of the 8259 PIC.

5.5 THE 8237 DMAC

The fourth special-purpose LSI device employed in the PC is the 8237 DMAC. As we have discussed, a DMAC is capable of becoming the master of the bus system. In that regard, it is extremely similar to a microprocessor. In fact, most DMACs are actually special-purpose microcomputer ICs with a dedicated microprogram. Figure 5.15 illustrates the pinout of the 8237 DMAC.

The PC employs the 8237-5 (5-MHz) high-performance four-channel DMAC. Figure 5.15 indicates that the control bus interface of the DMAC is different than the other devices that we examine in this chapter. First of all, the I/O read and I/O write signals are bidirectional. Remember that the 8237 will behave in two distinct modes. When it is being programmed by the system processor, the DMAC appears to be like any other I/O device and the I/O read and I/O write pins are inputs. On the other hand, when the DMAC takes control of the system as the bus master, the I/O read and I/O write signals become outputs and the memory-read and memory-write signals pins also become active.

Also notice that the lower 4 bits of the address bus are bidirectional; they are inputs when the 8237 is being programmed and outputs when it is functioning as the bus master. The other 12 bits of the data bus are provided by A_4 through A_7 and A_8 through A_{15}. The high byte of the address bus is multiplexed with

8259A Programmable Interrupt Controller

```
initialization command words:
020 - 020  INT w xxx1lisf   l=1 level trigr, =0 edge trigr
                            i=1 interval of 4, =0 of 8
                            s=1 single 8259, =0 multiple
                            f=1 init cmnd wrd 4, =0 none
021 - 021  INT w tttttxxx   ttttt= t7-t3 of intr. vect adrs
021 - 021  INT w 00000000   no slave devices
021 - 021  INT w 000sbbeu   s=1 spcl fully nested, =0 none
                            bb=0 non buffered mode
                              =1 non buffered mode
                              =2 buffered mode - slave
                              =3 buffered mode - slave
                            e=1 auto end intr, =0 nomral end
                            u=1 8088 mode, =0 8085 mode


operation command words:
021 - 021  INT w mmmmmmmm   =1 set, =0 reset mask for 7-0
020 - 020  INT w eee00111   eee=0 rotate in auto eoi - set
                               =1 non specific eoi
                               =2 no operation
                               =3 specific eoi
                               =4 rotate in auto eoi - reset
                               =5 rotate on non specific eoi
                               =6 set priority using lll
                               =7 rotate on specific eoi lll
020 - 020  INT w 0mm01prr   mm=2 reset special mask
                               =3 set special mask
                            p=1 poll, =0 no poll
                            rr=2 rd ir reg on nxt read
                               =3 rd is reg on nxt read
```

Figure 5.14   8259 PIC I/O addresses.

the 8 bits of the data bus. *Address strobe* (ADSTB) functions as the ALE signal to demultiplex the address/data bus.

As illustrated in Figure 4.1, when AEN (address enable) goes active-high, the 8288 system controller and the 74LS373 address bus buffers are taken to inactive-high and high-z output levels. This enables the 8237 to take control of the system address bus. Like all bus masters, the DMAC must have a ready input (to coordinate with slow memory and I/O devices), a clock input (driven by the 8284 at 4.77 MHz), and a reset input.

When one of the *DREQ* (DMA request) inputs is taken active-high, the DMAC requests control of the bus system by bringing HRQ (hold request) to an active-high level. The microprocessor relinquishes control of the buses and

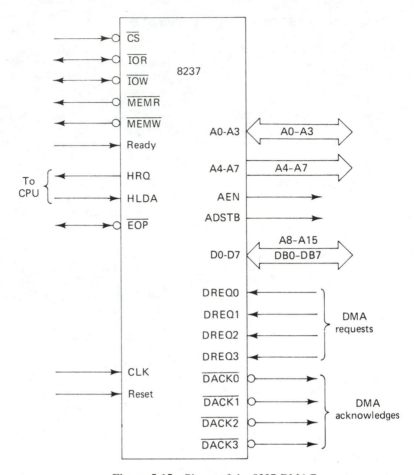

Figure 5.15   Pinout of the 8237 DMAC.

then responds by taking the 8237's HLDA (hold acknowledge) input to an active-high level. The 8237 then asserts the appropriate $\overline{\text{DACK}}$ (DMA acknowledge) output, which functions as a DMA-acknowledge chip-select signal for the I/O device-requesting service. Figure 5.16 illustrates a simplified block diagram of the DMA system operation. The address, data, and control buses can be driven by either the microprocessor or DMAC. Note that Intel uses the term *hold* as a description of a DMA operation. Thus in Intel terminology, a hold request is a DMA request and a hold acknowledge indicates that the microprocessor has taken its bus system to high-z.

Event 1. Let's assume that an applications program needs to read a sector of data from floppy disk storage. A DOS function call is invoked that instructs the floppy disk controller IC to initiate the transfer. The floppy disk controller requests DMA operation by bringing DREQ to an active level.

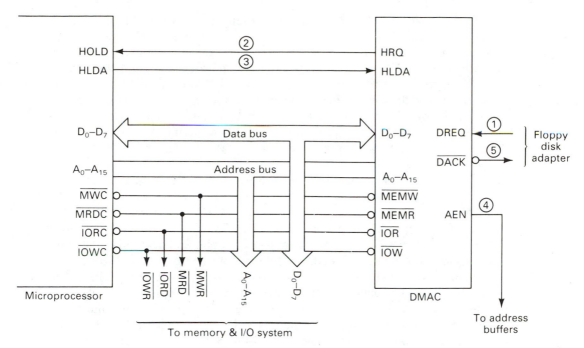

Figure 5.16   Simplified DMA operation.

Event 2. The DMAC must now ask the microprocessor to relinquish control of the bus system by taking HRQ to an active level. HRQ drives the DMA request (hold) input of the microprocessor.

Event 3. The microprocessor takes its buses to high-z and acknowledge that the requesting bus master can take control by driving HLDA to an active level.

Event 4. The DMAC asserts AEN to enable its address and data bus buffers.

Event 5. When a microprocessor talks to an I/O device, the chip-select signal is derived from the upper address bits by a TTL decoder. The DMAC outputs an address that points to the source or destination RAM locations—the I/O device involved in the DMA operation is never explicitly addressed. After the DMAC takes control of the system bus, it asserts the appropriate $\overline{\text{DACK}}$ output and the block-transfer operation begins.

DMA operations in the PC are complicated by a few factors. When the 8088 is operating in maximum mode, the HOLD and HLDA pins do not function. DMA operations must be accomplished by generating wait states. The DMA request from the DMAC is conditioned by a block of circuitry on the system board called the *wait-state logic*. This circuitry finds a time when the 8088 can be placed into a wait-state. The output of the wait-state logic drives the RDY input of the 8284 clock generator and also acknowledges the DMA request.

A second complication in the PC system is that a DRAM refresh cycle must occur once every 15.2 μs. Most DMACs are programmed to operate in *block-transfer mode*. In this mode an entire block of data is transferred between RAM and disk. A block-transfer operation would have control of the bus system for long periods of time; this would keep the DRAM refresh operation from occurring, and the contents of main memory would be corrupted. For this reason the 8237 DMAC is programmed in a single-byte transfer mode. An individual DMA request must occur for each byte of data to be transferred. The refresh operation uses the highest priority channel in the DMAC. Therefore, a refresh cycle will never be missed.

The third complication of DMA processing in the PC is that the 8088 has a 20-bit address bus and the 8237 has only a 16-bit address bus. How is the address bus of the 8237 extended to 20-bits so that the entire 1 MB of 8088 accessible memory can be addressed? A 74LS670 four-by-four register file with three-state outputs supplies the upper 4 address bits for each DMA operation. Remember that the 8237 DMAC has four independent channels. The 74LS670 contains four memory locations, each with a capacity of 4 bits. These 4-bit memory locations contain the high-order address bits for the appropriate DMA channel. The 74LS670 is I/O mapped into the PC system. The 8088 must write the correct 4-bit value for each of the DMA channels into the 74LS670. Whenever a 64-kB boundary is crossed, the 4-bit value in the 74LS670 must be incremented or decremented to point to the new 64-kB block. Figure 5.17 summarizes the I/O addresses and functions of the 8237 DMAC and 74LS670 register file.

Let's take a moment to understand how a dummy DMA request from Channel 0 of the 8237 is used to refresh the DRAM subsystem. The current row address is stored in the *current address* register. Each DMA request causes the current row address to be output by the DMAC. After each refresh operation, the contents of the current address register are incremented. This process continues until all 128 rows of DRAM have been refreshed. At that point the contents of the current row address register is reinitialized to zero and the 2-ms refresh cycle is repeated.

Because Channel 0 of the DMAC is dedicated to RAM refresh, if it malfunctions or is accidentally reprogrammed, the PC immediately crashes. The remaining three DMA channels are bused to the expansion slots. In theory they can be employed for any purpose; however, Figure 5.18 indicates their usage in standard practice.

All PCs have at least one floppy disk drive. You can assume that DMA Channel 2 is actually dedicated to this function. Likewise, if a hard disk is installed in the PC, DMA Channel 3 is normally employed. If the PC has a floppy and hard disk and is also connected to a *local-area network* (LAN), Channel 1 is used as the LAN DMA channel.

Some LAN schemes support a "disk-less" PC configuration that does not

8237A-5 DMA Controller

```
000 - 000   DMA rw (2 bytes) current address chanl 0
002 - 002                        "         "        "   1
004 - 004                        "         "        "   2
006 - 006                        "         "        "   3
001 - 001   DMA rw (2 bytes) current word count chanl 0
003 - 003                        "       "     "     "   1
005 - 005                        "       "     "     "   2
007 - 007                        "       "     "     "   3
008 - 008   DMA r rrrrtttt    read status register
                              rrrr = request by chanl 3,2,1,0
                              tttt = terminal cnt chanl 3,2,1,0
            w arlptchm        write command register:
                              a=1 DACK active high, =0 low
                              r=1 DREQ active high, =0 low
                              l=1 extended write, =0 late write
                              p=1 rotating priority, =0 fixed
                              t=1 compressed timing, =0 normal
                              c=1 ctllr disable, =0 enable
                              h=1 chanl0 hold enable, =0 disable
                              m=1 mem-mem enable, =0 disable
009 - 009   DMA w xxxxxrcc    r=1 set request, =0 reset request
                              cc= channel # 0-3
00A - 00A   DMA w xxxxxmcc    m=1 set mask, =0 reset mask
                              cc= channel # 0-3
00B - 00B   DMA w mmsattcc    mm mode =0 demand, =1 single
                                     =2 block, =3 cascade
                              s=1 adrs incmnt, =0 adrs decmnt
                              a=1 autoinit, =0 no autoinit
                              tt=0 verify, =1 write, =2 read
                              cc= channel # 0-3
00C - 00C   DMA w xxxxxxxx    start byte pointer w least sig byt
00D - 00D   DMA r             read last byte transferred
            DMA w xxxxxxxx    master clear
00E - 00E   DMA w xxxxxxxx    unmask all chanls, enab DMA rqts
00F - 00F   DMA w xxxxmmmm    m=1 set, =0 rst mask chanl 3,2,1,0
```

LS670 DMA page register control

```
080 - 080   DPG w   xxxxpppp   pppp=high 4 address bits chanl 0
081 - 081   DPG w   xxxxpppp      "   "         "     "    "   1
082 - 082   DPG w   xxxxpppp      "   "         "     "    "   2
083 - 083   DPG w   xxxxpppp      "   "         "     "    "   3
084 - 09F   DPG w              shadow of address 080 - 083
```

Figure 5.17 Summary of the 8237 DMAC and 74LS670 register file.

DMA channel	Common usage
0	RAM refresh
1	*Network interface
2	*Floppy disk interface
3	*Hard disk interface

*Bused to expansion slots

Figure 5.18 DMA channel assignment.

have any mass storage (i.e., no floppy or hard disk). In this situation all software and data are accessed via the network; special firmware installed on the network adapter enables the PC to boot from the system server instead of a local floppy. This is an exception to the statement that indicated that all PCs must have at least one floppy disk drive.

As is true with system interrupts, no two devices should attempt to use the same DMA channel. Before you install any adapter board into a PC, you must establish which interrupt and DMA channels are currently in use. If the adapter board to be installed requires an interrupt or DMA channel, it must be configured to use one that is not already employed by the system board or other adapter card.

Consider the simple task of installing a serial port into the PC. This port must be addressed as COM1: or COM2: and may use either interrupt 4 or 3. If there are presently no serial boards in the system, the settings of COM1: and IRQ-4 should be selected.

5.6 BLOCK DIAGRAM OF THE PC SYSTEM BOARD

We have now examined all of the major components that reside on the system board. Figure 5.19 is a block diagram of the system board that illustrates all the subsystems and their relationships to the data and address buses. Notice the absence of the control bus. Assume that the appropriate read and write lines are connected to the various memory and I/O devices.

CPU Subsystem

The 8088 microprocessor, 8284 clock generator, 8288 system controller, 8087 NDP, 8259 PIC, and the wait-state logic constitute the actual processor subsystem of the PC. You may wonder why the 8559 is included in this group of circuitry. The PIC essentially expands the interrupt processing capability of the system in the same manner that the 8288 expands the control bus capability.

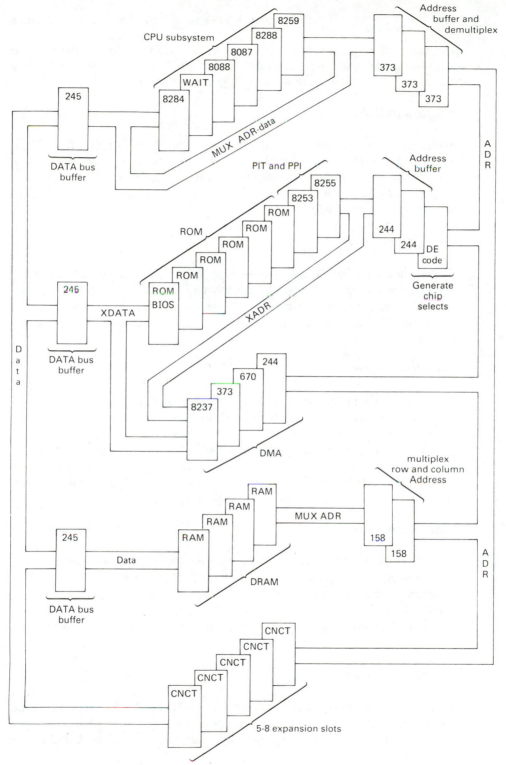

Figure 5.19 Block diagram of system board.

The wait-state logic also fits into this category. As was mentioned in the previous section, the wait-state logic is used to enable DMA access without employing the traditional hold and hold acknowledge pins of the 8088.

Address Buffers

Notice that two different types of TTL devices are used to buffer the address bus. The 74LS373 is a transparent latch; it not only buffers the address bus but also is used to demultiplex the address/data bus of the 8088. The 74LS244 is simply a three-state noninverting buffer; it is used to buffer the demultiplexed portion of the system address bus.

Data Bus Buffers

Because the data bus is bidirectional, the 74LS245 octal bus transceiver is employed as the data bus buffer. Remember that the three 74LS373s and one 74LS245 that are directly connected to the internal multiplexed address/data bus of the 8088 are taken to high-z when the DMAC gains control of the bus system.

ROM Subsystem

In the early PCs the ROM subsystem was created from five 8K-by-8 ROMs. There was also an extra socket for an additional 8K-by-8 ROM. On newer PC system boards, the sockets for these six 8K-by-8 ROMs are replaced by two sockets. The first one contains a 32K-by-8 ROM and the second socket contains an 8K-by-8 ROM. Notice that this is just a more efficient way of providing 40 kB of system ROM. The ROM contains the power-on self-test, BIOS, floppy and hard disk boot loaders, and the BASIC programming language.

DMA Subsystem

The 8237 DMAC, 74LS670 four-by-four register file, and the appropriate buffers constitute the DMA subsystem. The 74LS373 is used to buffer and demultiplex the address/data bus of the DMAC; the 74LS244 buffers the upper 4 bits of the DMA address as supplied by the 74LS670. The outputs of the two address buffers in the DMA subsystem must be a high-z during normal processing when the 8088 has control of the bus system.

DRAM Subsystem

Main memory is constructed from four banks of DRAMs. Each bank contains nine memory ICs—one for each bit of the data bus and an additional parity bit, which is used to ensure the integrity of the contents of the DRAM. The first PC employed 16K DRAMs. The system board had a capacity of 64K of RAM. A maximum of 596K of DRAM could be placed on memory-expansion boards.

The second generation of system board employed 64K DRAMs; it could hold a total of 256K of DRAM. A maximum of 384K could be placed on memory expansion boards. The latest generation of system board employs two banks of 256K DRAMs and two banks of 64K DRAMs. This total of 640K is the maximum that the PC hardware and DOS can support; no additional DRAM can be placed in expansion boards. The two 74LS158s are used to multiplex the lower 16 bits of DRAM address into an 8-bit row and 8-bit column address. We examine the DRAM subsystem in the next chapter.

Expansion Connectors

The earliest PCs had five expansion connectors; the newer PCs have eight expansion connectors. Remember that the older PCs also had only 63.5-W power supplies. In such a system, if 640 kB of DRAM and a hard disk subsystem are installed, the power supply may overload. We learn more about the PC expansion slots in the next chapter.

IMPORTANT CONCEPTS OF CHAPTER 5

- The 8255 PPI is used to interface the keyboard input, system-configuration switches, parity error signals, and timer-enable signals to the 8088.
- The first 256 I/O addresses are assigned to the system board in eight blocks of 32.
- Although the 8088 outputs a 16-bit I/O address, the PC processes only the first 10 bits.
- Cassette interface circuitry was found on the first two versions of the PC system board. This included a cassette connector on the back of the system unit and an enclosed cassette motor relay on the system board.
- The 8253 PIT provides three channels of fully programmable 16-bit negative edge–triggered down counters.
- Timer 0 is dedicated to providing a clock tick every 54.9 ms to update the TOD and decrement the floppy disk drive spindle motor delay.
- Timer 1 is used to provide a DRAM refresh interrupt each 15.2 μs. This timer must never be reprogrammed.
- Timer 2 is used in combination with a bit from the PPI to generate the speaker-drive signals. Once Timer 2 is programmed, it automatically cycles until reset by the system processor.

- NMIs can be externally masked by the resetting the NMI flip-flop. The system board and expansion RAM parity errors employ the NMI as well as the interrupt request from the 8087.
- The 8259 PIC manages a total of eight maskable interrupts.
- The 8088 acknowledges an INTR request by pulsing the $\overline{\text{INTA}}$ output of the 8288 twice. The first active-low pulse acknowledges the interrupt and freezes the interrupts-pending queue in the PIC. The second active-low pulse commands the PIC to place the appropriate interrupt type into the data bus, to be read by the 8088.
- The interrupt type is multiplied by four to derive the address of the service routine vector. This vector is 4 bytes long and is stored in low RAM. It consists of a 16-bit base address and 16-bit offset stored in Intel format.
- Interrupts 0 through 7 from the PIC generate interrupt types 8 through F.
- Interrupt 0 is used to signal the TOD clock tick.
- Interrupt 1 indicates that the keyboard input SIPO shift register has a byte of data to be read by the CPU.
- Interrupts 2 through 7 are bused to the expansion connector and are available for use by system adapter boards.
- The 8237 DMAC provides four channels of DMA. It has bidirectional control lines and can function as a bus master by directly transferring data between memory and mass storage.
- The normal hold and hold acknowledge pins of the 8088 are not functional when the 8088 is operating in maximum mode. DMA access is gaining by using a block of circuitry called wait-state logic to cause the ready input of the 8284 to go to an inactive level.
- Channel 0 *of the DMAC* is used in conjunction with Timer 1 to refresh one row of DRAM every 15.2 μs. This DMA channel must never be reprogrammed.
- DMA channels 1 through 3 are bused to the expansion connectors to be employed by interface adapters.
- An interrupt or DMA channel must never be shared by different expansion boards.
- The 16-bit address of the DMAC is augmented by a 4-bit output from a 74LS670 four × four register file.
- The DMAC address buffers must be at high-z during normal system processing.
- $\overline{\text{DACK}}$ is interpreted by the I/O device requesting DMA as the equivalent of an active chip select signal.
- The block diagram of the system board illustrated in Figure 5.19 is an important tool for understanding the relationship of the different subsystems on the system board.

6

THE DRAM SUBSYSTEM AND EXPANSION SLOTS

We have studied all the blocks illustrated in Figure 5.19 with the exception of the DRAM subsystem and the expansion slots. The knowledge of these two subjects will give you a complete understanding of the PC system board and lay the groundwork required to understand how memory expansion boards and other adapters communicate with the system processor.

6.1 CONCEPTS OF DRAM SYSTEMS

SRAMs are generally *byte-oriented* devices. Each unique address in a SRAM points to eight memory cells—one for each bit of data on an 8-bit bus. In contrast, DRAMs are usually *bit-oriented* devices. Each unique address in a DRAM points to only one memory cell. Eight DRAM ICs must be employed to create a block of system memory. Figure 6.1(a) illustrates the pinout of a 64K DRAM.

If a memory IC contains 64K unique locations, it must have 16 address inputs ($2^{16} = 64K$). The 4164 appears to have only half of the required address inputs. As illustrated in Figure 5.19, DRAMs have multiplexed address inputs. This enables DRAM ICs to be placed in much smaller packages. The 4164 DRAM is housed in a 16-pin DIP. If multiplexed addressing is not employed, it requires an additional 8 pins.

With each increase in semiconductor technology the capacity of DRAMs increases, not by a factor of two but actually by a factor of four; hence 16K DRAMs were replaced by 64K DRAMs. Likewise, 64K DRAMs have been

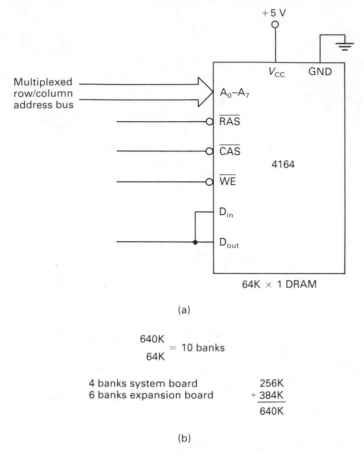

(a)

$$\frac{640K}{64K} = 10 \text{ banks}$$

4 banks system board   256K
6 banks expansion board   + 384K
                             640K

(b)

Figure 6.1   Pinout of 4164—64K DRAM.

replaced by 256K DRAMS in new designs. Very soon 265K DRAMs will be replaced by 1M DRAMs. This factor of four occurs because each time one physical address line is added to a DRAM (due the multiplexed address bus), it results in an additional two logical address lines. The addition of two address lines implies an increase of capacity by a factor of four.

Let's be careful not to confuse the multiplexed address/data bus of the 8088 microprocessor with the multiplexed address inputs of a DRAM. Figure 5.19 clearly illustrates that the 8088's address/data bus is demultiplexed with three 74LS373s. The two 74LS158s are used to multiplex the demultiplexed address bus of the system board into the row/column multiplexed address required by the DRAM subsystem. These two different types of multiplexed buses are not related. Let's discuss the pinout of the 4164 as illustrated in Figure 6.1(a).

Address Inputs

We see eight address inputs. We will discover how these lines are multiplexed to provide an internal 16-bit address that specifies one location within the 64K storage capacity of the 4164.

Remember that the memory cells within the DRAM are structured in a rectangular matrix of rows and columns. The lower 8 bits of the 16-bit address defines the row, and the upper 8 bits defines the column.

$\overline{\text{RAS}}$-(row-address strobe). $\overline{\text{RAS}}$ is a timing signal that is taken to an active-low level to indicate that the row address is presently residing on the address inputs.

$\overline{\text{CAS}}$ (column-address strobe). $\overline{\text{CAS}}$ is a timing signal that is taken to an active-low level to indicate that the column address is presently residing on the address inputs.

$\overline{\text{WE}}$ (write enable). $\overline{\text{WE}}$ is pulsed active-low to write the data bit residing on the data input into the memory cell specified by the 16-bit multiplexed address.

D_{in}/D_{out} (data in and data out).   Notice that the data-in and data-out lines are tied together. During a memory-write operation, this is an input pin; during a memory-read operation, it is an output pin. When the DRAM is not being accessed, this pin floats to high-z.

Power

The 4116 (16K DRAM) required $+5$ V, $+12$ V, and -5 V. The 4164 requires only $+5$ V. This not only makes the 4164 compatible with standard TTL power supplies but also releases two pins to be used as address inputs. This enables the 64K and 256K DRAMs to be housed in industry-standard 16-pin DIPs.

Figure 6.1(b) indicates how the 640K of system DRAM is placed into a total of ten 64K banks. On the versions of system board that exclusively employ the 64K DRAM, four banks (256K) reside on the system board, and an additional six banks (384K) can be placed on memory-expansion boards that are inserted into the PC expansion slots.

Figure 6.2(a) illustrates the internal symbolic negative edge–triggered latches that are used to demultiplex the row and column addresses. Let's examine the timing diagram of the DRAM read cycle as illustrated in Figure 6.2(b).

Event 1. The row address is placed onto the eight address inputs of the 4164 and $\overline{\text{RAS}}$ is taken to an active-low level. This causes the eight bits residing on A_o through A_7 to be stored in the row address latch.

Event 2. The address inputs of the 4164 are now driven by the column

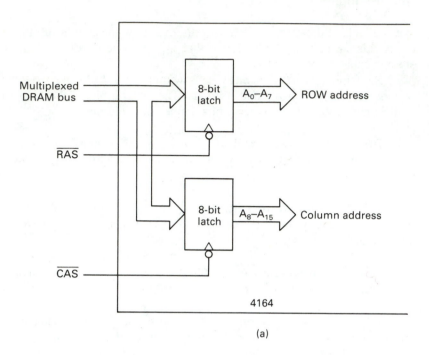

(a)

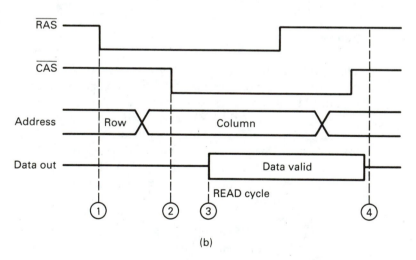

(b)

Figure 6.2   Using $\overline{\text{RAS}}$- and $\overline{\text{CAS}}$- to derive a 16-bit address.

address. $\overline{CAS}$ is taken to an active-low level and the column address is stored in the column address latch.

*Event 3.*The 4164 has now reassembled the 16-bit address. The bit of data residing at the specified address is placed onto the data output pin of the 4164.

Event 4. The data output pin is taken to high-z, and the $\overline{RAS}$ and $\overline{CAS}$ inputs return to inactive-high levels.

The next concept to tackle is how the 16-bit address is multiplexed onto the eight address inputs of the DRAM. Figure 6.3 illustrates a typical row/column multiplexing circuit. The 74LS157 is formally called a *quad 2-line to 1-line multiplexer*. Figure 6.3(c) shows that it can be simply modeled as a quad single-pole double-throw switch. When the select input (labeled $\overline{A}$/B on the IC) is low, the logic levels residing on the four A inputs are passed onto the four Y outputs. When select is high, the logic levels residing on the B inputs are passed onto the four Y outputs. Notice that the multiplexers in Figure 6.3(a) are always enabled because the enable pin (called the *strobe* in the function table) is tied to ground. Figure 6.3(b) is a function table that describes the operation of the 74LS157.

Figure 6.3(a) illustrates how two 74LS157s are used to create the multiplexed row/column address. The 8-bit row address (A_0 through A_7) is connected to the A inputs of both multiplexers. The 8-bit column address (A_8 through A_{15}) is connected to the B inputs of both multiplexers. The $\overline{row}$/column signal drives the select inputs of the multiplexers.

Once again, refer to the timing diagram in Figure 6.2(b). The 8088 places the 20-bit address onto its multiplexed address/data bus. On the falling edge of ALE the 74LS373s demultiplex and latch the 20-bit address. The upper 4 bits are used to drive address decoders. The lower 16 bits are connected to the inputs of the two 74LS157 multiplexers.

Initially the $\overline{row}$/column signal is at a logic 0 level. Therefore, the row address is driving the address inputs of the DRAMs. A timing delay circuit drives the appropriate $\overline{RAS}$ input to an active-low level. The falling edge of $\overline{RAS}$ latches the row address into the 4164.

A brief period later $\overline{row}$/column goes to a logic 1 level. The column address is now driving the address inputs of the DRAMs. After a slight delay to allow the address inputs to settle to stable logic levels, $\overline{CAS}$ is then taken to an active-low level. The falling edge of $\overline{CAS}$ latches the column address into the 4164 and the remainder of the read operation progresses as illustrated in the timing diagram.

The time-delay circuit in Figure 6.3(d) should help you visualize the $\overline{RAS}$, $\overline{row}$/column, and $\overline{CAS}$ sequence of signals. The 33-Ω resisters are used to match the output impedance of the 74LS157s with the input impedance of the DRAMs. This minimizes the period required for the address bits to settle to stable logic levels.

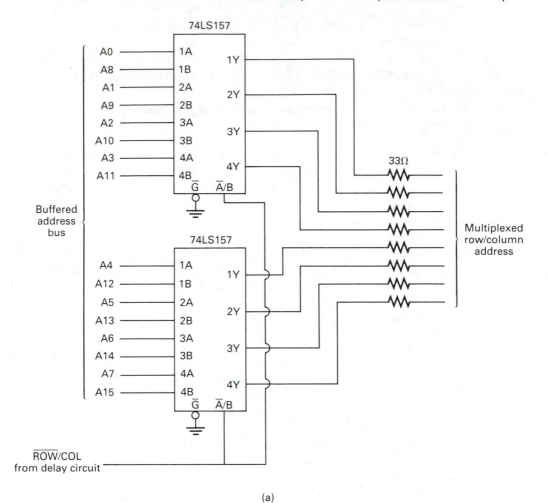

(a)

Strobe	Select	A	B	Output Y
H	X	X	X	L
L	L	L	X	L
L	L	H	X	H
L	H	X	L	L
L	H	X	H	H

Function table 74LS157

(b)

Figure 6.3   Using the 74LS158 to provide a multiplexed row/column address.

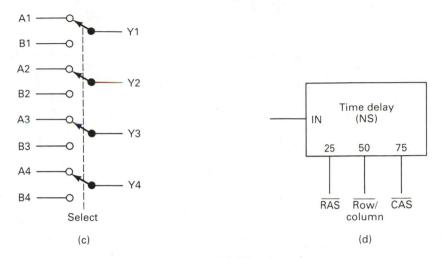

Figure 6.3 (Cont.)

If you refer to the schematics of the PC system board in the IBM *Technical Reference Manual*, you will notice that the system board actually employs the 74LS158 quad 2-line to 1-line multiplexer. The 74LS157 outputs true logic levels; the 74LS158 outputs complemented logic levels. As far as we are concerned, the 8088 places an address on the address bus, and the 74LS157 or LS158 multiplexes this address onto inputs of the DRAMs. The fact that the 74LS158 outputs a complemented address is actually of no consequence to the operation of the circuit.

Now that we understand the pinout of the 4164 and the row/column addressing scheme, we can examine how nine 4164s are connected to form 64K bytes of parity-checked DRAM. Refer to Figure 6.4. The outputs of the row/column multiplexers and the $\overline{WE}$ signal are connected to each DRAM chip on the system board. However, separate $\overline{RAS}$ and $\overline{CAS}$ signals are generated for each of the four banks of DRAMs on the system board. Within a particular bank of DRAMs only the data-in/data-out lines are connected to individual ICs. Thus each DRAM chip in a particular bank is used to store 1 bit of the 8-bit byte of data.

The ninth DRAM in the bank is used to store the output of a 74S280 parity generator IC. Using D_0 through D_7 as inputs, the 74S280 generates a logic 0 or logic 1 parity bit, which is stored in the parity DRAM. When a byte is read from DRAM, the 74S280 generates a parity bit and compares this bit with the bit that is read from the parity DRAM. If the two bits do not match, a *parity check 1* error is generated. This indicates a DRAM parity error has occurred on the system board.

The DRAMS in Figure 6.4 constitute one 64-KB bank of DRAM. To take the concept one step further, examine Figure 6.5. The nine DRAMs il-

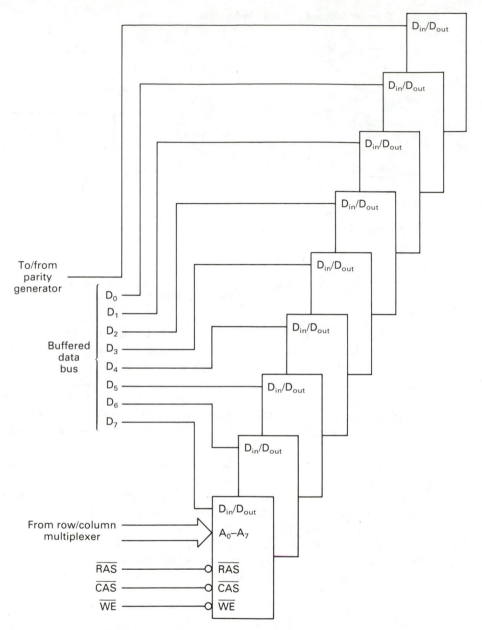

Figure 6.4 64K-bytes of parity checked DRAM.

lustrated in Figure 6.4 are condensed into a bank of DRAM. Each bank of DRAM in Figure 6.5 constitutes 64 KB of memory. Notice that the multiplexed address bus and $\overline{\text{WE}}$ line are directly connected to each DRAM. The buffered data bus is connected to each bank of DRAM, where each bit in the data bus is associated with a particular DRAM IC.

134

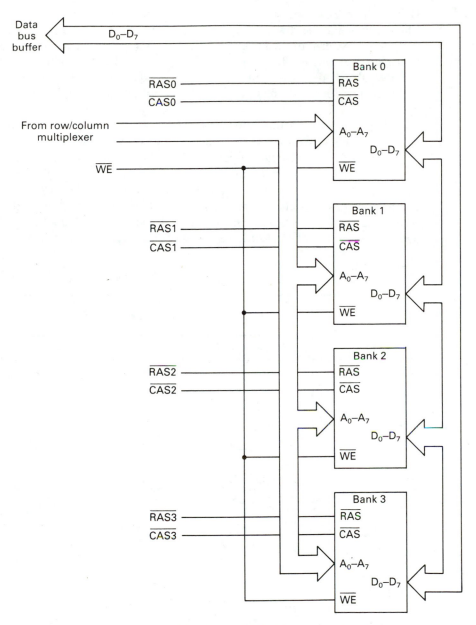

Figure 6.5 256K-bytes of DRAM on system board.

Separate $\overline{CAS}$ and $\overline{RAS}$ signals are generated for each of the four banks. During the refresh operation all four $\overline{RAS}$ signals go to an active-low level. This ensures that the row of memory cells addressed by the output of Channel 0 of the DMAC is refreshed in every DRAM on the system board. Figure 6.6(a) illustrates the simple refresh operation. The timing diagram simply illustrates that the DMAC places the current row address onto the address bus and $\overline{RAS}$ is pulsed low for a specified period. $\overline{CAS}$ is not taken active during a refresh cycle.

Figure 6.6(b) illustrates how four AND gates are used to make the four $\overline{RAS}$ inputs go active during the refresh cycle. On an AND gate a low level on either input will cause the output go to low. During a normal R/W operation $\overline{Refresh}$ is held at an inactive-high level. When Timer 1 of the PIT fires every 15.2 μs, DMA Channel 0 initiates a DRAM refresh cycle. The current contents of the DMAC's row counter are output onto the address bus and $\overline{Refresh}$ is taken to an active-low level. This causes the four $\overline{RAS}$ outputs to go active, and the four banks of DRAM have a row of memory cells refreshed.

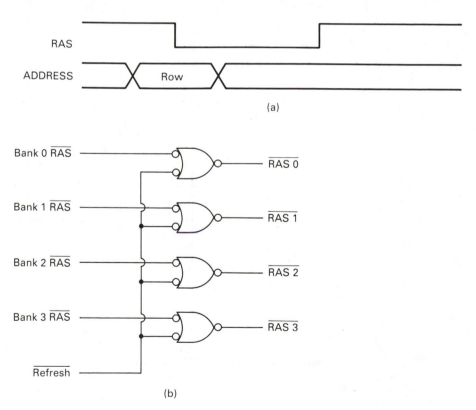

Figure 6.6   DRAM refresh-only operation.

6.2 THE EXPANSION SLOTS

Imagine that all the circuitry on the system board was compressed into one incredibly powerful microcomputer IC. What form would its bus system take? Like all microprocessors it would have the standard address, data, and control/status buses. But it would also have DMA capability and many interrupt-request lines. Keep this concept in mind as you examine Figure 6.7, which illustrates the signals that are bused to the expansion slots on the PC system board. The numbers in parentheses denote the edge connector pin number of each signal, as we see in Figure 6.8.

Address Bus and Data Bus

The address and data buses are the 20-bit demultiplexed address bus and 8-bit data bus as shown in Figure 5.19.

ALE

The 8288 outputs ALE as the timing signal used to demultiplex the address/data bus of the 8088. You may wonder why ALE is bused to the expansion slots—after all, the address/data bus is already demultiplexed. ALE is simply used to indicate the beginning of a memory or I/O bus cycle by the 8088. It provides a synchronization point to the expansion board.

Memory and I/O Control

These are the standard memory and I/O control signals that are output by the 8288 system controller (during 8088 bus cycles) and the 8237 DMAC (during DMA cycles).

Interrupt Requests

Remember that IRQ-0 and IRQ-1 are dedicated to the TOD and keyboard interrupts. Interrupt requests 2 through 7 are available for use by expansion boards, as indicated in Figure 5.9. Notice that the interrupt-acknowledge signal does not need to appear at the expansion slot because the 8259 PIC is the only device that needs to see the 8088's interrupt acknowledge.

DMA Request/Acknowledge

Remember that DREQ-1 through DREQ-3 are bused to the expansion slots. Likewise $\overline{\text{DACK}}$-1 through $\overline{\text{DACK}}$-3 must appear at the expansion slots. Figure 5.18 illustrates the typical uses of the DMA channels. Notice that $\overline{\text{DACK-0}}$ is bused to the expansion slot. Remember that this signal indicates that a DRAM

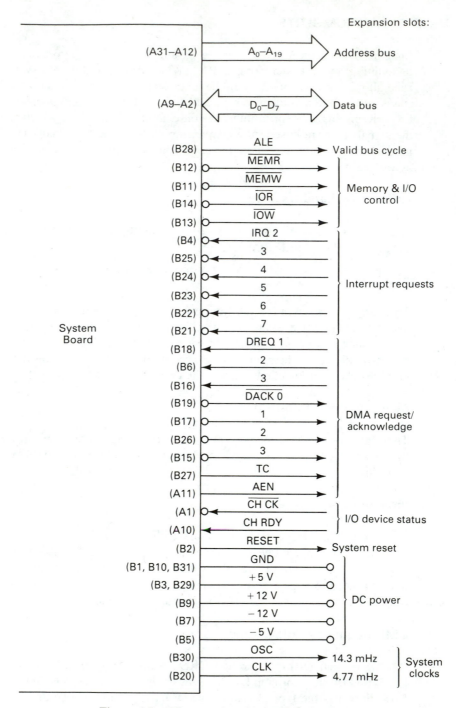

Figure 6.7 PC system board expansion slot signals.

refresh operation is in process. Expansion boards that contain DRAM must use this signal and the row address output by the DMAC to perform refresh simultaneously with the system board refresh cycle.

Terminal Count

TC is the inverted signal from the EOP pin of the 8237 DMAC. A positive pulse on TC indicates that the active channel of the 8237 has finished its DMA cycle.

Address Enable

Remember that the active-high signal address enable is used to indicate that a DMA cycle is in progress. This signal can be used to enable or disable buffers or determine the direction that signals flow through a bidirectional buffer. A good example of this function is that the memory or I/O control signals can be supplied by either the microprocessor or the DMAC. AEN is used to determine which control lines are bused out to the expansion slots.

I/O Device Status

These two pins are used to provide the 8088 with special status information.

I/O channel ready (CH RDY).   Remember that every microprocessor has a ready input. By pulling ready to an inactive level, a slow memory or I/O device can extend the bus cycle. CH RDY is used as a ready input for adapter boards. If a slow memory or I/O device that resides on an adapter board is accessed, circuitry on the adapter board will bring CH RDY to an inactive-low level for a predetermined number of CPU clock cycles. CH RDY will then return to an active-high level and the bus cycle will be completed.

I/O channel check ($\overline{\text{CH CK}}$).   Remember that two bits of Port C in the PPI are used to report DRAM parity errors. PC_7 is used to report system board parity errors and PC_6 is used to report expansion board parity errors. When a DRAM parity error occurs on a memory expansion board, $\overline{\text{CH CK}}$ is taken to an active-low level. This causes the NMI of the 8088 to go active. The system responds by reporting a *parity check 2* error and entering a halt state.

Reset

The active-high reset output from the 8284 clock generator is used to reset the circuitry on adapter boards during the system power-up sequence.

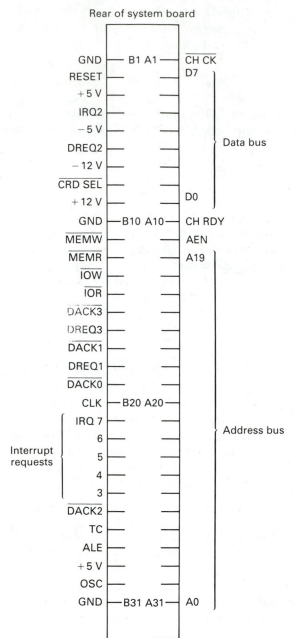

Figure 6.8 62-pin I/O slot edge connector.

DC Power

All adapter boards require well-regulated DC power. Five volts are used to power the microprocessor, memory, and TTL ICs. RS-232 serial ports require $+12$ V and -12 V. Floppy and hard disk drives require $+5$ V and $+12$ V. As indicated in the previous section, the original system board employed 16K DRAMs, which required -5 V. Since 16K DRAMs are no longer used, the -5-V DC output is rarely employed.

Notice that the expansion connector dedicates three pins for ground and two pins for $+5$ V. These two circuits must have extremely low resistance to accommodate high current requirements.

System Clocks

Two of the system clocks generated by the 8284 are bused to the I/O slots. As we have indicated, the 14.3-MHz clock is used by the display adapter and the 4.77-MHz clock is used to generate wait stares (utilizing the CH RDY input).

The signals illustrated in Figure 6.7 are terminated on five to eight 62-pin edge connectors. See Figure 6.8. Notice that the edge connector has two sides, identified as side A and side B. Each side has 31 pins. Looking at the I/O slots from the front of the system unit, side A appears on the right and side B appears on the left. Pins A-1 and B-1 are at the end of the I/O slot, which is adjacent to the rear of the system unit.

IMPORTANT CONCEPTS OF CHAPTER 6

- Generally speaking, SRAMs are byte-oriented and DRAMs are bit-oriented.
- DRAMs appear to have only half of the required address inputs because they employ a multiplexed address scheme.
- It is the responsibility of external circuitry to multiplex the address and create the correct $\overline{RAS}$, $\overline{CAS}$, and $\overline{row}$/column multiplexer timing signals.
- Most PCs employ 64K DRAMs. The latest version of the XT system board uses both 256K and 64K DRAMs. Soon 1M DRAMs will be employed in all new designs.
- The falling edge of $\overline{RAS}$ latches the contents of the address inputs into the row-select register.
- The falling edge of $\overline{CAS}$ latches the contents of the address inputs into the column-select register.
- When one memory cell in a DRAM is accessed, all cells that share the same row are automatically refreshed.

- Channel 0 of DMAC supplies the row refresh address and Timer 1 of the PIT initiates a DRAM refresh operation every 15.2μs.
- A refresh-only operation consists of driving the address inputs with the appropriate row address and pulsing $\overline{RAS}$.
- Separate $\overline{RAS}$ and $\overline{CAS}$ signals are generated for each bank of DRAM.
- 33-Ω resistors are used to minimize the ringing that occurs on the output lines of the row/column multiplexer circuits. This enables the row or column addresses to stabilize much more quickly.
- A 64-KB bank of DRAM consists of nine 64K DRAM ICs, one for each bit in the data bus, and an additional DRAM to support parity checking.
- The system board has the capacity for four banks of DRAM.
- A parity check 1 error designates a system board parity error.
- A parity check 2 error designates an expansion board parity error.
- The $\overline{CH\ CK}$ input on the expansion slots is used to report parity check errors on expansion memory.
- The expansion slots should be thought of as the outputs of a powerful microcomputer chip that supports all of the traditional aspects of three-bus architecture as well as advanced DMA and interrupt-processing features.
- Each expansion slot is a double-sided 62-pin edge connector.
- System DMA and interrupt channels are bused to the expansion slots as described in Chapter 5.

7

THE VIDEO DISPLAY

In the last chapter we analyzed the DRAM subsystem and the expansion slots. In this chapter we examine the monochrome display adapter that is employed by most PCs. The knowledge of the monochrome display adapter will provide the basic understanding of display systems that will enable you to easily comprehend the circuitry on the color graphics adapter (CGA) and the enhanced graphics adapter (EGA), which are the other popular display adapter cards for the PC.

7.1 THE RASTER-SCAN CRT DISPLAY

Most people are too well acquainted with the *raster-scan* CRT device called television. Raster-scan means that the picture is created by quickly "painting" a series of lines across the face of the CRT. Raster is taken from the Latin *rastrum*, which means *to rake*. On a raster-scan CRT the picture is raked across the screen. You will discover that this is a reasonably accurate metaphor of the actual process.

Characters produced by typewriters and daisy-wheel printers are continuous; they are constructed from unbroken lines. The characters created on video displays and by dot-matrix printers are not continuous but are formed from rectangular groups of adjacent dots. Figure 7.1 illustrates the letter *A* as it appears on a monochrome display.

Letters, numerals, and special symbols are created by illuminating selected dots in the rectangular matrix. The optimum dot-matrix character appears to be

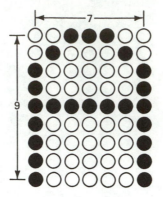

Figure 7.1 The letter "A" as constructed from a 7 × 9 dot matrix.

continuous, not actually a product of a finite number of dots. The major factors that affect the readability of dot-matrix characters are the size of each dot, the number of dots in the character matrix, and the distance between each dot. A comparison of 7 × 9 and 5 × 7 dot-matrix characters of equal physical size reveals that the first character is appreciably more readable and less fatiguing to the eye. The second character not only has fewer dots, but the dots must also be larger or further apart for the character to be of an equal size.

Each character is enclosed in a *character box*. The character box provides space between adjacent characters in the same row and between lines of characters. It also affords room for lowercase letters to descend below the base line of uppercase letters. The PC's monochrome display adapter places the 7 × 9 dot-matrix character into a 9 × 14 character box.

Figure 7.2(a) illustrates the screen capacity of the IBM monochrome display. It has 25 rows, each containing a a maximum of 80 characters. Therefore, the display has a capacity of 2000 (25 rows × 80 columns) characters. Figure 7.2(b) is an enlarged version of the five characters displayed in Figure 7.2(a). The dot capacity of the monochrome display can be described as 720 dots (80 characters × 9 dots per character) by 350 dots (25 rows × 14 dots per character).

Painting characters on a video display is similar to the process of painting a field (one full screen) of video information on a television. A CRT assembly is constructed from the following:

1. An electron gun
2. Horizontal and vertical deflection coils (called the *yoke*)
3. A phosphor-coated screen that glows when stuck by electrons

The electron gun fires electrons at the screen of the CRT. It is aimed by the magnetic fields produced by the vertical (up and down) and horizontal (left and right) deflection coils in the yoke assembly. The electron beam is initially

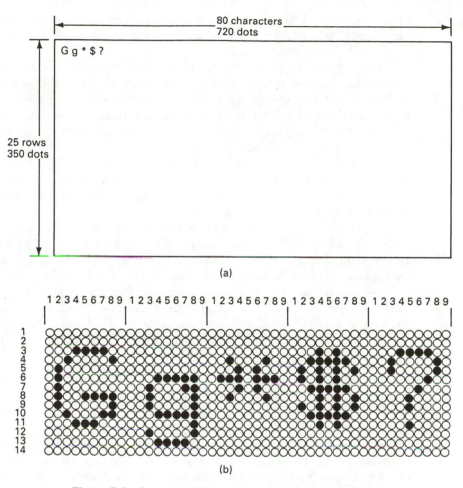

Figure 7.2   Screen capacity and dot generation of characters.

initially aimed at the upper left corner of the screen—the first column in the first row of dots.

The top row of each character is painted by moving the electron beam from the left to right. When the electron beam reaches the last dot in the first row, a signal called *horizontal sync* is asserted. Horizontal sync *blanks* (turns off) the electron beam and returns it to the first column in the second row of dots. The second row of dots is painted in a similar fashion. Notice that it takes 14 sweeps of the electron beam to paint the first line of 80 characters. This process continues until the last column in the last row of dots is painted.

A signal called *vertical sync* is then asserted. Vertical sync blanks the electron beam and returns it to the upper left corner of the screen, and the process of painting the *frame* of video information is repeated. The *persistence* of the human eye and the phosphor-coated screen is such that the screen must be *refreshed* at least 50 to 60 times each second to avoid detecting the flicker produced by the painting process.

The process of painting a frame of 2000 characters constructed from rectangular matrices requires a complex programmable IC called a *CRT controller* (CRTC). One byte of *video refresh memory* is required to hold the ASCII code of each character and a second byte is used to retain its associated *attributes* (blinking, underlined, reverse video, or intensified). If you are not familiar with the ASCII code, please read Appendix B.

To avoid confusion between the concepts of dynamic RAM, which requires a periodic refresh operation, and video refresh memory, whose contents are used to periodically refresh the video display, we use the term *display-RAM* as an alternative to video refresh memory.

A *character generator* is a ROM that contains the bit patterns to create each row of the 256 dot-matrix characters that can be displayed by the PC's monochrome display system. A PISO shift register is used to convert the 7-bit output (one bit for each column in the character) of the character generator into a bit stream to bias the control grid of the electron gun. A logic 1 causes the electronic gun to fire a sufficient number of electrons to illuminate a dot on the face of the CRT; a logic 0 suspends the firing of electrons. In this manner the dot patterns of each character are painted onto the screen.

7.2 THE 6845 CRT CONTROLLER

The 6845 CRTC is used in both the monochrome display adapter and the color graphics adapter. This extremely powerful, yet versatile, programmable LSI IC manages the entire display adapter in a fashion similar to the manner in which the 8088 controls the system buses. Figure 7.3 illustrates the simplified pinout of the 6845 as it is implemented on the monochrome display adapter. The 6845 is the only LSI device that we examine that is not manufactured by Intel. It is a product of Motorola Corp.

Data Bus Connection

D_0 through D_7 is the standard data bus connection that we have seen throughout this book. A 74LS245 is used to buffer the expansion slot data bus from the local data bus of the monochrome display adapter. The data bus connection to the display adapter is used to access the CRTC and the display-RAM for read and write operations.

RS

The 6845 has 19 internal registers. To address each register explicitly the 6845 would require a total of five address inputs. In order to fit the 6845 into a 40-

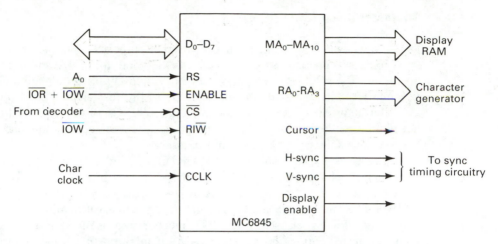

Figure 7.3   Simplified pinout of the 6845 CRTC.

pin package, a different register-addressing scheme had to be created. When RS is low, the 5-bit address of the selected internal register is written into the 6845's *address register*. Subsequent accesses to the 6845 bring RS to a logic 1 level, and the internal register pointed to by the contents of the address register is accessed.

Enable

The enable input is designed to be driven by the second phase of the clock output from a Motorola microprocessor. On the monochrome display adapter, enable goes active-high when either $\overline{\text{IOR}}$ or $\overline{\text{IOW}}$ from the expansion slot is at an active-low level. Simply put, the CRTC is enabled during I/O accesses.

$\overline{\text{CS}}$

$\overline{\text{CS}}$ is a standard active-low chip select that you have seen with all bus-connected devices.

R/$\overline{\text{W}}$

Intel ICs have $\overline{\text{IOR}}$ and $\overline{\text{IOW}}$ command bus inputs. Because Motorola microprocessors support only memory-mapped I/O, the 6845 has a R/$\overline{\text{W}}$ input. When $\overline{\text{CS}}$ is active-low and enable is active-high, the level on the R/$\overline{\text{W}}$ will determine whether the CRTC is being accessed for a read or write operation. R/$\overline{\text{W}}$ is driven by $\overline{\text{IOW}}$ of the expansion slot.

Character Clock (CCLK)

Digital circuits utilize clocks for many different purposes. The microprocessor synchronizes its operations to the system clock, as does the DMAC during DMA operation. The 8253 PIT employs its clock inputs as a timing reference to generate accurate system alarm clocks for DRAM refresh and the TOD update, as well as to produce interesting audible tones. The 8255 PPI and 8259 PIC do not require a clock input. Their operation is synchronized to commands and acknowledge signals from the microprocessor.

The clock signal required by the CRTC is called a character clock. We know that the character produced by the monochrome display adapter is 7 dots wide plus 2 extra dots to separate characters on the same line. A rising edge on the CCLK indicates to the CRTC that the time interval required to shoot 9 dots at the CRT has elapsed. The CRTC reacts to the rising edge on the clock input by incrementing the contents of its display-RAM address outputs— effectively pointing to the next character to be displayed for a 9-dot time interval.

Display Refresh Memory Address (MA_0 through MA_{10})

The 6845 has a total of 14 memory address outputs, which enables it to support a maximum of 16K of display-RAM. Although the PC's CGA employs 16K of display-RAM, the monochrome display adapter employs only 2K. Thus 11 address lines are implemented ($2^{11} = 2K$).

Consider the separate responsibilities of the 8088 system processor and the 6845 CRTC concerning the process of writing new characters to display-RAM and supporting the unrelenting effort of refreshing the video display.

We know that after a key is depressed and converted into an 8-bit parallel byte, IRQ-1 on the PIC is driven active-high. The 8088 services the interrupt request by acquiring the address of the keyboard service routine from the PIC and reading the contents of the keyboard shift register into an internal CPU register. If the application wants this keystroke to be displayed, a DOS or BIOS call is invoked. This causes the ASCII value of the keystroke to be written into a specific location of video-RAM on the monochrome display adapter.

It appears that the process of writing a character into the display-RAM is the responsibility of the system processor. However, once the character is written into display-RAM, the CPU is no longer involved. The 8088 is much too busy to participate in the high-overhead housekeeping chore of constantly refreshing the video display.

That is the important function of the 6845 CRTC. Once the ASCII code of the character is written into the display-RAM, the CRTC provides the correct address of the character that is currently being painted onto the screen of the CRT. This process is similar to that of the 8237 DMAC providing the current row refresh address of the DRAM subsystem.

Display-RAM must be *dual-ported*—accessible to both the system processor (or DMAC) and also to the CRTC. Later in this chapter we see that the mechanics of dual-porting display-RAM is similar to multiplexing row/column addresses in a DRAM system.

Raster Address (RA$_0$ through RA$_3$)

Remember that raster refers to the individual lines that constitute the CRT display. We know that a character on the monochrome display adapter requires 14 rasters—one for each row of the character box. (For that reason many people prefer to interpret the letters *RA* as row address.) The raster address defines which row of dots in the the character matrix is currently being painted on the screen of the CRT. In the next section we learn how the raster address outputs are employed.

Cursor

If you look closely at a computer video display, you will notice that the cursor moves freely about the screen and does not affect the character over which it is positioned. Therefore, the cursor is not a character generated from display-RAM but rather is an independent entity. The shape of the cursor can be programmed to be an underline or block that is steady or blinking. The present location of the cursor is kept in the *cursor register* of the CRTC. At the appropriate time the cursor output goes active and it is mixed with the video output to create a cursor at the desired location.

Sync Signals

The CRTC uses the CCKL as the timing reference to create the vertical sync (V-sync) and horizontal sync (H-sync) signals, whose functions were described in the first section of this chapter.

Display Enable

The display enable output goes active-high during the time that it takes to paint the 720 dots that constitute one line on the PC's monochrome display. It goes inactive-low to provide a CRT blanking signal when the electron beam is returning from the right side of the screen to the next row of dots of the left side of the screen. This period is called the *horizontal blanking*, or *fly-back*, interval.

7.3 BLOCK DIAGRAM OF A GENERALIZED DISPLAY SYSTEM

We have now covered the basics of raster-scan CRTs and the function of CRTCs. Figure 7.4 illustrates the simplified block diagram of a display system.

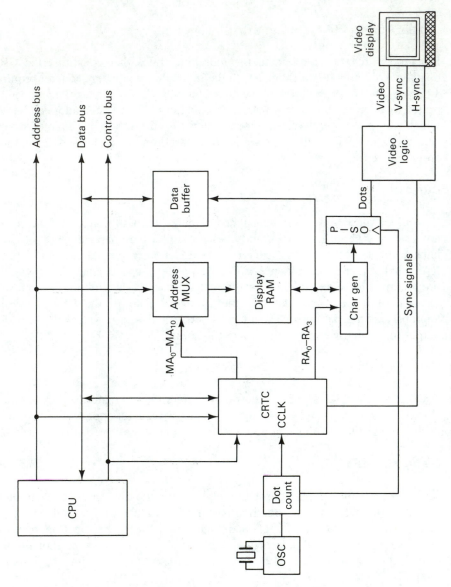

Figure 7.4 Block diagram of monochrome display adapter.

Bus System Connections

Notice that the system processor has the standard address, data, and control bus connections to the CRTC. Figure 7.3 indicates that only one address line is actually connected to the CRTC. The others are used to decode the CRTC chip-select signal. The data bus connection to the CRTC is used to program the device and read status registers. We also saw that the only control line connected to the CRTC was $\overline{\text{IOW}}$. The equivalent of the $\overline{\text{IOR}}$ signal is derived from a high level on R/$\overline{\text{W}}$, while $\overline{\text{CS}}$ and enable are at active levels.

Notice that the system address bus is also connected to the address multiplexer. Remember that the microprocessor writes characters to be displayed into the display-RAM. It also can read the contents of display-RAM to establish which character is currently displayed at a particular location of the video display.

The system data bus is connected to a bidirectional data bus buffer. This enables the CPU to access display-RAM for both read and write operations, as discussed in the previous paragraph.

Dot-Clock Generation

The dot-clock is a high-frequency clock signal that acts as the timing reference for shifting the output of the character generator into the video-processing logic. The character clock is derived from the dot-clock.

CRTC Address Outputs

Remember that the CRTC is responsible for providing the display-RAM address of the character that is currently being refreshed on the video display. A multiplexer circuit is employed to enable both the system processor and the CRTC to access the display-RAM.

Character Generator and PISO Shift Register

The character generator is a ROM that contains all the row patterns for the 256 characters that can be displayed by the monochrome display adapter.

Consider the action of refreshing one line of 80 characters. The CRTC provides the display-RAM address of the first character in the row and the raster address 0000. The output byte of the display-RAM and the raster address outputs of the CRTC are used as address inputs to the character generator. The seven dots describing the first row of the first character on the line are output from the character generator and placed on the inputs of the PISO shift register. On each rising edge of the dot-clock, one dot of video information is shifted into the video logic circuitry, where it is processed with cursor and attribute information and then drives the video output. This continues for seven rising edges of the dot clock. An additional two blank dots are appended to the character to form the 9-bit character box.

At this point the first row of the first character has been displayed. The CRTC outputs the address of the second character in the line and the actions described in the previous paragraph are repeated until the first row of all 80 characters in the current line have been displayed.

The CRTC once again outputs the address of the first character in the line and increments the raster address to point at the second row of characters—0001. The process described in the two previous paragraphs is repeated for the second row of dots. This action continues until all the rows of the 80 characters in the first line of the video display have been refreshed. The CRTC then moves onto the 80 characters in the second line on the video display. Notice that each character must be read from display-RAM a total of nine times until each row has been displayed. Then an additional five rows are used to form the character box. This part of the character box supports lowercase and the underline attribute of the video display.

Video-processing Logic

The video-processing logic is used to process the video dots and sync signals from the CRTC. The three outputs of the video-processing logic are used to drive the inputs of the video display.

7.4 BLOCK DIAGRAM OF THE MONOCHROME DISPLAY ADAPTER

We now have the background required to examine the actual block diagram of the monochrome display adapter, as illustrated in Figure 7.5. Other than additional detail, the major difference between Figures 7.4 and 7.5 is the manner in which the display-RAM subsystem is constructed. The monochrome display adapter has 4K of static display-RAM, which is mapped into the 1M memory space of the 8088 between the physical addresses of B0000H to B0FFFH. The even addresses in this 4K space are used to hold the ASCII code of the 2000 characters displayed in one screen; the odd addresses in this 4K space are used to hold the display attribute of the character in the adjacent even memory location. Simply put, if A_0 is a logic 0, then a character location is addressed; if A_0 is a logic 1, then an attribute location is addressed.

Figure 7.6 illustrates the format of the attribute byte. The function of the FG (foreground) and BG (background) bits are described in the table. The IBM monochrome display uses P-39 long-persistence green phosphor. In normal operation letters appear in a bright green color (foreground) against a black screen (background).

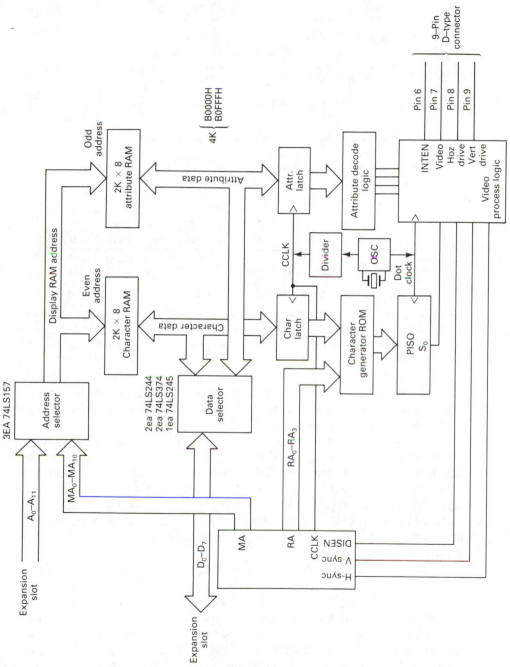

Figure 7.5 Block diagram of monochrome display adapter.

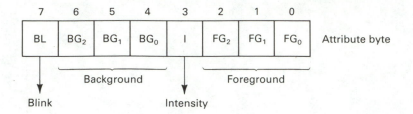

Background BG$_2$ BG$_1$ BG$_0$			Foreground FG$_2$ FG$_1$ FG$_0$			Function	
0	0	0	0	0	0	No display	
0	0	0	0	0	1	Under line	
0	0	0	1	1	1	Green on black	Normal
1	1	1	0	0	0	Black on green	Reverse video

Figure 7.6   Format of the attribute byte.

Also notice the additional two attribute bits. When B_3 is set the character is displayed with extra intensity. When B_7 is set the character blinks. It is important to remember that each character code in display-RAM has an associated attribute code.

The address selector is implemented with three 74LS157s in much the same manner as the row/address multiplexer that we examined in the last chapter. The data selector uses five ICs to multiplex the system data bus with the character display-RAM and attribute display-RAM.

On each rising edge of the character clock the contents of the character and attribute memory location addressed by the memory address outputs of the CRTC are latched into octal flip-flops. The character code is processed by the character generator and the attribute code is decoded by the attribute decode logic. The character dots from the shift register, the sync and display enable signals from the CRTC, and the outputs of the attribute decode logic are processed by the video-processing logic. This results in the actual drive signals to the video display.

You are familiar with H-sync and V-sync. As a matter of interest the frequency of the vertical sync signal usually matches the power line frequency. In the United States and Canada this is 60 Hz; in Europe it is 50 Hz. This minimizes the interference created when power line disturbances (hum) are modulated into the video frame. Contrary to usual practice, the monochrome display adapter has a 50-Hz (instead of a 60-Hz) refresh rate. This lengthens the video frame from 16.6 ms (60 Hz) to 20 ms (50 Hz).

The video output is a TTL signal that regulates the number of electrons that are fired at the screen of the CRT. The intensity output is derived from the intensity bit of the attribute byte. The intensity output goes to a logic 1 level and is mixed with the video output to create an intensified character.

7.5 THE CHARACTER GENERATOR AND DISPLAY-RAM

Figure 7.7 is a detailed view of the character-generator circuit. Notice that the character generator appears to be a standard 8K × 8 ROM. The low-address inputs are driven by RA_0 through RA_2 of the CRTC. The next eight address inputs are driven by the ASCII code of the character as read from display-RAM. Address line A_{11} is driven by RA_3. This input goes high after the first eight lines of the character have been written onto the video display. Finally, we see a signal labeled '' + Jumper.'' This signal is at a logic 0 level unless a test jumper point on the monochrome display adapter is shorted to ground. This causes A_{12} on the character generator to go high, and a new set of test characters are accessed in the character generator. (It appears that this function has never been implemented.) The $\overline{CE}$ (chip-enable or chip-select) signal is derived from decode circuitry each time a new character to be displayed is latched.

Figure 7.8 describes the configuration of the 2K × 8 character and attribute display-RAM systems. Figure 7.8(a) illustrates the pinout of the 2114 1K × 4 SRAM. This SRAM has 1K unique storage locations ($2^{10} = 1K$), each with four memory cells. In Chapter 6, we discovered that it required eight 4164s to

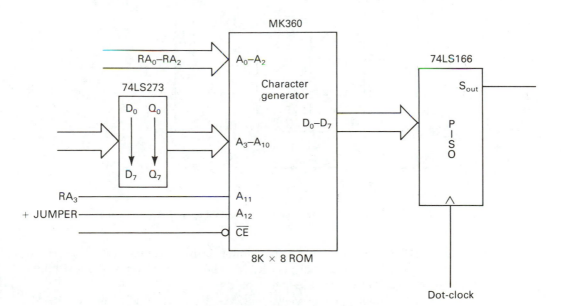

Figure 7.7   Character generator circuitry.

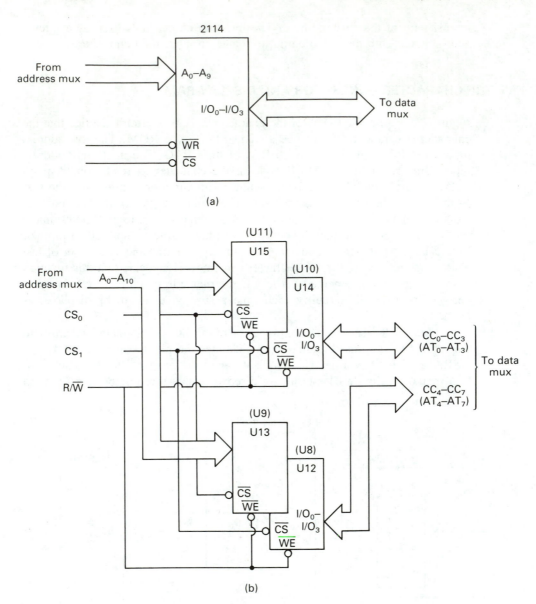

Figure 7.8   Character and attribute display-RAM system.

create a 64KB bank of memory. In a similar fashion, it takes two 2114 1K ×
4 SRAMs to create 1KB of display-RAM. The first 2114 holds the low nibble
and the second 2114 holds the high nibble.

From a pinout point of view, the 2114 is an extremely simple SRAM.
We see the required 10 address inputs, an active-low chip select, and a $\overline{\text{WE}}$

input that functions as a R/$\overline{\text{W}}$ input. We also notice that the 2114 does not have separate data-in and data-out pins, which is why the data pins are described as I/O.

Figure 7.8(b) shows the configuration of 2K of display-RAM in the monochrome display adapter. The 2K $\times$ 8 display-RAM systems for the character codes and the character attributes are identical. The IC designations U12 through U15 describe the four 2114s that constitute the character code display-RAM. The IC designations in parentheses (U8 through U11) designate the four 2114s that constitute the character attribute display-RAM.

The 10 low-order address bits output by the address multiplexer are bused to address inputs of U8 through U15. A_{10} is used to select the first or second 1K bank of SRAM. The $\overline{\text{WE}}$ line is also common to all eight 2114s. As we analyze the operation of the character code display-RAM system, keep in mind that everything we discover applies equally to the character attribute display-RAM.

U15 and U13 share a common chip-select line; they form 1KB of display-RAM. The same relationship is true for U14 and U12. U15 holds the low nibble and U13 holds the high nibble of the first 1K of display-RAM, and, once again, U14 and U12 share the same relationship for the second 1K of display-RAM. Essentially, U15 and U13 provide the character codes for the first 12½ lines (1000 characters) of the video display, and U14 and U12 provide the identical function for the second 12½ lines of the video display.

To reinforce the analysis of the display-RAM system, let's take a moment to consider a troubleshooting problem:

Symptom: The video display sometimes displays the wrong characters.

Example: When the capital *A* on the keyboard is struck, a capital *E* is displayed.

Solution: It appears that the character code display-RAM is malfunctioning. We have the choice of four possible SRAM chips that may be at fault: U12 through U15.

If the incorrect character appears in the first 12½ lines either U15 or U13 must be bad; if it appears on the second half of the display, either U14 or U12 must be bad.

For the sake of this example, let's say that the incorrect character appears on the third line of the display, indicating that the problem is in U15 or U13. We must now establish if the malfunction is occurring in the lower or upper nibble of the character code. Reference to the ASCII table in Appendix B yields the following codes:

$$A = 0100\ 0001$$
$$E = 0100\ 0101$$

The only difference is that B_2 is a logic 0 for A and a logic 1 for E. That probably means that B_2 in display-RAM for this position on the screen is stuck high. The malfunction occurs in the lower nibble of the code, so U15 should be replaced.

It is fairly common for particular bits in a SRAM to become stuck at logic 0 and or logic 1 levels. To troubleshoot to the bad 2114 SRAM chip, follow this procedure:

1. Is the screen displaying a character or attribute malfunction?

   U12 through U15 hold character codes, whereas U8 through U11 hold character attributes.

2. Does the malfunction occur on the top or bottom part of the display?

   For character code faults, U15 and U13 are associated with the top of the display and U14 and U12 are associated with the bottom of the display.

   For character attribute faults, U11 and U9 are associated with the top of the display and U10 and U8 are associated with the bottom of the display.

3. Comparing the ASCII code of the correct character or attribute with the one displayed, does the malfunction appear in the low or high nibble?

   For character code faults, U15 and U14 are associated with the low nibble and U13 and U12 are associated with the high nibble.

   For character attribute faults, U11 and U10 are associated with the low nibble and U9 and U8 are associated with the high nibble.

This simple troubleshooting procedure is not only a practical method of isolating display-RAM faults but also should help you understand how the display-RAM system functions.

7.6 THE IBM MONOCHROME DISPLAY

The four TTL level outputs of the monochrome display adapter board drive the IBM monochrome video display. The monochrome display consists of four units: a power supply, analog processing board, fly-back transformer, and CRT with deflection coils.

Caution: CRTs and their associated circuitry contain extremely high voltages that are a hazard to human life. Only trained and certified technical personnel should attempt to disassemble a video display and effect repairs.

Figure 7.9 illustrates a simplified block diagram of the monochrome display. Let's examine each block of circuitry.

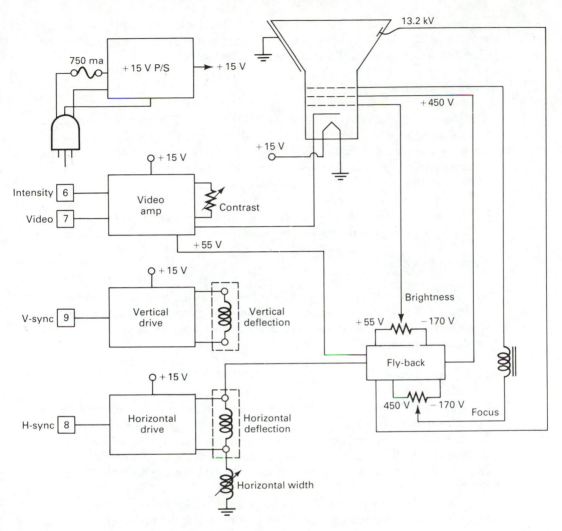

Figure 7.9   IBM monochrome display.

Low-Voltage Power Supply

This power supply converts standard 115-V, 60-Hz into a well regulated +15-V DC. This +15-V power supply is used to power ICs and transistors in the video amplifier, vertical drive, and horizontal drive circuits. The 750-mA fuse is not accessible from the outside of the monitor. To replace the fuse the entire case must be removed and the *pig-tailed* fuse desoldered.

The video amplifier, vertical drive, and horizontal drive circuits are located on the analog board. It is the function of these blocks of circuitry to convert the digital TTL level intensity, video, V-sync, and H-sync signals into analog signals that are capable of driving the CRT and yoke assemblies.

Video Amplifier

The video amplifier converts the intensity and video TTL inputs into a signal that is capable of driving the control grid of the CRT. The video amplifier circuitry contains a variable resister that functions as a contrast adjust. The contrast adjustment sets the range of brightness between the dark background of the CRT and the light characters that are displayed.

Notice that in addition to the $+15$ V, the video amplifier also requires $+55$ V to power the video output transistor. We examine the method in which this $+55$ V is derived during the the discussion of the fly-back transformer.

Vertical Drive

The vertical drive creates the waveform that drives the vertical deflection coil on the CRT yoke assembly. Although the vertical and horizontal coils are illustrated next to their associated blocks of circuitry, they are physically mounted on the neck of the CRT.

Horizontal Drive

The horizontal drive creates the current ramp that drives the electron beam across the face of the CRT, as illustrated in Figure 7.10. The sawtooth waveform illustrated in Figure 7.10 describes the current that flows through the horizontal deflection coil. When this current is passed through the deflection coil, a magnetic field is created that causes the electron beam to sweep horizontally across the face of the CRT.

When the amplitude of the sawtooth is at the lowest point, the electron beam is aimed at the left edge of the face of the CRT. As the amplitude of the sawtooth increases, the electron beam is deflected to the right. At the maximum amplitude of the sawtooth, the electron beam is aimed at the right edge of the face of the CRT. The electron gun is turned off (blanked) and the amplitude of the sawtooth quickly falls to minimum amplitude. This short period is called *fly-back* because of the extremely fast return of the electron beam to the start of the next line. The horizontal width (length of one line) is fine-tuned by a solid core inductor that is in series with the horizontal deflection coil.

Fly-back.   Electrons fired by the electron gun travel the length of the CRT and strike the phosphor coated screen. The energy transferred from the electron striking the phosphor coating of the screen causes the CRT to glow. To attract negatively charged electrons, the screen of the CRT must be charged to an extremely

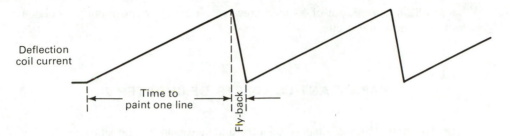

Deflection
coil current

Time to
paint one line

Fly-back

Figure 7.10   Idealized sawtooth waveform.

high positive voltage. The *anode* voltage of the monochrome display is 13.2 KV DC. The anode connector snaps into a hole near the front of the CRT.

Because the screen of the CRT behaves like a large capacitor, even after the video display has been disconnected from AC power, the anode voltage remains extremely high. Before removing the anode connector on any CRT, the video display must be disconnected from AC power and the anode connector must be shorted to ground several times until it no longer emits a spark. Because CRTs have a tendency to recharge themselves, the anode connector should be discharged prior to attempting reinstallation.

How is a 13.2-KV DC voltage generated to bias the anode of the CRT? That is the function of the fly-back circuitry. The fly-back block contains a *fly-back transformer* and the diodes and capacitors required to rectify and filter the output of several taps on the fly-back transformer. The fly-back transformer converts the extremely fast differential voltage of the fly-back signal into an AC voltage that is rectified and filtered to create +13.2-kV, +450-V, +55-V, and −170-V DC outputs. It is vibrations from the fly-back transformer that creates the characteristic high-frequency whine of video displays and television sets.

CRT

The CRT consists of many internal components. Every electron tube must have a *heater*. The heater is a resistive circuit in the back of the CRT that emits electrons to be fired by the electron gun. The heater in Figure 7.9 is powered by +15 V from the low-voltage power supply. A malfunctioning heater will render the CRT useless.

The *control grid* of the CRT regulates the number of electrons that are actually fired by the electron gun. The control grid is always biased by the output of the video amplifier. The next grid on the electron gun controls the brightness of the characters on the CRT. The following grid is used to accelerate the electrons toward the face of the screen. The last grid is the *focus grid*. It is used to ensure that the electron beam is not widely dispersed, a malfunction that results in blurred, out-of-focus characters. Notice the adjustments associated with brightness and focus.

IMPORTANT CONCEPTS OF CHAPTER 7

- The monochrome display adapter and associated monochrome display create high-quality 7 × 9 dot-matrix characters that reside in 9 × 14 character boxes.
- The monochrome display adapter contains 4K of static video-RAM.
- Each location on the video display is associated with 2 bytes of video-RAM.
- 2K of video-RAM is dedicated to hold the 8-bit ASCII character codes of the 2000 characters on the video display.
- 2K of video-RAM is used to store the character attributes associated with the 2000 character codes.
- Character codes are stored at even addresses and character attributes are stored at odd addresses.
- A CRT assembly consists of an electron gun, vertical and horizontal deflection coils, and a phosphor-coated screen.
- H-sync blanks the electron gun and returns the beam to the beginning of the next line.
- V-sync blanks the electron gun and returns the beam to the beginning of the frame.
- Video-RAM is dual-ported, enabling access by both the system processor and the CRTC.
- The system processor writes the character code and character attribute into video-RAM, but it is the responsibility of the CRTC to carry on the continuous process of refreshing the display.
- The character generator contains the dot patterns for each row of the 256 characters supported by the monochrome display adapter.
- A line of 80 characters is refreshed by painting each row of each character nine times.
- The CRTC provides the address and the raster code of the current character to be refreshed on the video display.
- The principal timing source for the monochrome display adapter is the dot clock oscillator. All other timing signals including the character clock and sync signals are derived from the dot clock.
- The character attribute code defines the foreground, background, intensity, and blink attribute of the associated character code.

- A PISO shift register converts the parallel output of the character generator into a serial bit stream to be processed by the video-processing logic.
- Troubleshooting incorrectly displayed characters is performed by comparing the ASCII code of the incorrect character with the correct character. This indicates which bit(s) are stuck.
- Troubleshooting incorrectly displayed attributes is performed in a manner similar to that for characters. Figure 7.6 should be used as an aid to create the bit patterns for the correct and incorrect attributes.
- Dangerous voltages exist on the CRT and associated circuitry. Video displays should be disassembled and repaired only by qualified technicians.
- The block diagram of the monochrome display consists of a low-voltage power supply, video amplifier, vertical and horizontal drive circuits, CRT, and fly-back transformer/high-voltage power supply.

8

THE FLOPPY DISK
SUBSYSTEM

In this chapter we study the most popular on-line mass storage subsystem employed in the PC. Floppy and hard disk drives store information in a random access format that enables any byte of data to be accessed within a minimum time interval. In magnetic tape storage, data is stored in a serial fashion along the entire length of the tape; the interval required to access a particular byte of data is proportional to where it is stored on the magnetic tape. Magnetic tape storage is extremely inexpensive, yet it is much too slow to be used on-line. Although a floppy disk is a removable type of media, its capacity is too limited to be used as a serious backup system for a large hard disk drive.

Another major difference between on-line and backup storage is that the computer's operating system can be loaded (booted) from an on-line but not a mass storage device. This implies that every computer must have at least one on-line mass storage device and that backup devices are employed at the discretion of the user—if important data is to be generated, then the user has a responsibility to see that it is backed up on some form of removable media.

8.1 THE FLOPPY DISK SUBSYSTEM

The interface between the monochrome display adapter and the monochrome display consists of only four inputs and no outputs. In terms of interaction with its system adapter, the floppy disk drive is much more complex than the monochrome display. Consequently, we start this chapter by examining the two interfaces of the floppy disk adapater—the interface to the PC expansion slot and the interface to the floppy disk drives. These interfaces are described in Figure 8.1. Let's examine the system bus connection with the floppy disk adapter, remembering the function of each line on the expansion slot as described in Chapter 6.

A_0 through A_9

The lower 10 bits of the address bus are used to create the chip selects for the *floppy disk controller* (FDC) IC and a drive-select *digital output register* (DOR). Address bit A_0 is also used to select specific registers within the FDC.

D_0 through D_7

The data bus connection is used to program and read status information from the FDC and write a control byte to the DOR. It also functions as the data path for DMA operations to transfer data directly between the FDC and system RAM.

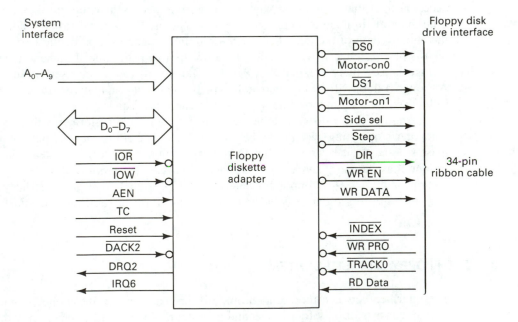

Figure 8.1   System and floppy disk drive interfaces.

I/O Read and Write Control

Like all intelligent LSI devices in the PC system, the FDC is I/O mapped. The $\overline{IOR}$ and $\overline{IOW}$ control signals are used to access the FDC for read and write operations.

AEN

Remember from Chapter 6 that AEN (address enable) goes to an active-high level to indicate that the DMAC has control of the system bus. The floppy disk adapter employs the DMA technique to transfer data between the FDC and system RAM. When AEN is active, the DMAC outputs an address that points to the source or destination of the data involved in the DMA transfer. Because the DMAC will also drive either $\overline{IOR}$ or $\overline{IOW}$ to active levels, AEN (along with $\overline{DACK-2}$) must be used to qualify when the contents of the address bus is selecting the FDC or addressing system RAM for DMA operations.

TC

After the FDC issues a command to the floppy disk drive, it waits for an active pulse on terminal count to indicate that the DMA transfer is complete.

Reset

The active-high system reset pulse is used to reset the contents of the DOR. One output line of the DOR is used to reset the FDC under program control. It is important that the processor system be able to reset the FDC under program control. If the floppy disk adapter gets hung up, a write command to the DOR will reset it to its default parameters.

DMA Request and Acknowledge

In Chapter 5 we learned that Channel 2 of the DMAC is utilized by the floppy disk adapter. When the FDC issues a floppy disk read or write command, DRQ-2 goes active-high to request the DMA transfer between the FDC and system RAM. $\overline{DACK-2}$ acknowledges that the DMAC has control of the system bus and that the data transfer can commence.

During a floppy disk write operation, the DMAC accomplishes a simultaneous read from RAM and write to FDC. To accomplish this complex operation, the DMAC must supply the address of the source of the data in RAM and simultaneously drive its $\overline{MEMR}$ and $\overline{IOW}$ outputs to active-low levels. The active level on the $\overline{DACK}$ input of the FDC will function as the equivalent of a chip select for this read RAM–write FDC operation.

A floppy disk read operation proceeds in the opposite manner. The DMAC performs a simultaneous FDC read–RAM write operation. The data rate on standard 5¼-in. floppy disk drives is such that a byte of data is available every $32\mu s$. This high-speed transfer can be accomplished only by DMA operation.

IRQ-6

We also saw in Chapter 5 that IRQ-6 is utilized by the floppy disk adapter. The FDC requests service whenever it completes a data transfer or a floppy disk drive system fault occurs.

You should not have been surprised with the descriptions of any of the system interface signals. We now turn our attention to the adapter's interface with the floppy disk drive(s).

The floppy disk drive adapter is connected to the disk drives by a 34-conductor flat ribbon cable. The adapter can support a total of four floppy disk drives; two drives can reside within the system unit, and two external floppy disk drives can be connected to the adapter via a 37-pin D-type connector on the rear of the system unit. The floppy disk drive adapter was designed when hard disk storage was cost-prohibitive. Because of the extremely inexpensive hard disk drives now available for the PC, external floppy disk drives are rarely employed.

Drive Select

$\overline{DS0}$ and $\overline{DS1}$ are active-low signals that are used to select which disk drive will respond to commands from the FDC. Because Drive 0 and Drive 1 share the same signal lines on the interface cable, only one drive can be selected at a time. The selected drive responds to the step and R/W commands on the interface cable, whereas the unselected drive ignores all commands.

This situation is similar to the bus systems that we have examined in this book. A controller selects one device that responds to commands; the remainder of the devices are inactive and ignore all activity on the bus.

Motor-On

On the original 8-in. floppy disk drives, when DC power was applied and a floppy disk was inserted, the *spindle motor* would automatically start and rotate the disk at a speed of 360 rpm (rotations per minute). A signal called *head load* was used to energize a relay that placed the R/W head in contact with the surface of the floppy disk.

Minifloppy disk drives rotate at a speed of 300 rpm. Unlike the original 8-in. floppy, 5¼-in. floppies do not rotate until the appropriate motor-on signal goes active. The reason for this is that minifloppy disk drives do not use a head-load relay; the R/W heads are in constant contact with the surface of the floppy disk. By enabling the spindle motor only when motor on is active, the life of the R/W heads is greatly increased.

Side Select

The floppy disk drives supplied with the original version of the PC were single-sided. Information was stored only on the bottom of the disk. Now all floppy disk drives are double-sided; data is stored on both the bottom (Side 0) and top (Side 1) of the disk. When side sel is low, Side 0 is selected for read or write access; when side sel is high, Side 1 is selected.

Step

In Chapter 1 we learned that data is stored on disks in concentric rings called *tracks*. The R/W head assembly is driven by a digital stepper motor. Each time a low pulse appears on the step output, the stepper motor rotates 3.6°. This rotation is converted by a metal band facility into 0.529 mm of linear movement. This is the distance between adjacent tracks on a double-density floppy disk.

Direction

Track 0 is the outermost track. When the Dir output is at a logic 0 level, the head assembly moves toward the center of the disk; when Dir is high, the head assembly moves to the outside of the disk.

Write Data and Write-Enable

The write data output carries the data and special clock information to be written onto the selected location on the floppy disk. The write operation occurs only when the write-enable output is at an active-low level.

Index

A small hole is punched into the floppy disk. The floppy disk drive uses an infrared LED and sensor to create an active-low index pulse for each revolution of the floppy disk. The floppy disk revolves at 300 rpm, so it completes five revolutions each second. This means that an active-low index pulse is generated once every 200 ms. This index pulse represents the beginning of the track that is currently under the R/W heads.

Write-protect

Floppy disks have a small cut out notch. If the notch is left uncovered, the floppy disk is write-enabled. To write-protect the disk, a piece of tape is used to cover the notch. When the disk is inserted into the drive, the piece of tape prevents the write-protect sense switch from closing. This causes an active-low write-protect signal to appear at the floppy disk drive adapter, and the write circuits on the floppy disk drive are also disabled.

Track 0

Floppy disk drives use an *open loop* system to position the R/W heads. The floppy disk does not provide positioning information to the disk drive. To find a reference point on the floppy disk, the floppy disk drive steps out the R/W head assembly until the Track 0 signal goes to an active-low level. This indicates that the heads are positioned over the first track on the floppy disk. All subsequent movement is referenced to this point. To protect the R/W head assembly from damage whenever Track 0 is true, step commands toward the outside of the disk are ignored.

Read Data

This is the serial stream of raw read data as it is recovered from the floppy disk. Read data is a composite signal consisting of the original data bits and clock information. The floppy disk adapter contains circuitry to generate a *data window* signal that is used to separate the read data from the clock information. We examine that circuit in a later section in this chapter.

8.2 THE FLOPPY DISK DRIVE ADAPTER

In terms of actual circuitry the floppy disk adapter is relatively simple. However, understanding the manner in which the floppy disk adapter creates data and timing signals to interface with the electromechanical floppy disk drive is complex. Any discussion about the floppy disk drive adapter should start with an examination of the 8272 FDC. The simplified pinout of the 8272 as implemented in the PC is illustrated in Figure 8.2. The Intel 8272 is equivalent to the *NEC 765*. In the IBM *Technical Reference Manual* and also in most publications, the FDC employed on the floppy disk drive adapter is usually referenced as the NEC 765.

The portion of the FDC above the dotted line illustrates the system interface as examined in Figure 8.1. Notice that the $\overline{RD}$ and $\overline{WR}$ lines are not driven directly from the command bus. Because the FDC employs DMA, either the system processor or the DMAC can drive the $\overline{RD}$ and $\overline{WR}$ inputs. Also notice that the reset input of the FDC is driven by the output of the DOR. Because of the modifications to the normal control lines of the floppy disk drives, the PC employs a 74LS273 octal flip-flop to send drive-select, motor-select, and reset signals under direct control of the system processor.

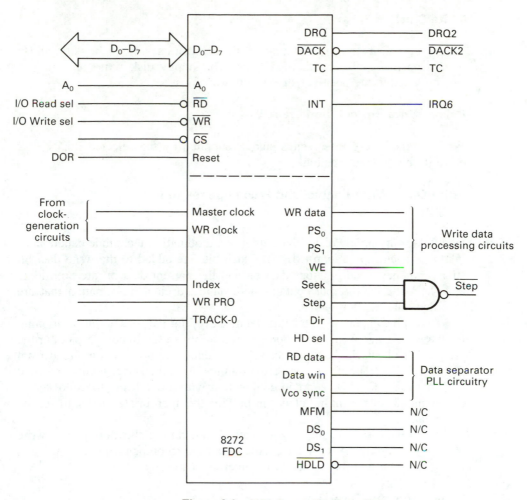

Figure 8.2   8272 floppy disk controller.

The 8272 was designed before 5¼-in. floppy disk drives were developed. It has many pins that are applicable only to 8-in. floppy disk drives. Double-density 8-in. floppy disk drives transfer data at 500 kilobits/s. In contrast, 5¼-in. double-density floppy disk drives transfer data at only a 250-kilobit/s rate. The clock frequencies specified in the 8272 data sheet apply to 8-in. floppy disk drives. Those clocks are divided by a factor of 2 to compensate for the slower transfer rate of 5¼-in. floppy disk drives.

Master Clock

The master clock is a symmetrical 4-MHz square wave derived from a 16-MHz crystal controlled oscillator.

Write Clock

This clock defines the write data rate of the FDC. It has a frequency of 500kHz with a positive pulse width of 250 ns. The floppy disk write operation is synchronized to the positive edge of this waveform.

Index, Write Protect, and Track 0

We examined these three status signals supplied by the selected floppy disk drive in the previous section.

Write Data, Write Enable, and Precompensation Outputs

Double-density floppy disk drives employ a modulation technique called *modified frequency modulation* (MFM). Clock bits are added to the write data bit stream whenever the previous data bit and the present data bit are both logic 0s. The write data output contains both data and clock information that are recorded onto the floppy disk.

The precompensation outputs define early, normal, or late bit positioning for the write data. Write-timing precompensation is used to compensate for the predictable playback shift that occurs when data and clock bits are read from the floppy disk. The precompensation outputs drive the select inputs of a dual 4-bit data selector that works in conjunction with a quad flip-flop, clocked at the frequency of the master clock, to provide the appropriate time shift for the write data.

The write-enable output goes active-high during the floppy disk write operation. This output is used to enable the write precompensation circuitry and is also bused to the floppy disk drive interface cable.

Seek, Step, and Direction

The active-high seek and step outputs are ANDed together to create an active-low step-pulse that causes the stepper motor in the floppy disk drive to rotate by 3.6° in the direction specified on the Dir output.

Head Select

A logic 0 selects Side 0 and a logic 1 selects Side 1 of the floppy disk for a read or write access.

Before we examine the next group of pins on the FDC, we must take a moment to understand how the data and clock information are combined to create the write data output to the floppy disk drive. Figure 8.3 illustrates the bit stream for single-density (FM) and double-density (MFM) data formats.

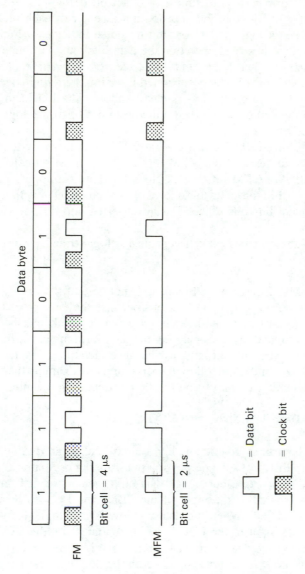

Figure 8.3 Data and clock bit stream for FM and MFM.

Figure 8.3 illustrates a byte of data as it appears on the write data output of the FDC. The crosshatched pulses represent clock bits, and the normal pulses represent logic 1 data bits.

The FM format is quite simple; a clock bit defines the leading edge of every 4µs bit-cell. The data bit appears in the center of each bit-cell. A logic 1 pulse indicates a logic 1 data bit and no pulse indicates a logic 0 data bit. During the floppy disk read operation the data bits must be separated from the clock information. That is the function of the *data separator*.

FM encoded data is easily separated by using the rising edge of the clock bit to fire one shot to create a 4-µs data window. The FDC samples the read data input in the center of the data window to establish the logic level of the data bit.

The MFM bit-cell is only 2 µs wide. This explains why the term double-density is used to describe the MFM format. Two MFM bit-cells appear in the same interval as one FM bit cell. A clock bit does not appear on the leading edge of each MFM bit-cell; this means that there is no explicit demarcation between adjacent bit-cells. Clock bits are inserted into the MFM stream.

> Only if the previous bit-cell contained a logic 0 and the present cell also contains a logic 0.

Referring to MFM diagram in Figure 8.3, notice that the first two logic 0s in the bit-stream do not generate clock bits because they are preceded by logic 1 data bits. The third and fourth logic 0s generate clock bits because each is preceded by a logic 0 level. Separating the data from the clock bits in an MFM bit-stream is an extremely difficult task because each bit-cell is not differentiated by a leading clock bit. In the following paragraphs we examine the block diagram of the data separator employed on the floppy disk drive adapter.

Read Data, Data Window, and VCO Sync

Floppy disk controller boards employ a circuit called an *analog phase-locked loop* (PLL). A PLL locks the output of a free-running oscillator to the frequency and phase of a varying input signal. The output data stream from the selected floppy disk is routed to the input of the PLL. The PLL outputs a valid data (data window) signal. When the data window is at a logic 1 level, the signal on the read data input of the FDC is valid. A logic 1 on the VCO sync output of the FDC is used to enable the PLL. Figure 8.4 illustrates the simplified block diagram of the *data separator* employed on the floppy disk drive adapter. Read data (consisting of data and clock bits) from the selected disk drive is conditioned by a digital one-shot circuit. The output of the one-shot circuit is applied to one input of the PLL and a standard data generator circuit that outputs a 250-ns data pulse. The PLL is composed of the three blocks enclosed in the dashed box.

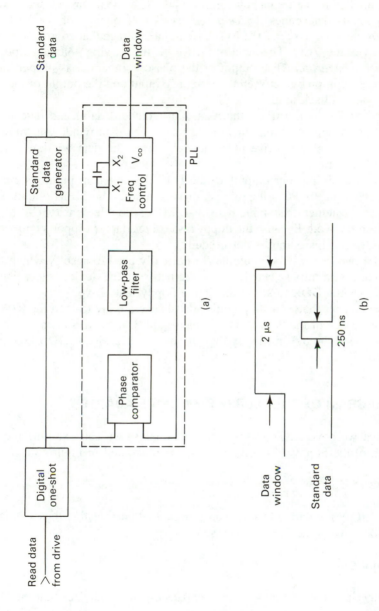

Figure 8.4 Data separator circuit.

The last component of the PLL is a *voltage-controlled oscillator* (VCO). A VCO is a free-running oscillator whose frequency can be fine tuned by a DC voltage applied to the frequency control input. The capacitor sets across the X_1 and X_2 inputs determines the *center* or *resting* frequency of the VCO. The output of the *low-pass filter* (LPF) is a small DC voltage that controls the output frequency of the VCO. The input of the LPF is the varying voltage output from the *phase comparator*. The output of the phase comparator is proportional to the difference in phase between the reference input and the output of the VCO, closing the feedback loop.

Figure 8.4(b) illustrates the read data (standard data) and data window inputs as they appear on the pins of the 8272. The data window is valid for a period of 2 µs. If a positive pulse appears under the data window, the read data bit is a logic 1.

The remaining four outputs of the FDC illustrated in Figure 8.2 are not implemented on the PC's floppy disk drive adapter. The MFM output is used to indicate whether the single-density (FM) or double-density (MFM) data format is employed. Because the floppy disk drive adapter supports only double-density drives, this output is not needed.

The two *device-select* outputs are normally used to specify which floppy disk drive is currently selected. As an alternative to the device-select lines, the PC employs the DOR to select the active floppy disk drive.

Remember that 8-in. floppy disk drives use a relay to load the R/W head onto the surface of the floppy disk. Because the R/W head is always in contact with the media on 5¼-in. floppy disk drives, the head load (HD LD) signal is not used.

8.3 BLOCK DIAGRAM OF THE FLOPPY DISK DRIVE ADAPTER

Now that we have studied its major components, we can examine the block diagram of the floppy disk drive adapter, as illustrated in Figure 8.5.

Command Bus

$\overline{\text{IOR}}$ and $\overline{\text{IOW}}$ are derived from decode logic that ensures that these signals are driven only when the FDC is accessed.

Terminal Count

Remember that the TC output on the expansion slots indicates that the DMAC has reached the terminal count in a DMA $\overline{\text{DACK-2}}$ operation. TC must be qualified with an active level on $\overline{\text{DACK-2}}$ to prevent the FDC from reacting to TC signals generated by channels 0, 1, and 3 of the DMAC.

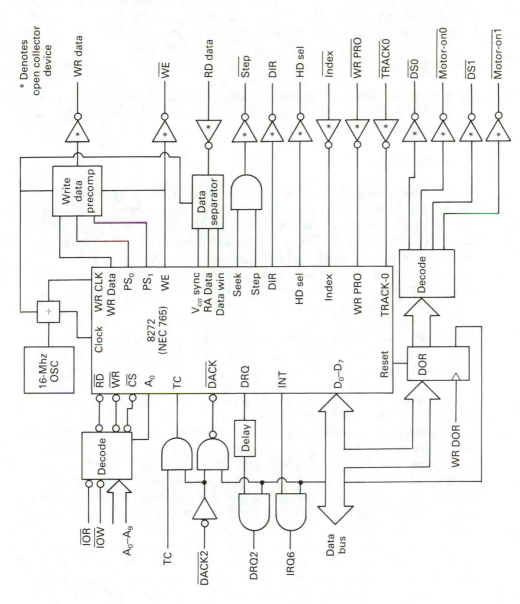

Figure 8.5 Block diagram of floppy disk drive adapter.

181

Interrupt and DMA Enable

Notice that 1 bit from the DOR is used to enable the gates that pass the interrupt request and DMA signals. This provides the capacity for the system processor to disable the operation of the floppy disk drive adapter.

Data Bus

The buffered data bus is routed to the FDC and DOR. The DOR is a write-only register that, in addition to floppy disk drive-select and motor functions, controls the reset signal to the FDC.

Clock Signals

All clock signals on the floppy disk adapter are derived from a crystal-controlled 16-MHz oscillator. The box labeled by a division sign is composed of several J-K flip-flops and an MSI counter that divides the 16-MHz output of the oscillator into clock signals of various frequencies (and duty cycles) that drive the master and write clocks of the FDC, the write-precompensation circuitry, and the data separator. The signals associated with the write data precompensation and data separator circuits were examined in the previous section.

Remember that the 34 conductor flat ribbon interface cable may be connected to two floppy disk drives that are housed within the system unit. We stated that this cable formed a circuit that is similar in concept to a bus system; several devices (floppy disk drives) receive commands from the bus master (floppy disk drive adapter).

In Chapter 2 you learned the reasons why standard TTL devices can not be used to construct a bus system. All outputs on the system bus must stay at a high-z level unless specifically addressed (chip selected) by the bus controller.

Instead of using three-state output devices, the floppy disk adapter/floppy disk interface drivers employ *open-collector* TTL circuits. An open-collector device is capable of outputting a logic 0 level but not a logic 1 level. The logic 1 output state of an open-collector TTL gate is equivalent to a high-z output. An external resistor must be provided to pull up the output of an open-collector device to a logic 1 level. Figure 8.6(a) illustrates the simple concept of open-collector devices.

Imagine the situation where we wish to select which floppy disk drive will provide the read data input to the floppy disk drive adapter. We know that the conductor that carries read data to the FDC is common to the read data outputs of both floppy disk drives. The $\overline{DS0}$/DS1 signal selects which open-collector NAND gate will be enabled. It is important to understand that open-collector devices have an active-low output level. The nonselected open-collector NAND will appear to be at a high-z level. When the selected NAND gate outputs a logic 1 read data level, it apparently goes to a high-z level, and the pull-resistor residing on the

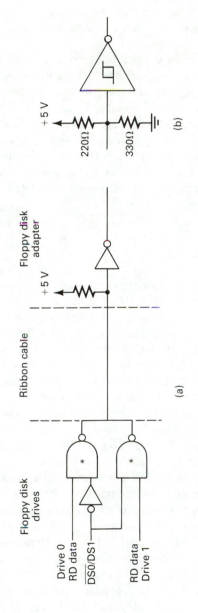

Figure 8.6 Open collector outputs on the floppy disk interface.

* = Open collector device

floppy disk adapter pulls the floating output to a logic 1 level; because open-collector devices are capable of outputting an active logic 0 output level, when the NAND sends logic 0 read data, +5 V is dropped across the pull-up resistor and a logic 0 appears on the input of the inverter on the floppy disk adapter. Consequently, both outputs can share the same line on the floppy disk interface cable.

Figure 8.6(b) illustrates the pull-up resistor network and *line receiver* that is employed on the floppy disk adapter. The combination of the 220-Ω and 330-Ω resistor network reduces the noise induced on the high-capacitance and unshielded interface cable.

The standard floppy disk interface cable dedicates four lines for drive-select signals and one line for the motor-on signal. Instead of employing the encoded drive-select and motor-on outputs of the FDC, the floppy disk adapter board decodes the output of the DOR to derive two drive-select and two motor-on signals. In the next section we discover why IBM chose to modify the standard interface.

8.4 THE FLOPPY DISK DRIVE

The floppy disk drive is an electromechanicanical device, which means it is constructed from electronic (ICs, transistors, resistors, and so on) and mechanical (motors, latches, switches, and so on) components. In most computer systems the electromechanical devices such as disk drives and printers suffer a much higher failure rate that the purely electronic systems. Furthermore, as mechanical devices wear and age, they need to be periodically aligned. In this section we examine the mechanical components and sensors on the floppy disk drive. Figure 8.7 illustrates the major components in the floppy disk drive.

The floppy disk drive contains two circuit boards. The large board mounted on top of the drive is called the *logic board*. It contains the interface, R/W and sensor-processing circuits. The *servo board* is mounted on the rear of the drive and contains the circuitry to rotate the spindle motor at a constant 300 rpm.

The second motor on the drive is a four-phase digital stepper motor that steps the R/W head assembly between tracks on the floppy disk. Each step pulse causes the stepper motor to rotate 3.6°. The rotational movement of the stepper motor is translated in the linear movement that drives the R/W heads by a metal band assembly. Notice the activity LED on the front panel of the drive. The LED illuminates to indicate that the drive is currently selected.

A floppy disk is inserted by lifting the front latch and sliding it along the guide rails. When the disk is fully inserted, the front latch is closed and it is clamped between the cone assembly and drive hub. The spindle assembly is driven by the spindle motor by means of a pulley and drive belt. The pulley has timing marks that are used with the aid of standard fluorescent lights to adjust the spindle speed to 300 rpm.

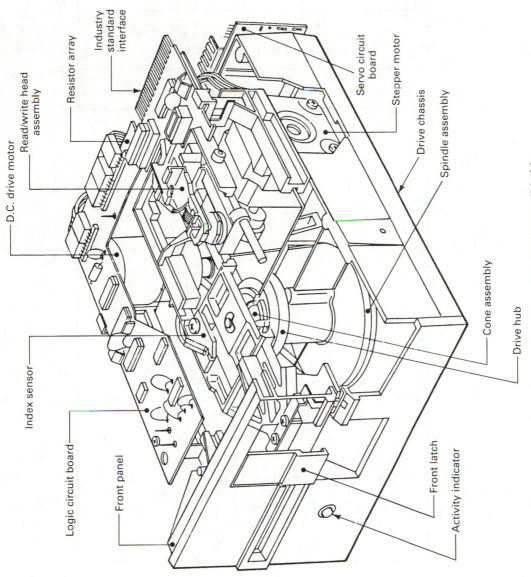

Figure 8.7 Pictorial view of the 5¼" floppy disk drive.

Industry
standard
interface

Resistor array

Read/write head
assembly

D.C. drive motor

Servo circuit
board

Stepper motor

Drive chassis

Spindle assembly

Index sensor

Logic circuit board

Front panel

Cone assembly

Drive hub

Front latch

Activity indicator

**DRIVE INTERFACE LINES
AND PIN ASSIGNMENTS**

Input Control Lines:
Controller-To-Disk Drive

Ground	Pin	Signal
1	2	Connector Clamp
3	4	Spare
5	6	Drive Select 3
9	10	Drive Select 0
11	12	Drive Select 1
13	14	Drive Select 2
15	16	Motor On
17	18	Direction Select
19	20	Step
21	22	Composite Write Data
23	24	Write Enable
31	32	Side Select

Output Control Lines:
Disk Drive-To-Controller

Ground	Pin	Signal
7	8	Index/Sector
25	26	Track 0
27	28	Write Protect
29	30	Composite Read Data
33	34	Spare

Figure 8.8   Drive interface cable pin assignments.

The floppy disk drive has two cable connections with the system. The 34-conductor flat ribbon cable slides easily onto the standard edge connector. A second cable provides DC power to the drive: +12 V, +5 V, and their associated grounds. Figure 8.8 and 8.9 illustrate the pinout of the interface and DC connectors on the floppy disk drive. In a standard configuration a maximum of four floppy disk drives can be attached to the controller interface cable. Figure 8.10 illustrates the programmable shunt employed on the Tandon floppy disk drive. This shunt has eight traces. To program the shunt, one trace is left shorted and the others are cut open. A drive can be programmed to react to device select 0, 1, 2, or 3. The MX (multiplex) option is used in systems that have only one drive, on which the control logic must always be enabled. When the Tandon drive is employed in the PC every trace on the programmable shunt is cut except for DS1. Both floppy disk drives in the PC system are programmed to react to an active level on DS1.

Many floppy disk drive problems that occur in new computers are due to incorrectly programmed shunts. IBM determined that it would prevent many setup problems by allowing both floppy disk drives to use the same programmable shunt configuration. Later in this section we see how this is possible.

In standard floppy disk systems one end of the 34-conductor cable is plugged onto the edge connector of the floppy disk drive adapter. One *insulation displacement connector* is clamped onto the controller cable for each drive in the system. Although every floppy disk drive has a 16-pin socket to install a *resistor terminator pack*, only the last drive on the *daisy chain* should have the terminator installed. The terminator contains the pull-up resistors required by the open-collector drivers of the floppy disk drive adapter. By placing the

D.C. POWER CONNECTOR PIN ASSIGNMENTS	
Pin	**Supply Voltage**
1	+12 volts D.C.
2	12 volts return
3	5 volts return
4	+5 volts D.C.
Pin	**Signal**
Ground lug 3/16-inch quick disconnect	Chassis ground from controller

Figure 8.9 DC power connector pin assignments.

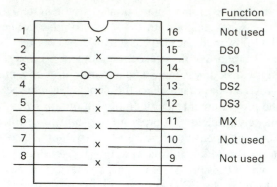

	Function
16	Not used
15	DS0
14	DS1
13	DS2
12	DS3
11	MX
10	Not used
9	Not used

x = Cut trace

Figure 8.10   Programmable shunt.

terminator on the last drive in the daisy chain, the *ringing* that results from digital signals propagating along the highly capacitive flat ribbon cable is greatly reduced.

On the standard floppy disk drive interface, pins 10, 12, and 14 carry the drive-select signals for drives 0 through 2. Remember that the floppy disk drive adapter board does not employ the encoded device-select outputs of the FDC. The DOR drives a decoder that outputs drive-select and motor-on signals for

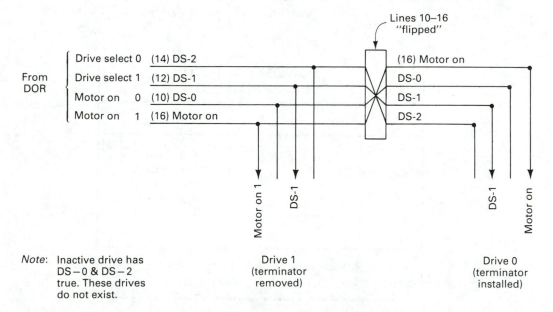

Note: Inactive drive has DS−0 & DS−2 true. These drives do not exist.

Figure 8.11   Floppy disk drive cable in the PC.

the two floppy disks that can reside in the system unit. Figure 8.11 illustrates how the drive-select and motor-on signals are implemented on the floppy disk interface cable.

Remember that the shunts on both drives are cut so that they respond to an active level on $\overline{DS1}$. This makes perfect sense for Drive 1, but how is Drive 0 accessed? Between the drives lines 10 through 16 of the interface cable are twisted in such a manner that the $\overline{DS0}$ output of the floppy disk drive adapter drives the $\overline{DS1}$ input of Drive 0. The same relationship is true for the motor-on signals. If the floppy disk interface cable in the PC system malfunctions, it must be replaced with an identical cable that has lines 10 through 16 swapped to drive the second connector. As you can see from Figure 8.11, one end of the interface cable is connected to the floppy disk drive adapter and the other end is connected to Drive 0 (where the terminator is also installed). Drive 1 uses the middle connector in the interface cable.

8.5 DISK DRIVE AND CONTROL ELECTRONICS INTERFACE

Floppy disk drives are the only components in the PC system unit that require periodic *preventative maintenance* (PM) and alignment. Figure 8.12 illustrates the sensor and control systems in the floppy disk drive. The drive motor servo circuit board outputs a DC voltage to drive the spindle motor. A drive belt connected between the pulleys of the spindle motor and spindle assembly rotates the floppy disk at 300 rpm.

The outputs of R/W heads 0 and 1 are connected to the control and R/W circuit board. The low-level currents induced into the read heads are preamplified by a *differential amplifier* and further shaped by circuitry to recreate the original signals that were output by the FDC during the write operation. We will see how the two outputs of the differential amplifier are used to provide disk drive alignment signals.

The write-protect switch senses the state of the R/W notch on the disk. If the switch cannot close because tape is covering the R/W notch, the internal write circuitry is disabled and the write-protect output goes active.

The activity LED illuminates whenever the floppy disk drive is selected by the controller. Sensing when the R/W heads are positioned at the beginning of a track requires the use of a transmitter and a receiver. The *index emitter* is an infrared LED that transmits a frequency of light beyond the visible spectrum. Each time the floppy disk completes one rotation, the index hole is positioned between the index emitter and the *index detector*. The index detector is an infrared phototransistor. When the base of the index detector senses the beam of the index emitter, an index pulse is generated. An infrared transmitter and receiver are employed to ensure that ambient visible light does not produce erroneous index pulses.

We have discussed how the digital four-phase stepper motor and metal

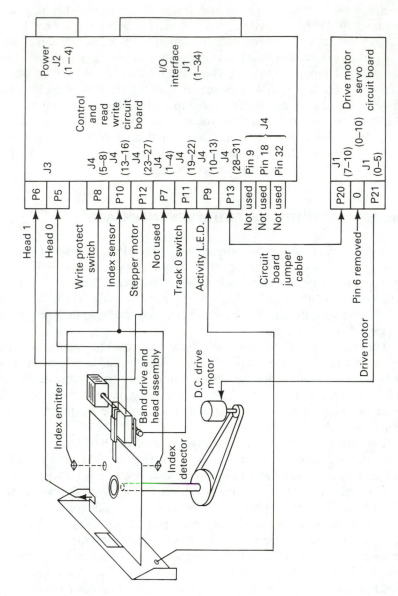

Figure 8.12   Sensor and control systems in floppy disk drive.

band assembly are used to move the R/W heads from track to track along the surface of the floppy disk. When the disk drive is initially accessed the FDC has no way of knowing where the R/W heads are positioned. The first instruction issued by the FDC is *recalibrate*. The direction output is specified to move the R/W heads toward the outside of the disk and the step line is pulsed until the Track 0 output goes to an active level. The FDC can now maintain the location of the R/W heads by incrementing or decrementing a track location register each time a step pulse is issued.

The exact positions of the Track 0 switch and *Track* 0 *stop adjustment* are extremely critical because all track locations are taken relative to the Track 0 indication.

8.6 FLOPPY DISK DRIVE ALIGNMENT ADJUSTMENTS

In the last section we examined the sensors and motor assemblies that require periodic alignment. Traditionally, floppy disk alignment required a *floppy disk exerciser*, an *analog alignment disk*, and a dual-trace oscilloscope.

The exerciser emulates the functions of a floppy disk drive adapter board. Through a combination of switches the technician can control the state of the spindle motor and step the drive to a specified track. The exerciser also contains test points to monitor the status of the write-protect and Track 0 switches, and index sensor. The analog alignment disk contains precisely recorded information that is used to align the R/W head positioning and index sensor. Figure 8.13 illustrates the three most important tracks on the analog alignment disk.

Track 1 contains an index pulse-to-data burst pattern. This enables the precise alignment of the index sensor to ensure that the start of the track occurs on the falling edge of the index pulse. Figure 8.14 illustrates the index adjustment. The differential outputs of the R/W head assembly are connected to Channels 1 and 2 of the oscilloscope. The actual signal from the R/W heads is the difference between the two differential outputs of the preamplifier. To display the read-back signal pattern, the oscilloscope is placed in the mode where Channel 1 is added to the inverted value of Channel 2. This results in the true data pattern.

The oscilloscope is externally triggered on the falling edge of the index pulse and the time base is set to 50 μs/division. The analog alignment disk is inserted into the drive and the exerciser is used to step the R/W heads to track 1.

The data burst should appear approximately 200 μs after the falling edge of the index signal. The tolerance is ± 100 μs. If the data burst does not appear in this range, the position index sensor must be adjusted. This is accomplished by loosening the index sensor retaining screw and carefully adjusting the position of the index sensor while watching the index pulse-to-data burst timing delay

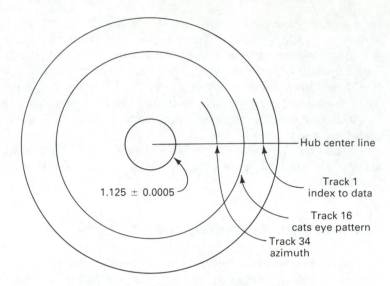

Figure 8.13   Analog alignment disk.

on the scope. After the adjustment is accomplished, the retaining screw must be retightened and the adjustment verified.

Track 16 of the analog alignment disk contains the *cat's eye pattern* that is used to perform the *radial alignment* of the R/W heads. This is the most common malfunction of floppy disk drives. A typical symptom of radial misalignment is the inability to read a floppy disk that was written on another disk drive. The need for *media interchangability* between floppy disk drives is extremely important. Figure 8.15 describes the concept of radial and azimuth alignment. The R/W heads should be perpendicular to both center lines of the floppy disk. The word *radial* refers to the radius of a circle. If a floppy disk drive is out of radial alignment, the R/W heads are not positioned over the center of the track, as illustrated in Figure 8.15(b).

Track 34 of the analog alignment disk is used to test for *azimuth alignment*, as illustrated in Figure 8.15(c). Azimuth misalignment occurs when the R/W heads are twisted and their sides are no longer perpendicular to the center lines of the floppy disk. There is no adjustment for azimuth realignment. If a disk drive is found to be out of azimuth alignment, the R/W heads are usually replaced.

Figure 8.16 illustrates the variations of the cat's eye pattern, which indicates the relative radial alignment of the disk drive. The oscilloscope is connected to the floppy disk drive in a manner similar to that of the index sensor–alignment procedure. The external trigger slope is changed, so that the scope is triggered on the rising edge of the index pulse. The analog alignment disk is inserted into the drive and the R/W heads are stepped out to track 16.

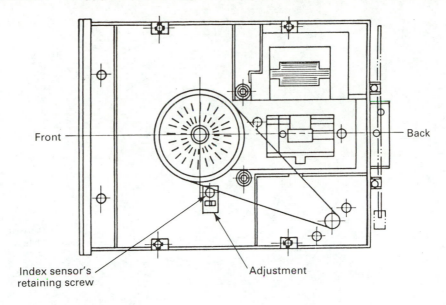

Front   Back

Index sensor's
retaining screw   Adjustment

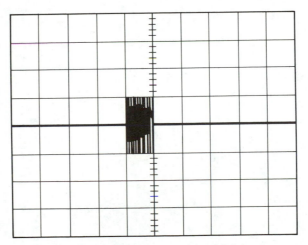

Time scale: 50 microseconds per division

Figure 8.14 Index sensor alignment.

The amplitude difference between the two cat's eye patterns that appear on the scope indicates the state of the radial alignment. Equal-amplitude cat's eyes signify a R/W head assembly that is perfectly aligned. The specification states that the smaller cat's eye may not be less than 75% of the amplitude of the larger cat's eye. If this is not the case, the drive must undergo radial

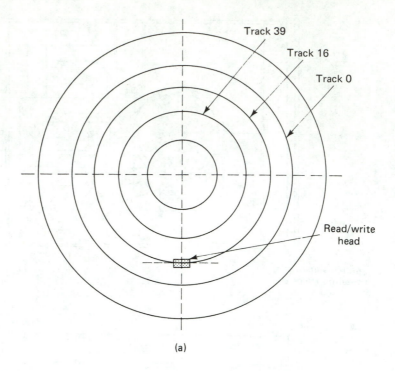

Track 39

Track 16

Track 0

Read/write
head

(a)

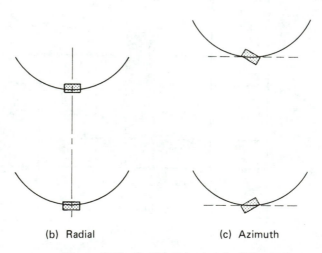

(b) Radial   (c) Azimuth

Figure 8.15   Radial and azimuth alignment.

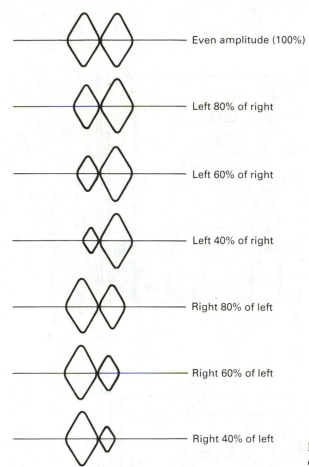

Even amplitude (100%)

Left 80% of right

Left 60% of right

Left 40% of right

Right 80% of left

Right 60% of left

Right 40% of left

Figure 8.16   Cat's eye patterns designating radial alignment.

alignment. Figure 8.17 shows the location of the three retaining screws that must be loosened prior to adjusting the radial alignment.

The *cam screw* at the end of the floppy disk drive is used to adjust the position of the R/W heads. The display on the scope should be monitored as the cam screw is carefully adjusted. When the two cat's eyes are of equal amplitude, the retaining screws are tightened and the radial alignment verified.

Figure 8.18 illustrates an adjustment that does not require the use of the analog alignment disk or an oscilloscope. A timing disk is affixed to the bottom of the spindle assembly. The outside ring has timing marks for 60-Hz operation, and the inner ring has timing marks for 50-Hz operation. To check the speed of the spindle motor the disk drive is turned on its side and the bottom of the spindle assembly is exposed to fluorescent lights. If the spindle assembly is rotating at exactly at 300 rpm, the timing marks appear to be stationary. If the

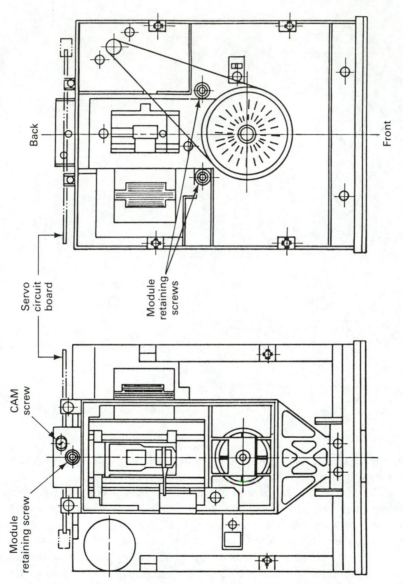

Figure 8.17 Retaining screws for radial alignment.

Back

Front

Servo
circuit
board

Module
retaining
screws

CAM
screw

Module
retaining screw

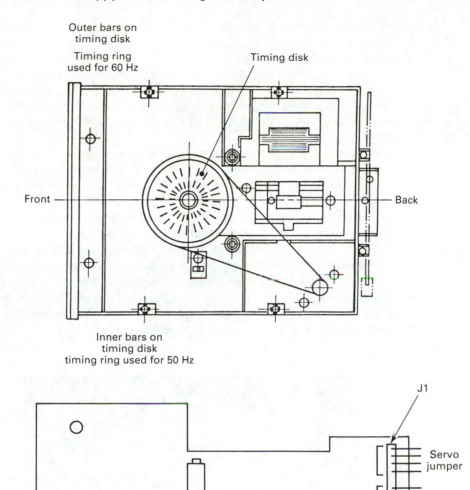

Figure 8.18   Spindle speed adjustment.

marks are slowly rotating, the variable resister should be carefully adjusted until they are stationary.

At the beginning of this section it was mentioned that employing an analog alignment disk and an oscilloscope was the traditional method of aligning floppy disk drives. Most oscilloscopes are bulky and difficult to use. In an effort to make it practical to align floppy disk drives in the field, a new generation of digital floppy disk alignment/exercisers was developed. Instead of employing an analog alignment disk to work with an analog measurement device (the oscilloscope), the new floppy disk drive alignment/exercisers employ a *digital alignment disk*. The oscilloscope is replaced by LEDs or digital readouts that specify alignment information. As an example, instead of seeing the analog cat's eye waveform on an oscilloscope, the digital alignment/exerciser displays the status of the radial alignment test by illuminating LEDs in a bar graph. Figure 8.19 is a photograph of the Lynx 470 floppy disk drive alignment tester/exerciser.

The Lynx 470 is powered from the disk drive under test. It enables all floppy disk alignment procedures and tests to be accomplished easily at the user's site. Because the floppy disk drive is the only component in the system unit that requires periodic mechanical alignment, a digital floppy disk drive alignment tester/exerciser and digital alignment disk are important tools that every microcomputer technician should carry in the field.

Dysan is the manufacturer of the industry standard analog and digital alignment disks. It has developed a product called the *Dysan Interrogator*. The Interrogator consists of a comprehensive disk drive alignment test and exercise program and a *Dysan Digital Diagnostic Disk* (DDD) that enables the technician to perform most tests and alignment procedures on a functioning disk drive without the need of a digital alignment tester/exerciser.

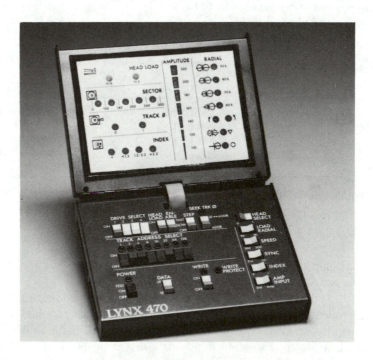

Figure 8.19 Lynx 470 floppy disk alignment tester/exerciser.

Periodically cleaning R/W heads was once a controversial procedure that is now widely accepted and practiced. After a few months of use R/W heads become coated with the oxide material from floppy disks. High-quality floppy disks have a fairly hard oxide surface, but inexpensive floppy disks often break down and quickly coat the R/W heads. This results in floppy disk read errors. Most head-cleaning kits consist of a fabric disk enclosed in a normal 5¼-in. floppy jacket. A packet of cleaning solution is dispensed onto the fabric disk and it is inserted into the floppy disk drive. The floppy disk alignment tester/exerciser is used to enable the spindle motor. While the R/W heads are in contact with the fabric disk, the cleaning solution breaks down the oxide coating and the spinning disk carries it away. In areas where floppy disk drives are exposed to dust or smoke or low-quality disks are employed, the R/W heads need to be cleaned at much shorter intervals.

There are two schools of thought on the subject of cleaning R/W heads. Some people believe that the abrasive nature of the fabric disk can damage the R/W heads and contribute to azimuth misalignment. They believe that the heads in disk drives should be cleaned only if the drives are producing read errors and the alignment checks indicate that all adjustments are within accepted tolerances.

The second school of thought believes that when cleaning disks are used in the proper manner they increase the life of the R/W head assembly. For this reason many people feel that the periodic cleaning of R/W heads prevent errors (and thus service calls).

IMPORTANT CONCEPTS OF CHAPTER 8

- The floppy disk drive adapter uses Channel 2 of the DMAC to transfer data directly between the floppy disk drive and RAM.
- Interrupt 6 is used to signal to the system processor that a floppy disk transfer is complete. This enables the 8088 to perform mandatory status-read operations on the FDC.
- The floppy disk drive adapter and floppy disk drive(s) are connected via a 34-conductor flat ribbon cable.
- The floppy disk interface utilizes open-collector TTL drivers to create the functional equivalent of a bus system. This enables one floppy disk drive adapter to control many floppy disk drives.
- The terminator (resistor pack) contains the pull-up resistors required by open collector outputs. It should be installed in the last drive on the control cable.
- The R/W heads on 5¼-in. floppy disk drives are always in contact with the surface of the floppy disk. Motor-on is used to minimize head wear by enabling the spindle motor only when the drive is selected.

- The Intel 8272 is equivalent to the NEC 765.
- Instead of employing the standard drive-select and motor-on signals of the FDC, the floppy disk adapter contains a digital output register.
- Both data and clock information are stored on the floppy disk.
- Double-density floppy disk drives employ MFM data encoding. A clock bit is appended to an MFM cell only if it contains a logic 0 and is preceded by a logic 0.
- The data separator consists of a PLL, LPF, and phase comparator. It is used to create a valid data window that enables the FDC to separate the data bits from clock information.
- The floppy disk drive has two printed circuit boards. The logic board contains the R/W amplifiers and control circuitry, and the servo board drives the spindle motor at a constant 300 rpm.
- A stepper motor is used to step the R/W heads from track to track.
- A metal band assembly translates the rotational movement of the stepper motor into linear movement.
- The spindle motor drives a pulley and drive belt that rotates the spindle assembly.
- Floppy disk interface cables use insulation displacement connectors.
- The R/W switch assembly senses the state of the R/W notch on the floppy disk.
- The infrared index transmitter and receiver produce an index pulse for each rotation of the floppy disk.
- The activity LED illuminates to indicate that the drive has been selected by the floppy disk adapter.
- The analog alignment disk is used in conjunction with an oscilloscope to provide signals for the standard alignment checks and adjustments.
- The index sensor alignment test ensures that the index pulse indicates the true start of a track.
- Track 16 of the analog alignment disk contains the cat's eye pattern. Equal-amplitude lobes in the cat's eye indicate correct radial alignment.
- Track 34 is used to verify azimuth alignment.
- Spindle-speed adjustment is accomplished by exposing the timing disk on the bottom of the spindle assembly to fluorescent light. The variable resistor on the servo board is carefully adjusted until the timing marks are stationary.
- A new generation of floppy disk drive tester/exercisers use digital technology. The analog alignment disk is replaced with a digital alignment disk, and the oscilloscope is replaced by LEDs on the exerciser.
- Cleaning R/W heads with a cleaning kit containing a wet solution often corrects intermittent read errors.

9

TROUBLESHOOTING
THE PC SYSTEM

The first eight chapters of this book have been directed at understanding the operation of the major components and subassemblies of the PC system. In this chapter we consider how to troubleshoot a malfunctioning system. The ROM resident POST executes initialization and test functions each time the system is energized. A group of diagnostic programs is contained on the IBM *Advanced Diagnostics Disk*. These programs enable the technician to test each subsystem and adapter in the PC system. We also survey the major types of test systems and test equipment that are commonly employed to troubleshoot microcomputer systems.

9.1 POST

Each time the PC is powered on, all the complex devices that we have studied in this book must be tested and initialized for the proper system operation. The POST is a collection of tests that reside in the same 8K ROM as the BIOS, which perform device verification and initialization. The information provided by the failure indication of the individual tests of the POST varies greatly. The POST produces four types of failure indicators:

1. When a test fails the 8088 is halted and the system simply "hangs." No information is output to the video display or to the system speaker. Test equipment can be employed that indicates the address in the BIOS firmware where the halt instruction occurs. The failing subsystem can be derived

by cross-referencing the address of the halt instruction to the listing of the BIOS firmware that is available in the IBM PC *Technical Reference Manual*.

2. A bit more helpful failure indication is a series of tones emitted by the system speaker. Sequences such as a long-short beep or a long-short-short beep indicate the general area of the subsystem failure. This failure indication can occur only after the 8253 PIT has been initialized.

3. A system error code is sent to the video display. This error code indicates the failing subsystem. For the sake of consistency, the POST and Advanced Diagnostics Disk employ the same set of error codes. For this error indication to occur, the majority of the system board and video display adapter circuitry must be initialized and functioning.

4. For specific RAM and keyboard errors, a message indicating the possible failing DRAM or key is sent in an encoded form to the video display.

In the Chapters 4 through 8 we studied the major LSI devices and subsystems that constitute the PC. You now understand the relationship of the system processor to the subsystems controlled by the DMAC, PIC, PIT, PPI, CRTC, and FDC. You also understand the interdependencies between the DMAC and PIT to accomplish the critical DRAM refresh function. Remember these important relationships as we examine the POST. Figure 9.1 lists the individual tests of the POST and their working and failure indicators. Figure 9.1 lists the fundamental tests in the order that they are accomplished in the 1501512 BIOS ROM. There have been three versions of the BIOS ROM. Figure 9.1 is intended to describe the general function of the POST. The BIOS ROM resides in the last 8K of the PC's 1-MB addressing space (F000:E000). The first bytes of the BIOS ROM contain the IBM copyright notice and the ROM part number. Always check the ROM part number and reference the appropriate BIOS listing before pursuing specific troubleshooting problems.

Figure 9.2 is a duplication of Figure 5.19. As we examine each test refer to Figure 9.2 to understand what support circuitry must be operational for the intelligent device or subassembly to properly function.

8088 Internals

This test simply verifies that the registers of the 8088 function properly. If a malfunction is detected, the processor executes a halt instruction at address FE0AD and the system hangs.

Notice that to verify the 8088 internals, a good part of the system board must be functioning. The 8088 reads instructions from the BIOS ROM—this indicates that the clock generator (8284), system controller (8288), and internal processor bus system must be functional. The address decoder and address/data buffers of the ROM subsystem must also be functional.

Power-On Self-Test

Order of Tests	Description	Indications Working	Failure
1	8088 Processor Test	None	Halts at FE0AD
2	BIOS ROS Checksum	None	Halts at FE0AD
3	Timer-1 Test	Speaker Clicks	Halts at FE0F8
4	Initialize Timer-1 for Refresh	None	None
5	Test DMAC Channel-0	None	Halt at FE12D
6	Initialize Channel-0 of DMAC For Refresh	None	Halt at FE15C
7	Verify First 16K of DRAM	None	System Hangs
8	Initialize PIC	None	None
9	Determine System Configuration and Manufacturering Mode Test	None Load and Execute Manfact. Test	None
10	Initialize CRTC and Verify Video-RAM	Cursor Appears	Beep 1-Long 2-Short
11	Test PIC	None	Display "101" Then Halt at FE35C
12	Verify PIT Channel-0 TOD	None	Display "101" Then Halt at FE35C
13	Keyboard Test	None	Display "301" If a key is stuck, display scan code.
14	Set Interrupt Vector Table	None	None
15	Test for Presence of Expansion Unit	None	Display "1801"
16	Check Remaining System RAM and Verify Refresh Operation	Display "XXX KB OK"	DMA Failure Display "101", then halt at FE35C. RAM Failure Display "BBbb 201"
17	Check for Optional ROM	None	Display "ROM"
18	Check BASIC ROM	None	Display "ROM"
19	Verify Disk Drive Adapter	Motor-On	Display "601"
20	Initialize Printer and Serial Ports	None	None
21	Display Error Message	Clear Screen	If Error, Beep short-short, then Display "Error Resume=F1"
22	Enable NMI	None	Display "Parity Check 1" or "Parity Check 2" Then Halt at FF8EF
23	Boot DOS From Diskette	DOS Prompt	Boots into ROM BASIC

Figure 9.1 The IBM power-on self-test.

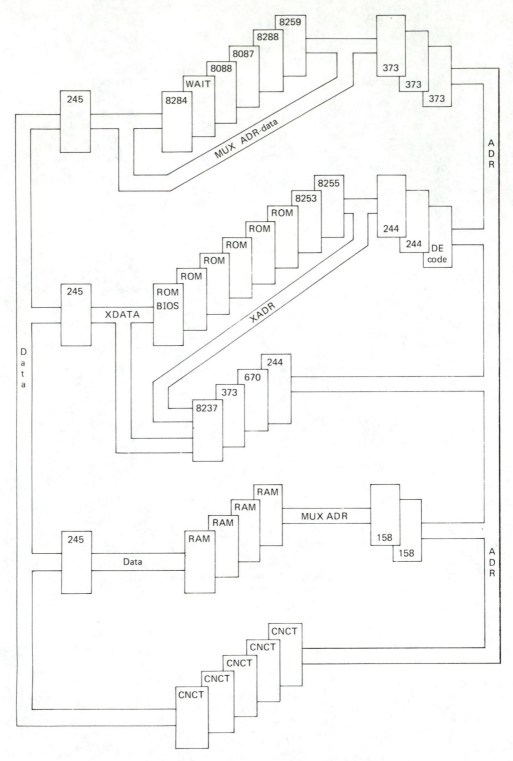

Figure 9.2 Block diagram of PC system board.

BIOS ROS Checksum

The IBM term for ROM is *read-only storage* (ROS). This check adds all the locations in the BIOS ROM to ensure that they equal zero. If any other sum occurs, this is an indication that the BIOS ROM is corrupted and the processor halts at FE0AD.

If the processor internals and ROS checksum tests pass, the intelligent devices in the system can be tested and initialized. Also of extreme importance is the understanding that before the system DRAM can be used, refresh operation must be tested and initialized. This entails the proper operation of Timer 1 of the PIT and Channel 0 of the DMAC.

Verify and Initialize Timer 1 for Refresh Operation

This test verifies that the PIT functions correctly and then initializes Timer 1 to perform a DMA request every 15.2 µs. If a test of the 8253 internals fails, the processor halts at FE0F8. An important working indication is that a faint click occurs at the speaker when the PIT is reset. Note that the sound is a "click," not the usual "beep" that is a function of the output of Timer 3 as illustrated in Figure 5.6

Test the DMAC

An internals test is performed on the 8237 DMAC. If a failure occurs, the processor halts at FE12D.

Program DMAC Channel 0 for DRAM Refresh Operation

Channel 0 of the DMAC and the 74LS670 Register File is initialized for refresh operation. If a stray interrupt (not requested by the PIT) occurs, the processor halts at FE15C. After the initialization and verification of refresh operation, the DRAM subsystem can be accessed.

Verify First 16K of DRAM, Clear DRAM, and Auto-Size System RAM

Remember that the original PC used 16K DRAMs. The first bank of DRAMs provided 16KB of R/W storage. Consequently the POST RAM operations process DRAM at 16K intervals. This test performs a *checkerboard* R/W examination of the first 16K of DRAM. This consists of writing alternate AAH (1010 1010), 55H (0101 0101), FFH, 01H, and 00H patterns to ensure that each bit can toggle.

In Chapter 5 you learned that the system switches indicate how much

RAM resides on the system board. The POST uses the setting of these switches to indicate the maximum RAM that resides on the system board. The remaining RAM in the system is *auto-sized*. The starting address of DRAM that resides on expansion boards must be set to immediately follow the last DRAM address on the system board. In this manner all DRAM in the PC system exists in a continuous block.

A bit pattern is written to RAM and then read back. When the two bit patterns no longer match, it is assumed that the end of the system RAM has been found. As a result, if a bad DRAM IC resides in the third bank on the system board, the POST may find only 128K of system RAM. The incorrect output of the malfunctioning DRAM in the third bank may make the POST draw the false conclusion that the end of system RAM has been found. This is not true for the earlier version of the BIOS ROM. The system switches were read and it was assumed that they indicated the true size of system RAM. If a bad DRAM IC existed, a memory error was reported, describing the bank and bad bit. We explore the techniques of troubleshooting RAM failures in a later section.

If a RAM malfunction is detected within the first 16K, the processor enters a program loop where the failing bit pattern and the byte 04H are alternately output to Port B of the PPI. The system will loop continuously and appear to hang. This infinite program loop produces excellent signals to troubleshoot the system board with an oscilloscope.

Although the last three banks of DRAM on the system board and the DRAM on all memory-expansion boards employ DIP sockets, IBM chose to solder the first bank of DRAM ICs. This means that the discovery of this POST error does not result in the easy fix of simply pulling out a bank of nine DRAM ICs and replacing them with chips that are known to be good. The bad chip must be derived from the output of the PPI or by using an IC comparator tester.

Great caution should be taken when desoldering any IC on the system board. The new IC should never be resoldered directly onto the system board; an IC socket should be soldered in place of the bad IC and the new IC simply inserted into the socket.

Initialize PIC and Set Temporary Interrupt Vectors

The PIC is initialized and a temporary set of interrupt vectors is written to low memory, as described in Chapter 5. No pass or failure indications occur.

Determine System Configuration

Now that the low-level chores have been accomplished, the system-configuration switches are read and stored into a specific location in low RAM. As you remember, the original PC system board had two banks of configuration switches, and the newer versions of the system board have only one bank of switches.

The second bank of switches on the original system board were used to indicate how much expansion memory was installed. Because the new BIOS ROM auto-sizes memory, these switches are no longer needed.

Two of the most important parameters established in the system-configuration check are the type of video display adapter(s) employed and the number of floppy disk drives in the system. The monochrome display adapter, which we examined in Chapter 7, has 4K of video-RAM. The color graphics adapter has 16K of video-RAM. Memory space is allocated in the system memory map so that both types of adapters can be concurrently installed in the PC. Two of the configuration switches are used to indicate the default video adapter that is connected to the primary system display. Through DOS commands, the secondary display can be enabled as the system console device. Although two video adapters and displays can be simultaneously connected to a PC, only one is active at a time.

Check for Manufacturing Mode

The keyboard easily connects to the rear of the system unit. It is a convenient means of loading a manufacturing test. If the keyboard ROM returns the value of AAH after a keyboard-reset operation, this indicates a normal, functioning keyboard. If the keyboard returns a value of 65H, this indicates that the keyboard contains the manufacturing mode test. The test is loaded into low RAM (as if it were coming from normal keyboard input), and execution is transferred to the first byte of the test. This test is used by IBM only in the manufacturing environment.

Initialize CRTC and Verify Video-RAM

Now that low RAM has been verified and temporary interrupt vectors are pointing to service routines, the CRTC on the video adapter designated by the configuration switches will be tested and initialized. These tests entail the 6850 CRTC internals, a R/W test on the video-RAM, verification of horizontal sync timing, and a ROM checksum on the character generator.

If an error occurs during any of these tests, the system speaker will beep long-short-short. If the cursor appears before the long-short-short beep, the character generator on the video adapter failed the checksum test. The processor does not halt due to a video adapter failure. The POST continues executing.

Remember that a malfunction in the R/W test of the video-RAM causes a video adapter error to occur. After the execution of the POST is complete and the system boots, examine the video display for the incorrect character or attribute. The bad memory IC can be established by following the procedure outlined in Chapter 7.

Now that the video adapter has been initialized, all further POST error descriptions are directed to the system display. These error indications provide much more information than simply halting the processor or emitting tones from the system speaker.

Test PIC

Although the PIC has been initialized, it has not been entirely tested. If a 8259 internal register fails or a spurious interrupt occurs, the error message 101 is displayed and the processor halts at FE35C.

The error code 101 is reserved to describe failures that occur on the system board. Remember that the video adapter was just initialized on the previous test; this is the first POST system board error that will cause 101 to be displayed.

Verify TOD Timer

The verify TOD timer tests the interval between Timer 0 interrupts to ensure that the TOD clock is functioning correctly. If the interval is too long or short, a 101 error is displayed and the system halts at FE35C.

Once the PIT is programmed, it will continue functioning independently of the system processor. If a 101 system error is displayed, verify that the output of Timer 0 is a symmetrical square wave with a period of 54.9 ms. This will enable you to distinguish between a PIC and a PIT 101 error.

Keyboard Test

As an alternative to returning the ASCII code of the depressed key, the PC keyboard returns a *scan code*, which describes the physical position of the depressed key as well as the status of the shift, control, and alternate keys. Returning a scan code instead of an explicit ASCII code results in the flexibility of remapping the keyboard to any arbitrary character set. The scan codes of each key position are listed in the IBM *Technical Reference Manual*.

If a keyboard error occurs, 301 is sent to the video display. If a key is found to be stuck in the closed position, the keyboard error code will be preceded by the two-digit hexadecimal scan code of the malfunctioning key. To isolate the malfunctioning key, the scan code is cross-referenced to the listing in the *Technical Reference Manual*.

Microcomputers and terminals have traditionally employed mechanical SPST key switches on their keyboards. The PC employs a *capacitive matrix* keyboard in which the individual key switches cannot be easily replaced. The removal of the key cap reveals a spring that is attached at the far end to an oval flapper. If the spring slides off of the nub on the flapper, it will appear that the key is stuck closed. Reseating the spring on the flapper nub (with a connector pin-puller or similar tool) solves most key switch problems.

If coffee or soda is spilled onto a keyboard, remove the key caps of the affected keys and carefully swab out the springs and flappers with a cotton swab and freon or alcohol solution. If a keyboard error occurs, the processor does not halt, but continues executing the POST.

Set Interrupt Vector Table

The temporary set of interrupt vectors is replaced by the operational set of vectors.

Test-Expansion Chassis

The original PC system board had only five expansion slots and a small 63.5-W power supply. With the addition of a video adapter, floppy disk drive controller, and a memory-expansion board, the slots could become quickly filled. The expansion chassis supports an additional five expansion slots and a power supply. The system board and expansion chassis communicate via a transceiver board installed in each system.

This test checks to see if a transceiver board is installed in an expansion slot. If a transceiver board is found, the communications between the system unit and expansion chassis is tested. An expansion chassis error causes 1801 to be sent to the video display. This would indicate that one of the transceiver boards, the interconnecting cable, or the power supply in the expansion chassis is not correctly functioning.

The use of expansion chassis is extremely limited. They are most often employed in laboratory environments where data acquisition and process control experiments that require dozens of channels of I/O are conducted.

Check System RAM in Excess of the First 16K
and Verify DRAM Refresh Operation

When the first 16K of system RAM was verified, the system RAM was auto-sized. This test verifies the system RAM beyond the first 16K. If a RAM error occurs, 201 is displayed. The RAM fault error code is preceded by the bad bank and bit of the DRAM failure, where BB stands for the bad bank and bb represents the bad bit position. In a later section we further explore DRAM troubleshooting procedures on the PC system.

If a DMA request of Channel 0 does not occur within 15.2 μs, the system board error 101 is displayed and the processor halts at FE35C.

In the original BIOS ROM the progress of the DRAM verification test was not displayed. If the remaining system RAM passed, the POST simply executed the next test. In the newer versions of the BIOS ROM, the progress of the DRAM check is displayed in 16K intervals. In this manner the total amount of RAM discovered during the auto-size procedure and verified by the DRAM check is displayed. If this amount of RAM does not match the amount that is actually installed in the system, a DRAM error probably occurred during the auto-size, which the processor misinterpreted as the end of system RAM. The Advanced Diagnostics Disk enables the technician to test RAM that was not found by the auto-size portion of the POST.

Check for Optional ROM

A portion of the system memory map is allocated for optional ROM. This ROM usually takes the form of the ROM on a *hard disk drive adapter*. The hard disk drive adapter performs the same function for hard disk drives that the floppy disk drive adapter performs for the floppy disk drives. The original BIOS ROM did not support hard drives as a boot device. Newer BIOS ROMs look for this optional ROM starting at memory location C8000H. A valid optional ROM is designated by having the checkerboard pattern 55H, AAH in its first two memory locations. The third location has the size of the ROM divided by 512K. Thus an 8K ROM has 55H, AAH, and 10H in its first three locations. There are many different manufacturers of hard disk drive adapters for the PC system. The manufacturer of the ROM for the hard disk drive adapter is indicated in the copyright notice following the three mandatory identification bytes.

The hard disk controller ROM contains the BIOS routines and POST that is specific to the hard disk drive system. A hard disk error is indicated by a code of ''1700.''

When a hard disk drive adapter is installed in a system that has the original BIOS ROM, the system must booted from the floppy disk. The manufacturer of the disk drive adapter usually supplies a program that enables systems with the older BIOS to recognize the hard disk subsystem. The new BIOS ROM tests for the hard disk drive controller ROM and modifies the system boot procedure, as is examined in a few paragraphs.

If a checksum error occurs, the failing address is displayed, followed by the word ROM. The address range of the hard disk drive-adapter control ROM is C8000 to CA000.

The original system board had six 8K ROM sockets. One socket was utilized by the BIOS ROM, and four ROMs stored the BASIC programming language interpreter. One socket was empty. The newer versions of the system board have two ROMs, one 8K BIOS ROM and one 32K BASIC ROM. There are no empty ROM sockets on the new system board.

Checksum BASIC ROM

A checksum operation is performed on the four 8K ROMs on the original system board or the 32K ROM on the newer system boards. The error indication is the same as the the optional ROM test.

Verify Floppy Disk Drive Adapter

The verify floppy disk drive adapter test verifies the internals of the FDC and the floppy disk drive system. The activity LED on drive A will illuminate during this test. If an error occurs the code ''601'' will be displayed.

Initialize Printer and Serial Ports

The initialize printer and serial ports routine checks the standard addresses for the presence of a maximum of two printer ports (LPT1: and LPT2:) and two serial ports (COM1: and COM2:). If the ports exist, they are initialized and mapped into the system device-allocation table.

Display Error in Progress Message

If a POST error occurred that did not cause the processor to halt or enter a continuous loop, the message Error Resume = F1 is displayed. This alerts the user that the system is functioning but an error did occur during the POST. By pressing the F1 key, the next test in the POST is executed. If no errors have occurred, the speaker emits a single short beep and the video display is cleared.

Enable NMI

Remember that the main use of the NMI is to report parity errors in the system board and expansion RAM. The enable NMI test enables parity checking. That does not necessarily mean that a bad parity DRAM will immediately create a parity error. If the bad parity DRAM is in one of the banks of RAM that is not currently accessed by the processor, a parity error will not be generated. Parity errors in high RAM usually occur when a large application program is loaded. At that point the processor begins to access high RAM for read operations, and the parity error occurs. Remember that Parity Check 1 refers to the system board RAM and Parity Check 2 refers to RAM that resides on expansion boards.

Often a bad parity DRAM will be found during the DRAM verification test of the POST. The appropriate error code is written to the video display but appears only for a split second. When parity checking is enabled, the error message written by the DRAM verification test is overwritten by a parity check error. To see the error code that describes the bad parity DRAM chip, you must reboot the system and carefully watch the upper left corner of the video display for the fleeting error message.

Boot DOS From Floppy or Hard Disk Drive

Within the BIOS ROM is a routine for software interrupt 19 (Int 19), called the *bootstrap loader*. If no optional ROM was detected to indicate the presence of the hard disk drive controller, program execution is transferred to Int 19 of the BIOS ROM, and the first two sectors of track 1 of the floppy disk in drive A are read into low RAM. These sectors contain the programs called ibmbio.com and ibmdos.com. These programs enable the remainder of DOS to be accessed.

If the bootstrap load is successful, execution is transferred to the location in low RAM that contains the bootstrap program from the floppy disk. If, after several retries, the bootstrap module cannot be loaded from the floppy disk drive, program execution is transferred to ROM BASIC and the BASIC logo appears on the video display. This is a throwback to the concept of using a cassette as a mass storage device and having the PC boot directly into BASIC.

If the optional hard disk controller ROM has been detected, the vector for Int 19 does not point to the BIOS ROM bootstrap loader but rather to the bootstrap loader in the hard disk controller ROM. The routine first attempts to boot from a floppy disk in drive A. If it is unsuccessful, then it attempts to read the boot loader from the first hard disk drive in the system, designated as drive C. If both the floppy disk and hard disk access attempts are unsuccessful, then the system transfers execution to ROM BASIC.

PC systems that contain hard disk drives are usually booted from the hard disk. The exception to this is if the hard disk has not yet been partitioned or formatted at the DOS level or the boot tracks have been damaged. By booting via a floppy, the hard disk can be examined to determine the nature of the malfunction.

9.2 THE ADVANCED DIAGNOSTICS DISK

In the *Guide to Operations* manual, which IBM supplies with each system unit, is a diagnostics disk designed for use by nontechnical personnel to verify system failures. IBM also sells the *PC Maintenance Manual*, which contains the *Advanced Diagnostics Disk* (ADD) and *wrap-back plugs* (also called *loop-back connectors*) that are used to test the LPT and COM ports. The ADD is designed to be employed by technical personnel to troubleshoot a system malfunction to the subassembly level.

Remember, for the ADD to be of any assistance the system must be bootable from the floppy disk drive and the video display subsystem must be at least partially operational. If the system does not pass the POST and a halt instruction is executed, the indications issued by the POST will be your only clue to the malfunctioning subassembly.

The ADD is often used to find *intermittent failures* that cannot be reliably reproduced by the user. The most important function of the ADD is to differentiate between software and hardware failures. Picture the situation where a user experiences an apparent malfunction each time the printer is accessed. The problem may lie in the setup of the word-processing program, the printer port, the printer, or the setup of the printer. If the ADD verifies that the hardware within the PC (including the printer port) is correctly functioning and the self-test on the printer passes, then the malfunction is most likely in the setup of the printer or the word-processing program.

To start the diagnostics routines the ADD is placed in drive A and power is applied to the system. After the system boots, a menu is displayed, offering four choices. Two of the choices are standard system utilities—format a blank disk and copy a disk. The other two enable the user to enter the diagnostics program and boot DOS.

When the "run diagnostics routines" option is selected, the floppy disk is accessed and, after a short interval, a screen listing the installed devices in the system is displayed. This screen is derived from the information that is gathered by the POST. The installed devices include the system board, keyboard, the total amount of system RAM, one or more video display adapters (remember that the PC supports multiple display adapters), the number of floppy disk drives, the number of printer and serial ports, the existence of the IBM Graphics Printer, the number of hard disk drives, and the existence of the expansion unit. Preceding each item on the list is the leading digit of the error code for that item.

If the installed device list is correct, you may proceed to the next menu. If it is incorrect, you are given a list from which you should select the missing devices. As you add a device the appropriate error message is displayed. If the POST does not find an installed device, that usually indicates that the device is not functioning. It could also indicate that it is set up incorrectly. Always check the jumpers and switches on a board before you declare that it is bad. If a second serial or printer port is not recognized, ensure that it is addressed correctly and that the proper interrupt has been selected (as discussed in Chapter 5).

Consider the case where the system memory is auto-sized in the POST. We said that a bad DRAM can cause the POST to think that it has reached the end of the installed system RAM. If the system has 512K of RAM but the POST and diagnostics show only 128K, the most likely cause is that a bad DRAM IC resides in Bank 2. (The banks of DRAM are labeled starting with Bank 0.) You should enter the true amount of installed RAM. This will enable the diagnostics to test all the installed DRAM.

Once the installed devices listing is correct, the diagnostics program will proceed to the system checkout menu, which will enable you to set the number of times a diagnostics routine is to be run. Usually the option to run a test once is selected. If a machine appears to have an intermittent memory problem, you may select the test to run several times and instruct the routine to stop when an error is detected. The next menu lists the possible diagnostic routines and directs the technician to chose which device should be tested.

System Board Test

The system board diagnostic routine verifies the operation of the components on the system board, including ROM checksums.

System Memory Test

Because the auto-size portion of the POST may misinterpret a DRAM fault as an indication of the end-of-system memory, the system memory test aids in identifying the the malfunctioning DRAM chip. Before you run this test ensure that the diagnostics has displayed the correct system memory size. Figure 9.3 illustrates the physical layout of the four banks of DRAMs on the system board and the individual IC error designations.

The other six banks of DRAMs in a fully configured 640K system reside on an expansion board. If the diagnostic detects a DRAM read failure, it will print the 201 error message and the bank and bit of the failure. This information is encoded as illustrated in Figure 9.3. The banks are labeled 0 through 9, and each bit within a bank has a unique error code. If the first location of the DRAM in bit 3 of bank 2 fails, the error message:

Failing Address-Space/Module 20000 08

will be displayed. The first five hex digits reveal the address of the failure. In a system employing 64K DRAMs, the bank of the failing DRAM is easy to derive. Remember that 64K has a hex value of FFFF. Thus the range of addresses in bank 0 extends from 00000H through 0FFFFH; bank 1 addresses are from 10000 through 1FFFFH, and bank 2 addresses are from 20000H through 2FFFFH. Thus the first hex digit in the error message can be interpreted as indicating the bad bank, and the remaining four digits indicate the failing location within the 64K address space of the particular DRAM.

If the first location of a DRAM is bad, be suspicious—always ensure that it is properly inserted into the DIP socket; one or more legs may be bent under or hanging over the socket.

The last two hex digits in the error code point to the bad bit or bits within the specified bank. Take the two hex digits and expand them into their 8-bit binary form. A logic 1 in a bit position indicates a bad bit. Thus the error code:

08 → 0000 1000

indicates that bit 3 is bad. The error code

60 → 0110 0000

indicates that bits 5 and 6 are bad. This explains why IBM chose to utilize what may, on first inspection, appear to be an overly complicated method of designating failing bits. Because the parity bit-error code does not have any logic 1 bits, it can not be detected in the presence of other failures.

The memory diagnostic normally halts when a failure occurs. Thus after one bad DRAM IC is replaced, the diagnostic may find others that were not discovered in the first run. Replacing DRAM ICs that may have failed due to a power surge or came from the same run of bad ICs takes great patience.

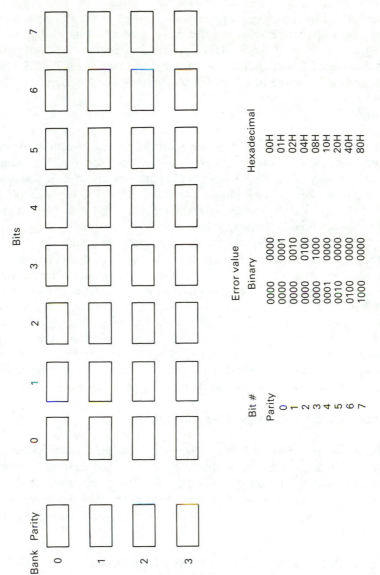

Figure 9.3 DRAM layout on system board and error designations.

Simply replace the bad DRAM as indicated and rerun the diagnostics. Continue this procedure until no further failures occur.

In our examination of the POST we discussed that a DRAM failure in the first 16K will force the processor to enter an infinite loop. This type of failure can be verified by monitoring the output of Port B of the PPI with an oscilloscope. The scope will display the distinctive pattern of the failing bit pattern alternated with 04H. If the POST fails after the speaker click but before any audible or visual failure indications, observe the signals on Port B of the PPI for the indication of the first 16K DRAM failure exercise loop.

Keyboard Test

This test displays the pattern of the keyboard on the video display. As each key is depressed, the corresponding key on the video display blinks. This test is used to find keys that are stuck open. (We have already studied how the POST indicates that a key is stuck closed.) If a key is stuck open, pull off the key cap and closely examine the spring and flapper. Look for an indication of dirt, dust, or spilled liquids in the keyboard.

The 301 POST error, without an accompanying scan code, may indicate that the keyboard cable has an open line. The ends of the keyboard cable are constantly flexed; it is fairly common for an open to occur where a wire meets the pin in the connector. Often this problem is intermittent and will occur only if the keyboard cable is flexed. To verify the continuity of the wires in the keyboard cable, the keyboard cover is removed by extracting the two screws on the bottom of the keyboard cover, and the cable is easily snapped out of the connector. The black wire terminated in a lug and attached to the keyboard cover retaining screw is the keyboard ground wire. Carefully check each wire in the cable for continuity with an ohmmeter, as illustrated in Figure 9.4.

Display Adapter and Video Display Test

Depending on the type of display adapter(s) installed in the system, this diagnostic provides a submenu of tests. These tests are designed to verify the character generator, character attributes, video-RAM, color output of the color graphics adapter, and various display configurations. The monochrome display adapter has the error code of 400 and the color graphics adapter has the error code of 500.

Floppy Disk Drive Adapter and Floppy Disk Drives

This diagnostic verifies the operation of the floppy disk drive adapter, interface cable, and floppy disk drive(s).

If a floppy disk drive is exhibiting intermittent failures or diminished performance, this test can provide a few of the functions of the floppy disk

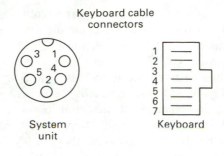

Keyboard cable
connectors

System
unit

Keyboard

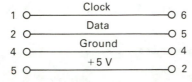

Figure 9.4 Keyboard cable
and connectors.

drive exerciser/tester that we discussed in Chapter 8. The system should be booted from a working floppy disk drive and the drive under test installed as the second drive in the system. The floppy disk tester/exerciser portion of the diagnostics performs a sequential seek, random seek, verify floppy disk, and spindle-speed test.

A severe limitation of this diagnostic is that it does not enable the technician to place the R/W heads over a specified track. Without this ability, the ADD cannot be used explicitly to verify radial alignment. Nonetheless, these tests do allow the technician to evaluate the performance of a floppy disk drive in a controlled environment.

RS-232 Serial Ports

We know that a maximum of two RS-232 serial ports can be installed in the PC system. These ports, designated COM1: and COM2:, are used to connect the PC with modems, printers, mice, bar code readers, graphics tablets, and dozens of other common RS-232 devices.

There are two major aspects to testing a serial interface adapter. First, the internal operation of the serial interface adapter must be verified. This is accomplished by writing control words and invoking the *internal loop-back test* function of the serial communications LSI device called the *UART (universal asynchronous receiver/transmitter)*. The serial adapter in the PC employs the 8250 UART.*

*For more information on RS-232 serial communications refer to Byron W. Putman, *RS-232 Simplified: Everything YOU Need To Know About Connecting, Interfacing and Troubleshooting Peripheral Devices*. Englewood Cliffs, N.J.: Prentice-Hall, Inc., 1987.

The second portion of verifying a serial port is called an *external loop-back test*. The serial port loop-back test connector supplied with the advanced diagnostics is plugged into the RS-232 port under test. This test connector loops the transmitted data from the UART back into the received data input. Thus the output drivers and line receivers are tested, as well as the ± 12-V output of the power supply which is used to power the RS-232 line drivers and receivers. Figure 9.5 illustrates the configuration of the serial loop-back connector. Remember that the + 12-V output is used by the floppy and hard disk drives and also by the serial ports on the PC. However, the − 12-V output is usually employed only by the serial ports. A failure of the − 12-V output of the power supply may not be detected unless an RS-232 port is installed in the PC. The error code 1100 indicates a COM1: failure, and 1200 indicates a COM2: failure.

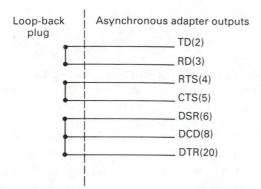

Figure 9.5 Serial loop-back connector.

Hard Disk Drive

Most new PCs are equipped with a hard disk drive. The typical capacity of hard disk drives are 10, 20, and 30 MB. When the POST discovers a ROM at C8000, it assumes that a hard disk controller and hard disk drive are installed in the system.

The ADD provides several hard disk controller and drive tests. The ADD also contains a low-level format program for the hard disk drive. Because hard disk drives have such great storage capacities, the low-level format program is used to discover and mark bad sectors on the disk surface that can not be reliably used to store data. The partition and format functions supplied by PC-DOS do not physically reformat the hard disk but only initialize the disk (erasing the pointers to previous files) and prepare it to accept new DOS files.

The ADD also contains a program called *shipdisk*. When a system with a hard disk drive is to be transported, the R/W heads must be stepped to a reserved *parking track*, or a track that does not contain data. This ensures that the bouncing and jarring of the heads against the surface of the coated or platted hard disk platter will not cause read errors.

Error code	Subassembly
100	System board
200	Memory
300	Keyboard
400	Monochrome and printer adapter
500	Color graphics adapter
600	Floppy disk drive system
900	Printer adapter
1100	COM1: serial port
1200	COM2: serial port
1300	Game adapter
1400	IBM dot-matrix printer
1500	SDLC COM adapter
1700	Hard disk dirve system
1800	Expansion chassis

Figure 9.6   Summary of error codes.

Figure 9.6 illustrates the summary of error codes for the most common adapters in the PC system.

9.3 BOARD SWAPPING AND COMPONENT-LEVEL REPAIR

The most rudimentary level of microcomputer troubleshooting is to simply swap a malfunctioning system with a known-good-unit (KGU). Obviously, this method of troubleshooting requires no technical knowledge, and it is extremely expensive to hold entire spare systems in inventory.

The other extreme is to attempt to repair each system malfunction to *component level*. This method demands the efforts of a highly skilled technician, the assistance of many pieces of specialized test equipment, a large spare parts inventory, and a great deal of time.

Between these two extremes is the option to repair a malfunctioning PC to the subassembly level. Here, subassembly is defined as a printed circuit board, power supply, disk drive, or other unit that can be easily removed and replaced. The logic behind this approach is simple: Before visiting the site of the malfunction, the technician can consult with the user who reported the malfunction and determine the possible failing subassemblies.

In the light of our study of the POST and ADD, this approach should seem to be a good compromise. Often with the assistance of only a *DMM (digital multimeter)* and the ADD, a technician can quickly and efficiently get a customer up and running, which is the single most important goal of any service technician. If the problem indicated a possible floppy disk drive failure, the technician would bring a spare drive and interface cable, a floppy disk drive adapter, a floppy disk alignment tester/exerciser, or a floppy disk drive evaluation program such as the Dysan Interrogator, and a head-cleaning kit.

The technician now returns to the shop with the bad subassembly. How will this board, power supply, monitor, floppy disk drive, hard disk drive, or keyboard be repaired? It's simply a matter of economics. There are three basic methods of repairing a bad subassembly:

1. In-house component-level repair
2. Third-party depot repair
3. No repair—throw away bad subassemblies.

Let's discuss the test equipment, parts, turnaround time, float inventory, and personnel requirements of each method just listed.

In-House Component-Level Repair

Repairing the majority of subassemblies in-house requires skilled technicians, standard test equipment (DMMs, oscilloscopes, logic probes and pulsers, IC comparators, and so on), specialized programmable automated test systems, and a large stock of standard and custom integrated circuits, switches, and other components.

In-house component-level repair is often limited to large service organizations where the investment of the parts inventory and specialized test systems can be amortized over a considerable volume of subassemblies., Automated test systems range in cost from $10,000 to $150,000. It also requires many days and months of labor to write the test programs for each subassembly to be repaired.

In an effort to make in-house component-level repair available to small organizations, several manufacturers have created microcomputer subassembly test systems that do not require a large investment in software development and also sell for under $10,000. The Fluke 9010A illustrated in Figure 9.7 is a general-purpose programmable microprocessor troubleshooting system.

In addition to the base 9010A system, a microprocessor pod to emulate the processor in the system under test must be purchased. A complete PC troubleshooting system from Fluke consists of the 9010A, 8088 pod, and a set of traced fault diagnostic programs on microcassette tape. Fluke also sells a test-development system that runs on the PC. This enables technicians and test engineers quickly to develop test programs for the 9010A. To troubleshoot other microcomputer systems, the appropriate pod is purchased and the test software must be developed in-house or obtained from Fluke or a third-party test-software development house.

Figure 9.8 illustrates the Dair Computers Aid/88 troubleshooting system. This system sells for under $3000. Unlike the Fluke 9010A, which is a general-purpose programmable test system, the Aid/88 is specifically designed to test and repair the IBM system board. It contains built-in tests that verify the operation of the bus system and memory. Furthermore, it uses the POST to pinpoint system board failures by displaying the address of the halt instruction.

Figure 9.7 Fluke 9010A micro troubleshooter.

Figure 9.8   Dair Computers Aid/88.

As we discovered in the first section of this chapter, by cross-referencing the halt address to the POST listing, the circuit failure can be localized to an intelligent IC, decoder or address/data bus buffer. The Aid/88 is an extremely cost-effective means of getting started in the PC repair business.

Third-Party Depot Repair

There are hundreds of depot board repair vendors for PC boards. For a *flat-rate* fee or *time and materials* (T/M), these companies repair malfunctioning printed circuit boards. They usually employ large and expensive high-throughput automated test systems to achieve a reasonable repair rate.

Imagine the following cycle for a subassembly in the *float inventory* of a PC maintenance firm. A PC under maintenance contract suffers a failure. The user calls the maintenance organization to report a problem and provides a detailed description of the system's symptoms and error indications. In this case, let's assume that the user explains that the system fails to boot off the floppy disk drive and displays a 601 error. With this knowledge the technician takes a floppy disk adapter, a control cable, a floppy disk drive, and a floppy disk drive alignment tester/exerciser to the customer's site.

The technician tries booting the system from the ADD and gets the 601 error. The technician removes the cover of the system unit and verifies the following:

1. +5 V and +12 V appear on the power connector of the floppy disk drive.

2. The controller cable is snug on both the floppy disk drive and adapter sides.

3. The correct connector of the controller cable is plugged onto drive A. (Remember that this will be the connector *after* the twist of the wires on the controller cable.)

4. The terminator and option header are correctly installed in drive A.

If cleaning the R/W heads with the wet-solution kit has no affect, the technician then substitutes the good floppy disk drive adapter into the system and the system boots and functions correctly.

We now have one bad floppy disk adapter to repair and one less good floppy disk adapter in float inventory. On the IBM floppy disk drive adapter, there are no ICs in sockets. This makes it difficult to swap suspect chips. The technician should visually inspect the board to check for burned ICs or other obvious failures. The *fingers* on the edge connector should also be inspected for excess corrosion.

If none of these checks reveals a problem, the board is sent off to a depot repair service. *Turnaround* defines the length of time it takes for the depot to repair and return the bad board. If the depot has a long turnaround time (4 to 6 weeks) the maintenance firm must carry a larger spare-parts inventory. It is obvious that a shorter turnaround time enables the maintenance firm to purchase a smaller spare-parts inventory. Thus a premium is placed on depot repair services that guarantee a 1- or 2-week turnaround.

In actual practice, most maintenance organizations apply some form of screening, where easy and cheap fixes are accomplished in-house and more difficult problems are passed on to the depot.

Don't Repair Bad Subassemblies—Throw Them Away

Many overseas companies manufacture and market IBM PC compatible subassemblies for prices that are comparable to depot repair costs for the equivalent IBM subassemblies. If the customer is agreeable to having non-IBM subassemblies used in his or her machine, then this is a viable alternative to depot repair.

To avoid copyright infringement the circuitry on these overseas "clone" boards does not exactly match that of their IBM counterparts. These boards are not usually supported by depot repair because each would require a slightly different test program. The options are to effect the easy repairs in-house and keep the unrepairable units for spare parts, or send the clone board back to the U.S. distributor for repair.

The same considerations are now true for floppy and hard disk drives. The newer generation of half-height floppy disk drives is sold at the price of depot repair for a standard floppy disk drive. If an in-house fix with a floppy disk drive alignment tester/exerciser is easy and quick, the drive can be turned around and returned to float inventory. If not, it can be kept for spare parts and replaced with a new overseas half-height unit.

The sealed R/W head–disk platter assembly in a hard disk drive is called the *head disk assembly (HDA)*. When a head crash occurs or the system unit is moved without parking the heads, the surface of the disk platter and possibly the R/W heads are damaged. This is usually indicated by a 1701 fixed disk read error. Because the inside of the HDA must not be exposed to any smoke or dust particles, it can be opened and repaired only in a *clean room facility*. The repair costs of an HDA are often as much or more than simply purchasing a new drive. Be extremely cautious when purchasing a new hard disk drive from a manufacturer other than IBM that it is compatible and matches the same specifications as the original drive.

IMPORTANT CONCEPTS OF CHAPTER 9

- The POST verifies and initializes the intelligent devices, DRAM subsystem, and I/O ports each time the system is energized.
- The POST error indications vary from simply halting the system processor to describing the location of the bad DRAM IC or stuck key.
- Before the DRAM subsystem can used, Timer 1 of the PIT and Channel 0 of the DMAC must be tested and functioning.
- A checksum operation verifies the contents of a ROM.
- If an error occurs in the first 16K of DRAM, the processor enters an infinite loop that alternately outputs the bad byte pattern and 04H to Port B of the PPI.
- The first bank of DRAM ICs are soldered, not placed in DIP sockets.
- The default system configuration is determined by reading the configuration switches, auto-sizing the DRAM, checking for optional ROM, and determining the existence of serial or parallel ports.
- During the auto-size portion of the POST, a DRAM fault may be interpreted as the end of RAM. The ADD is used to find the bad memory device.

- System board faults exhibit a 101 error.
- The most common form of optional ROM is the firmware for the hard disk drive subsystem at C8000H.
- If the optional ROM at C8000H is detected, the bootstrap loader vector is pointed at the firmware in the hard disk drive adapter.
- If a noncatastrophic POST error occurs, the message F1 = Resume is output to the video display.
- Parity error checking is enabled near the end of the POST.
- The ADD and loop-back plugs are used to verify a hardware failure to the subassembly level.
- Intermittent errors are found by instructing the ADD to run a diagnostic routine until an error occurs.
- The first menu on the ADD has the user verify the system configuration as determined by the POST. Devices can be added or removed to correct the configuration.
- DRAM faults are indicated by a ''201'' error code and the ORed pattern of the bad bit codes.
- A keyboard error is indicated by ''301.''
- All aspects of installed video display adapters can be tested by the ADD routines. The monochrome display adapter has an error code of 400 and the CGA an error code of 500.
- The operation of RS-232 serial ports (COM: ports) and parallel printer ports (LPT: ports) is verified with a loop-back test.
- The heads on a hard disk drive should be parked with the shipdisk program prior to moving the system unit.
- The ADD provides fundamental programs to test and exercise floppy and hard disk drives.
- Component-level repair on PCs requires skilled technicians, standard test equipment, and automated test systems.
- Depot repair facilities use powerful automated test systems to repair PC subassemblies.
- Many subassemblies manufactured overseas are competitively priced with the depot repair services for the equivalent IBM subassembly.
- A float inventory is the stock of spare parts used to replace bad subassemblies found at the customer's site. After the malfunctioning subassembly is repaired (in-house or at a repair depot), it becomes part of the float inventory.
- An HDA should be disassembled only in a clean room. It is often more costly to repair an HDA than to purchase a new drive.

APPENDIX

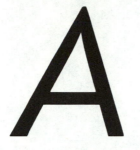

*THE BINARY AND
HEXADECIMAL
NUMBER SYSTEMS*

A.1 INTRODUCTION TO DIGITAL SIGNALS

When most people are asked to name a waveform they think of the sine wave. The sine wave is the fundamental waveform; all other waveforms are derived from various phase and frequency combinations of the sine wave. Another common waveform is the square wave. Let's take a moment to contrast these two waveforms, as illustrated in Figure A.1. The amplitude of the sine wave is continuously changing. Following that line of thinking, we can say that the amplitude of any given sine wave has an infinite number of possible values. These values exist between the positive and negative peaks. The sine wave is an *analog signal*. The term *analog* refers to a waveform whose amplitude changes in a continuous fashion.

The amplitude of a square wave consists of only two values, a high value and a low value. These amplitude changes occur discretely, that is, in steps. The square wave is called a *digital waveform*. This appendix describes the number systems that are associated with the digital waveforms and circuitry found in microcomputers. The use of the term *digital* indicates that a numeric value can be assigned to each level of the waveform. Our decimal number system is based on the fact that human beings have 10 fingers. In essence, a square wave has only two "fingers." It should seem logical that digital electronics supports a base-2 number system. The digits in this system are 0 and 1. The digit 0 is assigned to the low part of the square wave and the digit 1, to the high part of the square wave.

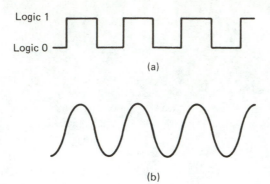

Figure A.1   Square wave and sine wave.

A.2 NUMBER BASES AND COUNTING

The base-2 number system is called the *binary number system*. The base of a number system describes the number of unique digits in that system. In our decimal number system there are 10 unique digits, 0 through 9. In the binary number system there are two unique digits: 0 and 1.

All number systems, regardless of their bases, function identically. We should take a moment and review the decimal number system. Most number systems operate with a *weighted code*. Weighted codes use place values. Refer to the example of a three-digit decimal number in Figure A.2. Notice that the place value of the rightmost column is equal to the base raised to the 0 power. The next column's place value is equal to the base raised to the first power; the value of the last column is the base raised to the second power. This process can continue indefinitely to represent a number of any size.

Consider the act of counting. We start with the first digit in the number system. This digit is always the quantity 0. Each time we increment the count, we use the next digit in the system to represent the new, updated count. What happens when we run out of unique digits? When we have employed all the digits in our number system, we must restart the counting procedure with zero. To ensure that the objects we have already counted are not lost or forgotten, a *carry* is generated. This carry is added to the value in the next column.

$$10^2 \quad 10^1 \quad 10^0$$

$$5 \qquad 3 \qquad 7$$

$$10^0 \times 7 = 7$$
$$10^1 \times 3 = 30$$
$$10^2 \times 5 = \underline{500}$$
$$537$$

Figure A.2   What does the number "537" really represent?

A decimal number is called a *digit*. The term digit indicates one of the 10 fingers. A binary number is called a *bit*. The word *bit* is a contraction of Binary digIT. Notice the counting table illustrated in Table A.1. On every count the LSB toggles, 0 to 1 or 1 to 0. The next column toggles on every other count; the column after that, on every four counts. Finally, the most significant

	2^3	2^2	2^1	2^0	Decimal equivalent
		Comments:			
0000					0
+___1					
0001				0 + 1 = 1	1
+___1					
0010			0 + 1 = 1	1 + 1 = 0	2
+___1					
0011				0 + 1 = 1	3
+___1					
0100		0 + 1 = 1	1 + 1 = 0	1 + 1 = 0	4
+___1					
0101				0 + 1 = 1	5
+___1					
0110			0 + 1 = 1	1 + 1 = 0	6
+___1					
0111				0 + 1 = 1	7
+___1					
1000	0 + 1 = 1	1 + 1 = 0	1 + 1 = 0	1 + 1 = 0	8
+___1					
1001				0 + 1 = 1	9
+___1					
1010			0 + 1 = 1	1 + 1 = 0	10
+___1					
1011				0 + 1 = 1	11
+___1					
1100		0 + 1 = 1	1 + 1 = 0	1 + 1 = 0	12
+___1					
1101				0 + 1 = 1	13
+___1					
1110			0 + 1 = 1	1 + 1 = 0	14
+___1					
1111				0 + 1 = 1	15

Table A.1   Binary counting table.

column toggles once every eight counts. The frequency at which the column toggles indicates its place value.

A.3 BINARY ADDITION AND SUBTRACTION

Infrequently you will need to add or subtract two binary numbers. The best tool to use for this purpose is a handheld calculator that supports multiple number bases. In this section we learn to add and subtract binary quantities manually.

Binary addition is as easy as counting. All you must remember is these four rules:

$$
\begin{aligned}
0 + 0 &= 0 \\
1 + 0 &= 1 \\
1 + 1 &= 0 \qquad \text{and a carry of 1} \\
1 + 1 + 1 &= 1 \qquad \text{and a carry of 1}
\end{aligned}
$$

Study the addition examples illustrated in Figure A.3. Examine example A.3(d). The least significant column creates a carry. This carry is added to the next column, where two 1s are already to summed. This is a situation where the last addition rule is applied:

$$1 + 1 + 1 = 1 \qquad \text{and a carry of 1}$$

Before we attempt binary subtraction, let's review the methods that we employ in decimal subtraction. The act of subtraction is closely tied to the concept of the *borrow*. The borrow in subtraction is analogous to the carry in addition. The major conceptional problem experienced with the borrow is, How much is really being borrowed? Refer to the following subtraction problem:

$$
\begin{array}{r}
54 \\
- \ 8 \\
\hline
46
\end{array}
$$

When we attempt the subtraction it is obvious that we must borrow from the 10s column. The value that we borrow is therefore equal to 10. Adding our borrow to the value in the 1s column yields 14. Eight subtracted from 14 is 6. This process may seem painfully obvious, but it is important that you consciously

$$
\begin{array}{llll}
\text{(a)} \quad 1001 & \text{(b)} \quad 1110 & \text{(c)} \quad 1010 & \text{(d)} \quad 0011 \\
+ \ \underline{0011} & + \ \underline{1000} & + \ \underline{0111} & + \ \underline{0111} \\
\quad 1100 & 1 \ 0110 & 1 \ 0001 & \quad 1010
\end{array}
$$

Figure A.3   Binary addition examples.

$$
\begin{array}{cccc}
1010 & 1101 & 1000 & 1110 \\
-\ \ \ \ 1 & -\ \ \ 11 & -\ \ 100 & -\ 1101 \\
\hline
1001 & 1010 & 0100 & 0001
\end{array}
$$

Figure A.4 Binary subtraction with elementary borrows.

understand the details of a borrow operation. Consider the following subtraction problem:

$$
\begin{array}{r}
504 \\
-\ \ \ 8 \\
\hline
496
\end{array}
$$

This time we cannot borrow from the adjacent digit. We must first borrow 10s from the 100s place and then borrow 1s from the 10s place.

We have seen that one of the rules of binary addition is $1 + 1 = 0$ and a carry. The operation of borrowing is the inverse of the operation of carrying. The following subtraction problem illustrates the manner in which you should approach a binary borrow.

$$
\begin{array}{r}
10 \\
-\ 1 \\
\hline
01
\end{array}
=
\begin{array}{r}
\not{1}0^{1+1} \\
-\ 1 \\
\hline
01
\end{array}
$$

This first binary subtraction does not require a borrow:

$$
\begin{array}{r}
1101 \\
-\ \ 100 \\
\hline
1001
\end{array}
$$

The binary subtraction problems illustrated in Figure A.4 require only elementary borrows. This subtraction problem illustrates a complex binary borrow:

$$
\begin{array}{r}
1100 \\
-\ \ \ \ 1 \\
\hline
1011
\end{array}
$$

A.4 CONVERTING BETWEEN NUMBER SYSTEMS

Occasionally you will be required to convert between decimal and binary. Many digital devices manipulate information in groups of 4 bits called a *nibble*. Because of this, the binary representations of the decimal numbers between 0 and 15 should be memorized. Infrequently, you will be required to work with numbers outside of this range. You will need an algorithm to accomplish the conversion. An algorithm is nothing more than a procedure, or recipe, for solving a mathematical problem.

We have stated that the place value of any column is equal to:

$$\text{Place value} = \text{number's base}^{(\text{column number} - 1)}$$

The place values of the first eight columns of a binary number are expressed in Table A.2. Take a moment to consider Table A.2. An important skill that a digital technician must possess is the ability to recognize patterns. You may have noticed that the place value doubles for each successive column. In the decimal system the place value increases by a factor of 10 for each successive column. This is a key concept in understanding number systems. How do we apply this information to the problem of *binary-to-decimal number conversion?* We merely sum all the place values for those columns in the binary number that contain a 1. For example, consider the conversion of the binary number 1001 1101, as illustrated in Figure A.5. Note that an 8-bit binary number is commonly broken into nibbles to improve its readability.

Decimal-to-binary conversion is much more difficult than binary-to-decimal conversion. One of the greatest difficulties in learning an algorithm for decimal-to-binary conversion is that technicians perform these operations so infrequently that they often simply forget the technique. (As was stated previously, the best method of any conversion is to employ a calculator that supports multibase arithmetic.)

We now examine a slow and inefficient, yet extremely intuitive, means of performing decimal-to-binary conversion. The following is a word description of our algorithm:

The first step we perform is to find the largest place value that is less than or equal to the number that we wish to convert. We assign a 1 to that bit position and subtract the place value from the number. We repeat this process until the number we wish to convert is reduced to zero.

Column number	Formula	Place value
1	2^0	1
2	2^1	2
3	2^2	4
4	2^3	8
5	2^4	16
6	2^5	32
7	2^6	64
8	2^7	128

Table A.2 Binary-to-decimal place values.

Column values

	128	64	32	16	8	4	2	1
Binary number	1	0	0	1	1	1	0	1
to convert								

$$
\begin{array}{r}
128 \\
+\ 16 \\
+\ \ 8 \\
+\ \ 4 \\
+\ \underline{\ \ 1} \\
157
\end{array}
$$

Figure A.5   Binary-to-decimal conversion of 1001 1101.

As an example, convert 89 into binary. First, we list the binary column numbers for reference:

Place Values
128   64   32   16   8   4   2   1

Step 1. 64 is the largest column value that is less than or equal to 89. We will place a 1 in that bit position and subtract 64 from 89.

The intermediate binary result is 0100 0000.
The decimal value left to convert is $89 - 64 = 25$.

Step 2. 16 is the next column that is less than or equal to the value to convert. We place a 1 in that bit position and subtract 16 from 25.

The intermediate binary result is 0101 0000.
The decimal value left to convert is $25 - 16 = 9$.

Step 3. The next place value that is less than or equal to the value to convert is 8.

The intermediate binary result is 0101 1000.
The decimal value left to convert is $9 - 8 = 1$.

Step 4. The decimal value of 1 will obviously fit into the first column of the binary number.

The final binary result is 0101 1001.

Step number		Intermediate binary result
1.	167	
	− 128	
	39	1000 0000
2.	39	
	− 32	
	7	1010 0000
3.	7	
	− 4	
	3	1010 0100
4.	3	
	− 2	
	1	1010 0110
5.	1	
	− 1	
	0	1010 0111

Figure A.6 Decimal-to binary conversion of 167.

As a second example, the decimal-to-binary conversion of 167 is illustrated in Figure A.6.

A.5 INTRODUCTION TO THE HEXADECIMAL NUMBER SYSTEM

Consider a typical 16-bit microprocessor address:

$$1011\ 0001\ 1111\ 0101$$

Attempting to describe an address that is 16 bits wide can be extremely confusing. In groups of 16 (or even 8), strings of 1s and 0s have a tendency to blur together. In the first part of this appendix we examined the binary number system, which is used to describe the actual outputs of digital circuits. Because of the long data bytes and addresses that describe microprocessor circuitry, another number system is required, which efficiently compresses these long strings of 0s and 1s into an easily readable form.

This new number system should meet the following criteria:

1. It must have the capacity to manage long groups of bits in an easily readable form.
2. Conversion between native binary and this new number system must be trivial.

There is a number system that uniquely meets these criteria; it is called the *hexadecimal* system. The prefix *hex* is Greek word for six; *decimal* means 10. The hexadecimal number system has a base of 16 (6 + 10). Although a number system with a base of 16 may seem awkward or clumsy, you will find that hexadecimal numbers are extremely easy to understand and manipulate. If a technician is going to work with microprocessor circuits, a fluent command of hexadecimal is required.

A number system with a base of 16, by definition, must have 16 unique counting symbols. The first 10 are borrowed from the decimal system and the last 6 are taken from the alphabet.

$$0, 1, 2, 3, 4, 5, 6, 7, 8, 9, A, B, C, D, E, F$$

What is the simple relationship between binary and hexadecimal numbers? You know that 4 binary bits can represent 16 unique numbers. Because the hexadecimal number system has 16 symbols, any group of 4 binary bits can be represented by one hexadecimal symbol. Table A.3 illustrates the relationship of each binary nibble to its equivalent hexadecimal symbol. Notice that the first 10 lines in Table A.3 appear to be a standard binary-to-decimal conversion. The last 6 binary combinations are represented by letters. Reconsider the 16-bit address that we examined at the beginning of this section.

$$1011 \quad 0001 \quad 1111 \quad 0101$$
$$B \qquad 1 \qquad F \qquad 5$$

The string of 16 bits can be represented by 4 hexadecimal symbols. To convert any string of binary bits into a hexadecimal number, start with the least sig-

Binary	Hexadecimal
0000	0
0001	1
0010	2
0011	3
0100	4
0101	5
0110	6
0111	7
1000	8
1001	9
1010	A
1011	B
1100	C
1101	D
1110	E
1111	F

Table A.3 Binary nibble to hexadecimal symbol.

nificant bit and form groups of nibbles. If the last nibble has less than 4 bits, pad the missing bits with zeros and convert each nibble into the corresponding hexadecimal symbol. To avoid ambiguities, the letter H is often appended to the end of a hexadecimal number.

For example,

$$1011\ 0011\ =\ B3H$$
$$10\ 1001\ 1111\ =\ 29FH$$
$$1100\ 0101\ 1010\ 1011\ =\ C5ABH$$

Converting from hexadecimal to binary is also an elementary task; each hexadecimal symbol is simply expanded into its equivalent binary nibble.

A.6 HEXADECIMAL-TO-K CONVERSION

It is often required to translate an address in hexadecimal to its value in K's of memory. You already know that 1K of memory is equal to 2^{10}, or 1024, bytes. Table A.4 is a tool to aid in this conversion technique.

The first column in Table A.4 denotes the powers of 2 (from highest to lowest) for a 16-bit address. The second column indicates the decimal equivalent of each power of 2. The third column shows the K value of each decimal number in the second column. Finally, the last column describes the hexadecimal equivalent of the previous columns.

Powers of 2	Decimal	Value in K's	Hexadecimal
2^{15}	32,768	32	8000
2^{14}	16,384	16	4000
2^{13}	8,192	8	2000
2^{12}	4,096	4	1000
2^{11}	2,048	2	0800
2^{10}	1,024	1	0400
2^{9}	512	1/2	0200
2^{8}	256	1/4	0100
2^{7}	128	1/8	0080
2^{6}	64	1/16	0040
2^{5}	32	1/32	0020
2^{4}	16	1/64	0010
2^{3}	8	1/128	0008
2^{2}	4	1/256	0004
2^{1}	2	1/512	0002
2^{0}	1	1/1024	0001

Table A.4   Powers of 2, decimal, value in K's, and hexadecimal conversion.

Let's assume that you need to know the hexadecimal equivalent of a memory location at 13K.

Step 1. Break 13K into values that are listed in Table A.4

$$13K = 8K + 4K + 1K$$

Step 2. Sum the hexadecimal equivalents of the individual values derived in step 1.

$$13K = 2000H + 1000H + 0400H = 3400H$$

An important part of the memory-mapping procedures discussed in this book involves the process of hexadecimal-to-K conversion.

A.7 HEXADECIMAL CONVERSION

Consider the place values of a four-digit hexadecimal number:

Place value

X $\qquad$ X $\qquad$ X $\qquad$ X

$16^3 = 4,096 \qquad 16^2 = 256 \qquad 16^1 = 16 \qquad 16^0 = 1$

To convert a hexadecimal number to its decimal equivalent, you must first convert the hexadecimal symbol in each column to its decimal equivalent. Multiply the decimal equivalent of each symbol by the place value of the column. Finally, sum all the products from the multiplication; the result is the decimal equivalent of the hexadecimal number. As an example, let's convert A3F9H to its decimal equivalent.

Step 1. The decimal equivalent of each column is

10   3   15   9

Step 2. Multiply each of these column values by the proper place value:

$10 \times 4096 = 40,960 \qquad 3 \times 256 = 768$

$15 \times 16 = 240 \qquad 9 \times 1 = 9$

Step 3. Sum the products from Step 2.

40,960
768
240
+   9

41,977

This procedure is identical with the binary-to-decimal conversion procedure. The only difference is the place values.

Decimal-to-hexadecimal conversion follows the same procedure as decimal-to-binary conversion. Once again, we use Table A.4 as an aid. The first

Convert 45,346 to hexadecimal.

	Intermediate value	*Hexadecimal sum*
Step (1)	45,346	
	$-\underline{32,768}$	8000H
	12,578	
	$-\underline{\ \ 8,192}$	$+\underline{2000H}$
	4,386	A000H
	$-\underline{\ \ 4,096}$	$+\underline{1000H}$
	290	B000H
	$-\underline{\ \ \ \ 256}$	$+\underline{0100H}$
	34	B100H
	$-\underline{\ \ \ \ \ 32}$	$\underline{0020H}$
	2	B120H
	$-\underline{\ \ \ \ \ \ \ 2}$	$+\underline{0002H}$
	0	B122H

Check: Reconvert B122H to decimal.

$$11 \times 4096 = 45056$$
$$1 \times\ \ 256 = \ \ \ 256$$
$$2 \times\ \ \ 16 = \ \ \ \ \ 32$$
$$2 \times\ \ \ \ \ 1 = \underline{\ \ \ \ \ \ 2}$$
$$45,346_{10}$$

Figure A.7   Decimal-to-hexadecimal conversion.

step in the conversion process is to find the largest decimal number (column 2 of Table A.4) that is smaller than or equal to the number to be converted. This value in column 2 is subtracted from the decimal number that we are converting. The hexadecimal equivalent, in column 4, becomes the first value in a hexadecimal sum. We continue to subtract decimal numbers from the intermediate value and sum their hexadecimal equivalents until the intermediate value is equal to 0. Figure A.7 illustrates the conversion of 45,346 to hexadecimal.

The conversion in Figure A.7 requires six subtractions to reduce the decimal number to 0. Notice how the hexadecimal column is summed to produce the converted hexadecimal number. The second part of Figure A.7 is a reconversion from the hexadecimal sum to the original decimal quantity.

A.8 HEXADECIMAL ADDITION AND SUBTRACTION

The hexadecimal addition during the decimal-to-hexadecimal conversion does not generate carries. A hexadecimal carry is generated when an addition causes a hexadecimal result that is greater than F. All carries, in any number system, are handled in the same manner. The base of the number system is subtracted from the result that produced the carry. The result of this subtraction is the new answer for the column that produced the carry and a one is added to the next significant column.

It is difficult to add directly in hexadecimal. When performing an addition, the hexadecimal symbols A through F are converted into their decimal equivalents. Each column is then added. If a column total that is greater than 15 occurs, 16 (the base value of the hexadecimal number system) is subtracted from that answer. The result of the subtraction is the answer for that particular column and a carry is added to the next significant column. If a result of 10

Problem: 7CH   *Note:* Parentheses indicate
            ; 58H   decimal numbers.

Step 1 Convert hexadecimal values to decimal.
              7 (12)
            + 5   8

Step 2 Add columns.
              7 (12)
          +   5   8
            (12) (20)

Step 3 Perform carry.
                 (12)   (20)
    carry   +   1   − (16)
                 (13)   4

Step 4 Reconvert all numbers to hexadecimal.
              Answer = D4H

Figure A.8   Hexadecimal addition with carry.

through 15 occurs at any column, that number is converted into the proper hexadecimal symbol. Figure A.8 illustrates a hexadecimal addition example.

The most important part of hexadecimal subtraction is the borrow. When a borrow occurs in decimal subtraction, the value of 1 is subtracted from the next significant column and the value of 10 is added to the column that required the borrow. In a subtraction operation of any base, the value that is added to the column that requires the borrow is always equal to the base of the number system. Therefore, a hexadecimal borrow will result in a value of 1 being subtracted from the next significant column and the value of 10H (16 decimal) being added to the column that required the borrow.

When we added hexadecimal numbers, hexadecimal symbols were converted to their decimal equivalents. We perform hexadecimal subtraction in the same manner. Figure A.9 illustrates a hexadecimal subtraction example.

You must practice until you feel confident with the hexadecimal number

Problem:

$$\begin{array}{r} \text{ABH} \\ -\ \underline{\text{5EH}} \end{array}$$

Step 1 Convert hexadecimal values to decimal.

$$\begin{array}{r} (10)\,(11) \\ -\ \underline{5\ \ (14)} \end{array}$$

Step 2 Perform borrow.

$$(10) - 1 = 9 \rightarrow \begin{array}{r} 9\,(27) \\ -\ \underline{5\,(14)} \end{array}$$

Step 3 Subtract.

$$\begin{array}{r} 9\,(27) \\ -\ \underline{5\,(14)} \\ 4\,(13) \end{array}$$

Step 4 Convert decimal numbers to hexadecimal.

Answer = 4DH

Check:

$$\begin{array}{r} \text{5E} \\ +\ \underline{\text{4D}} \end{array} = \begin{array}{r} 5\,(14) \\ +\ \underline{4\,(13)} \end{array} = 9\,(27) = \text{ABH}$$

Figure A.9 Hexadecimal subtraction with borrow.

system. Hexadecimal is the most widely used number system in the microprocessor world. Data bytes and memory addresses are usually designated in hexadecimal. When a group of memory locations are "dumped" onto the video display, they are shown in hexadecimal form. Experienced microprocessor technicians can convert between binary and hexadecimal in their heads. Hexadecimal-to-K conversion is also extremely common, as is hexadecimal addition and subtraction. The least used hexadecimal skill is converting between hexadecimal and decimal. Remember that binary and hexadecimal are closely related, whereas in the digital world, decimal is an unnatural number base.

IMPORTANT CONCEPTS OF APPENDIX A

- The amplitude of an analog waveform has an infinite number of values.
- The square wave is a digital waveform.
- Because a square wave essentially has two fingers, it is best described by the binary number system.
- Most number systems use weighted codes that assign a place value to each column.
- The hexadecimal number system is a convenient shorthand method of symbolizing a binary nibble with one symbol.
- Memory addresses are usually expressed in hexadecimal. The capacity of memory systems is expressed in K's. Hexadecimal-to-K conversion is quite common.

THE ASCII CODE

B.1 STANDARD DIGITAL CODES

In the English language there are 96 common symbols that represent:

- Lower- and uppercase letters of the alphabet (a, b, c, A, B, C, . . .)
- Numerals (0, 1, 2, . . .)
- Punctuation marks (., ?, :, (, . . .)
- Arithmetic operators (+ , − , = , . . .)
- Unit symbols (%, #, $, @, . . .)

The outputs of a digital circuit can be used to represent these symbols. Each symbol is assigned a unique combination of logic 1s and 0s. Before a computer and peripheral can communicate, they must agree on the *digital codes* that are used to represent each symbol. The implementation of a standard digital code guarantees that computers and peripherals will recognize a common character set.

Although there are many standard codes employed in the computer industry, *ASCII (American Standard Code for Information Interchange)* is the most popular and widely recognized. ASCII is a 7-bit code in which 2^7 (128) characters are represented.

Later in this appendix we see that the IBM PC employs an 8-bit version of extended ASCII. The first 128 characters in the PC's ASCII code are identical with standard ASCII. The last 128 characters are unique to the IBM PC and compatibles. These extra codes are used to represent block graphics symbols and foreign language alphabets. The IBM *Technical Reference Manual* illustrates the characters associated with IBM's 8-bit ASCII.

Before we examine ASCII let's take a moment to think about the keys on a typewriter. The action of most keys is to cause a symbol to be printed by striking an embossed hammer against an ink ribbon and paper. However there are many keys on a typewriter that cause an action to occur rather than print a character. The return key causes the paper carriage to return to the first column of the left margin and also feeds the paper forward by one line. The backspace key moves the carriage back by one character. The tab key moves the carriage from its present position to the next tab stop. These are examples of *control keys*—keys that cause an action to occur rather than to print a character.

B.2 THE ASCII CODE

Figure B.1 illustrates the ASCII table. The ASCII table is rectangular matrix of 16 rows by 8 columns depicting a total of 128 unique elements. ASCII is a 7-bit code representing 32 control characters and 96 printable characters. For convenience, each row and column is labeled in both hexadecimal and binary.

The 96 standard printable characters illustrated in Figure B.1 are generated by pressing the appropriate key or the appropriate key while holding down the shift key. Computer keyboards have all the keys of a conventional typewriter and also have several special keys. A key labeled Ctrl is the *control key*. While holding down the control key, another key is pressed to create one of the 32 control codes in Figure B.1. The control codes in column 0 are generated by holding down the control key and pressing the appropriate key in column 4. Holding down Ctrl and pressing @ generates the code for an ASCII NUL. The standard notation for that control sequence is ˆ@, where the ˆ stands for the control key. Thus ˆG generates the code for an ASCII BEL and a ˆN generates the code for an ASCII S0. In a similar manner the control codes for the second column are generated by holding down the Ctrl key and pressing the appropriate key in column 5. A ˆS generates the ASCII code for a DC3 and a ˆQ generates an ASCII DC1.

The control codes are further broken into four groups: format effectors, communications controls, information separators, and miscellaneous. We examine first the format effectors, which provide analogous functions to the control keys of a conventional typewriter.

Format Effectors

BS (backspace) 08H—ˆH.   The BS character causes the cursor on a video display or the print head to move back one space. A backspace can be described as either *destructive* or *nondestructive*. A destructive backspace moves the cursor

		Col.	0	1	2	3	4	5	6	7
Bit 7			0	0	0	0	1	1	1	1
Bit 6			0	0	1	1	0	0	1	1
Bit 5			0	1	0	1	0	1	0	1
Bit 1	Bit 2	Bit 3	Bit 4	Row							

Row	Bit 4	Bit 3	Bit 2	Bit 1	0	1	2	3	4	5	6	7
0	0	0	0	0	NUL	DLE	SP	0	@	P	`	p
1	0	0	0	1	SOH	DC1	!	1	A	Q	a	q
2	0	0	1	0	STX	DC2	"	2	B	R	b	r
3	0	0	1	1	ETX	DC3	#	3	C	S	c	s
4	0	1	0	0	EOT	DC4	$	4	D	T	d	t
5	0	1	0	1	ENQ	NAK	%	5	E	U	e	u
6	0	1	1	0	ACK	SYN	&	6	F	V	f	v
7	0	1	1	1	BEL	ETB	'	7	G	W	g	w
8	1	0	0	0	BS	CAN	(	8	H	X	h	x
9	1	0	0	1	HT	EM	)	9	I	Y	i	y
A	1	0	1	0	LF	SUB	*	:	J	Z	j	z
B	1	0	1	1	VT	ESC	+	;	K	[	k	{
C	1	1	0	0	FF	FS	,	<	L	\	l	|
D	1	1	0	1	CR	GS	-	=	M	]	m	}
E	1	1	1	0	SO	RS	.	>	N	^	n	~
F	1	1	1	1	SI	US	/	?	O	_	o	DEL

Figure B.1 The ASCII code.

251

back one space and also erases the character under its final position. Typewriters use a nondestructive backspace; the carriage is simply moved back one position. Printers use a nondestructive backspace, whereas video displays make use of both types of backspaces.

HT (horizontal tab) 09H—ˆI.   The HT character is the equivalent of the tab key on a typewriter. On receiving an HT character, the cursor or print head moves to the next tab position. Tab positions on video displays and printers, just like tab positions on typewriters, are programmable. When applications programs are invoked, a *default set* of tab positions is used. Most applications allow the user to redefine (reprogram) the tab positions. It is the responsibility of the program to calculate the next tab position when it receives an HT character from the keyboard. Computer keyboards have a tab key that usually generates ˆI.

One should exercise caution with tabs on printers. In an initialized (power-up) state, many printers do not have a set of default tab positions and consequently ignore HT characters. A sequence of special characters must be sent to the printer to program the tab positions prior to normal printing operations.

LF (line feed) 0AH—ˆJ; CR (carriage return) 0DH—ˆM.   When the return key on a typewriter is pressed, two actions occur—the carriage returns to the first print column and the paper is advanced to the next line. On the video display of a computer or terminal, CR returns the cursor to the first column of the present line and LF moves the cursor down by one line or the paper up by one line (thus the term *line feed*). The column in which the cursor or print head is residing prior to the receipt of the LF is not changed. The action of a typewriter return key is a combination of CR and LF. Breaking a traditional typewriter return into two distinct actions results in a greater flexibility for output to video displays and printers. A *new-line character* is defined as sending a CR/LF sequence.

Commands are usually terminated by a CR. For example, to get a listing of the programs and files on a floppy disk, we might type in the command: dir ⟨CR⟩;, where ⟨CR⟩ indicates that the execution of the command will begin after the CR key is pressed. On the PC's keyboard the carriage return key is labeled *enter*.

Printers usually wait to receive a complete line of characters before starting the printing process. A CR indicates to a printer that it has been sent all the characters in the line and can proceed with printing.

FF (form feed) 0CH—ˆL.   The FF character has distinctly different meanings if sent to a printer or to a video display. Printer paper comes in the form of continuous sheets (bordered by pin feed holes) that are folded into pages and placed into a cardboard box. Each page is called a *form*. Form feed instructs the printer to execute the appropriate number of line feeds to bring the beginning of the next form in line with the print head. This operation implies that printers must know the number of lines per form and decrement the line count each time a LF character is received.

When sent to a video display, ˆL causes the cursor to move one space to the right in complementary fashion to a backspace.

VT (vertical tab) 0BH—ˆK.   VT also has different meanings to a printer and a video display. When sent to a printer, VT provides a function similar to that of the HT character. A VT character causes a printer to line feed to the next programmed vertical tab position.

When sent to a video display, ˆK causes the cursor to move up one line. This is the complementary operation to a line feed.

Most computer keyboards have four keys with arrows—up, down, left, and right. These *cursor-control* keys are used to move the cursor to any position on the display. Early computer keyboards did not have cursor-control keys. Instead ˆH, ˆJ, ˆL, and ˆK key sequences were used to move the cursor around the screen.

Cursor	Control Keys
Left	ˆH
Down	ˆJ
Up	ˆK
Right	ˆL

Communication Control Characters

The communication control characters are:

SOH	(start of header)
STX	(start of text)
ETX	(end of text)
EOT	(end of transmission)
ENQ	(enquiry)
ACK	(acknowledge)
DLE	(data link escape)
NAK	(negative acknowledge)
SYN	(synchronous idle)
ETB	(end of block)

These control characters are used during complex synchronous communication and data transfer protocols. The study of these topics is not relevant to the material in this book. Exceptions to this are the EXT (03H), EOT (04H), and SUB (1AH) characters.

The EXT character is generated with ˆC. On most computers typing ˆC *interrupts* the currently executing program and returns the user to the command level of the operating system.

EOT (ˆD) is used by the UNIX operating system, typically to indicate that the user has completed input and the program should continue execution. This is called an *EOF* (end of file) character.

SUB (ˆZ) is used by the popular CPM/80 and PC-DOS microcomputer operating systems as the last byte in a data file. When a program running under PC-DOS reads the byte 1AH, it knows that the end of file has been reached.

Information Separator Codes

The information separator codes are:

> FS   (file separator)
> GS   (group separator)
> RS   (record separator)
> US   (unit separator)

As with the communications control characters, in this book we have no general interest in the information separator codes.

Miscellaneous Codes

Many of the characters in the miscellaneous group have universally accepted meanings. We examine the most important of these control characters.

NUL (null) 00H—ˆ@.   NUL is often used to pad the beginning of a transmission of characters. This is required in situations where a receiving device (most often a printer) appears to miss the first few characters in a message. NUL is also used as a termination character when programming video displays and printers.

BEL (bell) 07H—ˆG.   When a video display receives a BEL character, it generates a tone. BEL is used to gain a user's attention to indicate an illegal entry or an important event.

DC1—DC4 (device control) ˆQ—ˆT.   These four codes are used to control the operation of video displays and printers. Of special interest are DC1 (ˆQ) and DC3 (ˆS). DC1 is called *X-ON* and DC3 is called *X-OFF*, where *X* is an abbreviation for transmission. Consider the typical situation where the computer is sending information so quickly that it is scrolling off the top of the video display before it can be read. A ˆS (X-OFF) sent to the computer causes it to stop sending data to the video display; a ˆQ (X-ON) indicates that the computer can resume data transmission. This use of X-ON and X-OFF is called *flow control*, or *software handshaking*.

Although X-ON is the most correct and formal way to indicate that the data transmission may resume, in general practice the first key depressed following X-OFF restarts the data transmission.

The most popular use of flow control is to reconcile the differing speeds of computers and printers. Because computers are electronic devices, they process data at an extremely fast rate. Printers, on the other hand, are electromechanical and are thousands of times slower than the computers from which they receive data. How can we be sure that the computer is not sending data so quickly that the printer is overrun and loses or garbles characters? All printers have a small amount of *buffer memory*. When the buffer is almost full, the printer transmits X-OFF to the computer. The computer reacts by suspending data transmission and patiently waits to receive an X-ON character from the printer to indicate that it should resume sending data. In this manner a lightning-fast computer can converse with an excruciatingly slow printer with no loss of data.

ESC (escape) 1BH—ˆ[.   Another key that is unique to computer keyboards is the ESC (escape) key. To exploit all the functions available on video displays and printers, there must be more than the 32 control codes of the ASCII code. The concept of an *escape sequence* is quite simple. When a video display or printer receives an ESC code, it interprets the next one or more printable characters as a command instead of data. This effectively creates an infinite number of unique commands. Modern printers have many features that are programmed or invoked via escape sequences.

Many applications that run on the PC use the ESC key to exit from a menu environment to a working environment. ESC can be thought of as an emergency stop button. Pressing ESC usually brings the user into a command environment.

DEL (delete)—7FH.   There is one special control character that does reside in columns 0 or 1 of Figure B.1. The DEL character is all logic 1s (111 1111). The history behind this goes back to the days of *paper tape*. From the early 1960s through the 1970s, paper tape was used to store digital data. ASCII characters were represented by the presence or lack of holes punched in the tape. No hole represented a logic 0, whereas a hole represented a logic 1. To delete a character all the holes must be punched out; thus the code of all logic 1s to represent a delete character. Many computer systems and documentation call the DEL character by its common alias, *rub-out*. Expect to see both DEL and RUB-OUT used to reference ASCII 7FH.

Like other control codes that we have examined, DEL has many uses. On a video display it is used to delete the character that is presently residing under the cursor. (This should not be confused with the BS, which moves the cursor one space to the left and then possibly deletes that character.)

B.3 PRINTABLE ASCII CHARACTERS

The remaining 95 characters (96 minus DEL) represent letters, numerals, punctuation marks, arithmetic operators, and unit symbols that can be represented on a video display or printer. The codes for these characters were not selected at random. ASCII is a well-thought-out and practical code that enables programs to accomplish common translations of letters and numerals.

ASCII 20H is the space. A space should not be mistaken for a NUL. When a computer or terminal is energized, every location in the display memory is initialized to ASCII 20H. The display is actually exhibiting 24 lines by 80 columns of the ASCII space character. ASCII 20H is used to provide spaces between characters and blank lines on video displays.

Digits and Letters

Consider column 3 of the ASCII table, which contains the digits 0–9. Notice that the least significant nibble of the codes representing the decimal digits are the binary representation of the digits themselves. To determine whether a certain character is a decimal digit, its code can be tested to fall between 30H and 39H. If the bits in the most significant nibble are reset to logic 0s, the actual value of the digit is recovered. Also notice that the only difference between the upper- and lowercase letters is the most significant nibble. This makes translating between upper- and lowercase a trivial chore.

Words can be alphabetized by ordering their ASCII codes from the lowest (starting with A at 41H) to the highest (ending with Z at 5AH). In a program that alphabetizes by ASCII code, a word starting with a capital letter will always appear before a word starting with a lowercase letter. In this manner programs written in BASIC can have a conditional statement in the form of:

$$\text{If A\$} > \text{B\$ then} \_ \_ \_ \_ \_$$

The ASCII values of the characters comprising the string variables are being compared. Thus A < B and Z < a.

Extended 8-Bit ASCII

As we mentioned at the beginning of this appendix, the IBM PC utilizes an 8-bit version of extended ASCII. These additional 128 characters, symbols, and block graphics are supported by dot patterns in the character generators on the monochrome display adapter and color graphics adapter. The additional 128 characters are accessed from the keyboard by holding down the alternate key and entering the three-digit (in decimal) ASCII code via the numeric keypad.

Not all printers will print these additional 128 characters. Check to ensure that the printer is IBM graphics compatible. Also remember that unlike most keyboards, the PC's keyboard does not send the ASCII code of the depressed key. It merely sends a scan code, which defines the physical position of the depressed key. It is a function of the software to map the scan codes into the appropriate ASCII character definitions.

IMPORTANT CONCEPTS OF APPENDIX B

- ASCII is a universally accepted 7-bit code representing 32 control codes and 96 printable characters.
- Each ASCII character is usually represented by two hexadecimal digits.
- Each of the 32 control codes is generated from the keyboard by holding down the Ctrl key while depressing another key, whose code appears in the sixth or seventh column of the ASCII table.
- The combination of the CR and LF characters is called a new-line character and is used to emulate a typewriter carriage return.
- A sheet of computer paper is called a form. A FF character advances the paper in a printer to the first line of the next form.
- Control codes can be used to move the cursor up, down, right, or left.
- The ˆ symbol is used to represent the control key. Thus ˆC means ''hold down the Ctrl key while depressing the C.''
- ˆC is used to interrupt a program that is currently executing.
- ˆD is used as an EOF marker in Unix, and ˆZ is used as an EOF marker in CP/M-80 and MS-DOS.
- The DC1 and DC3 characters are popularly known as X-ON and X-OFF. X-ON/X-OFF flow control is used to reconcile RS-232 devices that send/ receive or process data at different speeds.
- The IBM BIOS routine does not support software handshaking.
- An escape sequence is defined as the ESC code followed by one or more pritnable characters. Escape sequences are used to generate an infinite number of commands for programmable peripherals.
- DEL is the last character in the ASCII code. It is often used to synchronize the bit stream.
- Extended 8-bit ASCII is used to represent block graphics characters, foreign language sets, Greek letters, and mathematical or engineering symbols. These 128 printable characters are unique to each make and model of computer.

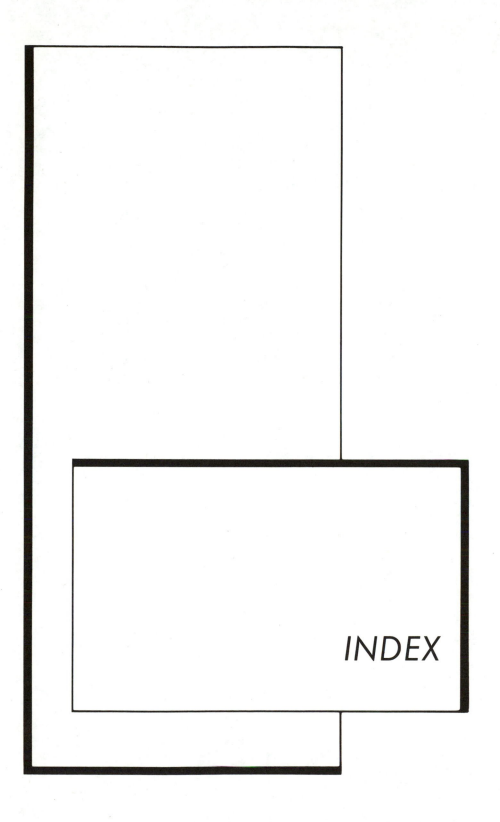

INDEX